Indiana University Uralic and Altaic Series
Volume 148
Larry Moses, Editor

Stephen A. Halkovic, Jr.

THE MONGOLS OF THE WEST

Research Institute for Inner Asian Studies
Indiana University, Bloomington
1985

THE MONGOLS OF THE WEST

ISBN 0-933070-16-0

TABLE OF CONTENTS

Chapter I

An Introduction to the History of
the Western Mongols

Countless tribal groups have moved across and lived on the steppe region of Central Eurasia known as Inner Asia. One group of western Mongol tribes called the Oirats played a major role in the history of this territory in the 17th and 18th centuries. During this time period the Oirats were also responsible for helping to shape events which effected the Russian Empire, the Ch'ing dynasty, and the territory of Tibet. They were a people who were to experience the policy of both Russia and China towards minority groups. Various tribes of this Oirat group would be able to freely choose whether to remain or move from the territory of either the Russian Tsars or the Ch'ing Emperors depending on Russian and Ch'ing responses. Much of the movement that was to take the Oirat tribes across these regions, however, was not dictated by outside forces but instead was brought about by internal Oirat tribal politics. For example, neither the Manchus nor the Russians caused the first migrations of the Oirats out of their home territory of Dzungaria. Instead it was the internal feuding amongst the Oirats themselves, which led to an exodus of Oirats out of Dzungaria across Turkestan and into the Volga steppe territory north of the Caspian Sea.

This type of transhumance by the various Oirat tribes did not begin in the 17th century nor did the reasons and motives behind these moves originate at this time. The early history of the Oirats or western Mongols demonstrates the great changes which can occur to a nomadic people in a relatively short time period. The Oirat were located west of Lake Baikal prior to the 13th century. They settled at the start of the 13th century in the Altai and quickly made the change from forest to steppe nomads.[1] The Oirats, although true Mongols, were set off from the eastern Mongols by the fact that they were not related to the line of Chinggis khan.

The legitimacy of rule for the Mongols was based on a relationship to Chinggis. With the fall of the Yuan dynasty, however, the prestige of the Chinggisid Mongols was on the point of collapse. When Ming advances continued even into the Mongol home steppeland at the end of the 14th century, the Chinggisid line reached such a low ebb that they were overthrown. The Oirat chieftain Ugechi killed the Chinggisid ruler Elbeq khan and seized power in 1399.[2] However, he was in turn overthrown by two rival Oirat leaders. The Oirats during this period were very conciliatory to the Ming court and in this way tried to gain advantageous treatment from the Ming.

The period from the end of the 14th century up to the mid-1430s in Mongolia was highly volatile. There were a number of changes in power between the Chinggisid and the Oirats. The Ming also changed allegiance several times, although it generally backed the Oirats.[3] The Ming policy seemed to have favored the Oirats because they were not viewed as legitimate rulers by all the Mongols, and were thus in a potentially weaker political position. If the Oirats seemed to be getting too powerful the Ming were ready and able to bring them down. During Yung-lo's reign the Ming did send several large-scale invasion forces against the Oirats, with varying degrees of success.[4]

After the Emperor Yung-lo died in 1425, the Oirats gained control and power was concentrated in the hands of Toghon.[5] Toghon, however, did not take the title of khan but put a descendent of Chinggis on the throne in order not to provoke popular discontent.[6] The Oirats now started to expand their base of operations from western Mongolia westward and took over the Chagatai territory on the Ili in Turfan and Kucha. In the process the Chagatai khan, Vais, was captured twice by Toghon.[7] To the east the Oirats were making both military and diplomatic advances. They had pressed the Ming to open up trading centers on the frontier. This the Ming finally consented to in 1438. Horses could be traded, but no weapons, copper, or iron could be traded to the Mongols.

When Esen succeeded his father Toghon as ruler of the Oirats in 1444, the western Mongols had already expanded into a large empire. Esen was to push the limits of their territory even farther. In 1445 he captured the Hami oasis, and in 1449, aggravated by not obtaining a Chinese princess for his wife as promised, and provoked by the low prices given in trade for horses by the Chinese, he attacked the Ming and inflicted a major defeat on the Chinese in the vicinity of Peking, their capital. Amazingly the emperor of China himself, Ying-tsung,

4

was captured during this battle.[8] The Oirats roamed freely over north China with their captive, plundering as they went. The Oirats campaigned even as far as Korea. Esen's intention in invading this region was not to try to subjugate Korea, but only to protect himself on that flank.

Esen was never able to take advantage of his great victory. He seemed almost more confused than the Chinese army had been. Instead of marching immediately against the capital which was entirely unprepared for an assault, he marched northward pillaging as he went. In the meantime the Chinese had immediately declared that a new emperor had taken the throne and that Ying-tsung was no longer emperor. In the end Esen was reconciled with the Chinese and released his prisoner in 1450.[9] Thus Esen, who held the emperor of China as prisoner and had the opportunity of taking the capital of Peking, was not able to take advantage of the situation.

As a result of the indecisive actions in China the eastern Mongols, who were already dissatisfied being under the Oirat yoke, rose up. Esen put the eastern Mongols down and killed the Chinggisid whom he had set up as puppet ruler. In 1454 he took the final step and decided to proclaim himself khan, and styled himself in Chinese fashion khan T'ien-sheng of the Great Yuan.[10] In the very next year Esen was killed by two of his own Oirat chieftains who were opposed to Esen making his rule hereditary. From this point on Oirat rule began to slip badly in eastern Mongolia, although the Oirats held power in western Mongolia to the Ili region and continued to be a force to be reckoned with between the Ili and the Caspian.

The eastern Mongols under Dayan khan (ruled 1478-1540) were able to unite and wrest control away from the Oirats on the Mongol homeland. The Oirats, who were a confederation of tribes and are always spoken of in Mongol texts as the Dörbön Oirat (Four Oirat), had once again broken up into factions during this period and thus weakened themselves. The problem of factional internal fighting was not just limited to the eastern Mongols. The Oirats suffered under the same handicap.

The eastern Mongols took advantage of Oirat dissension and even during the period of struggle for power after the death of Dayan khan various eastern Mongol chieftains were able to defeat separate elements of the Oirats. For instance, in 1552 Altan khan defeated the Khoid, one tribe of Oirats, and this victory opened up for the Khalkhas the Khangai Mountains which had been Oirat territory.[11] In only two more years the Khalkhas were nomadizing along the Selengge River Valley.

It was not only the Khalkha who were attacking the Oirat. The Ordos Mongols in 1562 and again in 1570 made attacks against the Oirat. The Oirats were constantly on the defensive towards the eastern Mongols in the latter half of the 16th century. In 1606 Laiqur khan of the Khalkha managed to bring the Oirats under subjugation and force them to pay tribute to the Zashaghtu Khan's house.[12] A turning point in Mongol-Oirat relations now occurred. Sholoi, who is also know as Altan khan, took command of the Khalkha forces. In a battle on the Irtysh

in 1623 the Oirat defeated Sholoi.[13] This Oirat victory allowed
the Oirats, who had suffered a series of defeats against the
Mongols, to finally gain a victory. However, the Mongols were
able to counter with several victories of their own. Slowly
the Oirat, who since Esen had been under eastern Mongol
control, now gained the upper hand over the Mongols and began
to push back the borders of their territory. The Oirats had
already in 1616 started a westward push and now they added to
this with an eastward and then a southern expansion.

Kho Örlökh, the leader of the Torghuut tribe of Oirats,
started to move his tribe across the Kirghiz-Kazakh steppes in
1616. For the next hundred years numerous groups of Oirats
followed this same migration route and settled on the lower
Volga steppe lands. While the strength of the western Mongols
was increasing that of the eastern Mongols was waning. By 1634
after the death of Ligdan khan, the ruler of the Chahar
Mongols, the Mongols of Inner Mongolia had come completely
under the power of the Manchus.[14] The strength of the Khalkha
Mongols was also sapped, having been split into a number of
khanates. Thus two major powers on the East Asian mainland were
emerging, the Oirats on the one side and the Manchus on the
other.

One further factor in the rise of Oirat power has to be
mentioned. The Oirats converted to Tibetan Buddhism at the
beginning of the 17th century. The conversion was to have
obvious major religious and cultural consequences for the
Oirats. It also had important political implications. The

Oirats because of their very zealous acceptance of Buddhism developed close relations with the Tibetan hierarchy. This inevitably led to a direct involvement in Tibetan politics. Thus, the sphere of Oirat control was drawn south into Tibet.

Since Altan khan's meeting with the Dalai Lama in 1578, there had been a great deal of cultural and economic activity between Tibetans and Mongols. With the death of Altan khan many groups of Mongols had entered Tibet ostensibly for religious purposes, but in reality to plunder the Tibetans. Since there was no unity in Tibet, the Tibetans could not keep the Mongols out.

The Khoshuts, a tribe of Oirats, developed a strong government around the Koke-nor area on the northeast borders of Tibet in the first half of the 17th century. Their ruler Gushi khan became a defender of the dGe-lugs-pa sect of Tibetan Buddhism, and in particular a champion of the Fifth Dalai Lama the leader of that group. By 1640 Gushi had put an end to the secular power in Tibet which was headed by the King of gTsang, who had opposed the Dalai Lama. Gushi then became the overall protector of the Dalai Lama's authority in Tibet. This foreign power in the form of the Khoshuts laid the foundation for a great age in Tibetan history. After Gushi's death in 1654 all real power gradually came into the Dalai Lama's hands and Gushi's two sons who succeeded him jointly were reduced to a nominal rule. The risk of letting in a foreign power, the Khoshut, to establish the Dalai Lama's regime seemed a risk well worth taking. Later when Manchu and Oirat were to fight over control of Tibet the risk was not to seem so worthwhile.

The greatest of the Oirat religious leaders was a member of this same Khoshut tribe. He was Zaya Pandita (1599-1662). Zaya Pandita created the Oirat Mongol script. This script is known as clear script since it settles the ambiguities of the Mongol script. He and his disciples translated over 200 Buddhist works into the Oirat script and thus made available a large mass of Buddhist doctrinal material.

Even such ardent fighters as the Mongols and Oirats did not fight each other all of the time. In 1640 a truce was reached between the leaders of the Khalkha Mongols and the Oirat. They jointly drew up a treaty in the form of a law code. This code fit the traditional nomadic culture. Crimes and punishments for those crimes varied according to the status of the person. This code contained religious, moral, customary, and political laws. It did not, however, successfully unite the Khalkha and Oirat Mongols.

A new Oirat power was on the rise in Tarbagatai, the Dzungars. These Dzungars were to produce a great ruler, one who was to recapture the Mongol capital of Karakorum, push out the Khalkhas and pose a serious threat to the Manchus--this was Galdan. It must be remembered that while Galdan was rising to power in the 1670s, the Manchus had their hands full with a large-scale rebellion. The Wu San-kuei rebellion was a most serious challenge to Manchu rule. At the same time internal fighting was going on among the Khalkha khans in Outer

Mongolia.

Galdan's rise to power also came out of dissension. Sengge, Galdan's elder brother, was assassinated in 1670 in a dispute over who was to rule the Dzungars. Galdan was studying in Lhasa at the time, but left to gain control of the Dzungars.[15] The causes of Galdan's struggle with the Khalkhas lie in the age-old clash of the eastern and western Mongols for supremacy of the Mongol race.

Galdan's clash with Tüsiyetü khan of the northern Khalkhas started with incidents in the 1670s, when Galdan fought for control over the Dzungars and Tüsiyetü backed Galdan's opponent. In 1687 open warfare broke out between the two. Tüsiyetü it seems made the first offensive moves. In retaliation Galdan launched his attack in 1688 on the Khalkhas. His success was complete leading even to the takeover of the Erdeni Dzu monastery at Karakorum. By 1690 Galdan had subjugated the territory of Khalkha.[16] This success was to be short-lived, however. Galdan was now at the height of his power, but he had gained such total control that he had pushed his fellow Mongols into the hands of the Manchus.

The Inner Mongols had pledged their support to the Manchus in 1634 and now even the Outer Mongols were forced to ask for Manchu support. The height of Oirat power in the east was to be marked by the final subjugation of the eastern Mongols to the Manchus. This event occurred in 1691 at an audience held at Dolon Nor--the Khandu (Shang Tu, Imperial City) of Qubilai,

between May 29th and June 3rd. All of the Khalkha Mongol
leaders, the Jasaghtu khan of the western Mongols, the Tüsiyetü
khan of the northern Khalkhas, the Sechen khan of the eastern
Khalkhas, the Sain Noyon khan of the middle Khalkhas and others
performed the ceremony of the three kneelings and nine
head-knockings.[17] The Khalkhas were then integrated into the
Manchu banner system to be split into even smaller groups and
thus even less likely to be able to be united.

As early as 1618, a group of Oirats led by the Torghut
prince Khɵ Ɵrlɵkh moved westward out of their homeland in
Dzungaria to the steppe lands north of the Caspian. Throughout
the rest of the 17th century various groups of Oirats migrated
out of Dzungaria and into the steppes north of the Caspian. The
Oirats who moved westward are called Kalmyks.

The Russians from the very beginning had a stormy
relationship with the Kalmyks. Khɵ Ɵrlɵkh for instance attacked
Astrakhan in 1640, but he was defeated and captured. Kalmyks
after this in 1655 made peace with the Russians. The Russians
used the Kalmyks in their wars against the Crimean Tatars, the
Kazakhs and the Kirghiz; however, the Kalmyks could not always
be relied upon to be loyal to the Russians.

Under the strong ruler Ayuuki, who reigned for 50 years
until he died in 1722, the Kalmyks had a quite independent
relationship with Russia. They supplied troops and fought
various common enemies, but they also were not above plundering
and attacking Russian provinces and possessions. In this way

Ayuuki's strength grew as did that of his subjects, the Kalmyks. The Kalmyks were not alone in failing to fulfill their promises, the Russians also were not always dependable allies. In 1715 the Sultan of Kuban, Bakhta Girei attacked the Kalmyks. When Ayuuki asked the commander of the Russian army for help, the commander replied that he could not fight without orders from the Tsar. This naturally made Ayuuki furious, but he was to get his revenge four years later, when the Russians asked for aid and Ayuuki responded, "I am not able to fight the Tatars of Kuban without orders from the Tsar." With a stable, strong leadership the Kalmyks were able to act independently and be their own masters.

The age-old weakness of all the Mongol tribes, lack of unity, was to prevent the Kalmyks from retaining their independence. The death of Ayuuki signalled the start of contention over the succession. Not only were the leading Kalmyk nobles involved, but the Tsarina and the Manchu emperor also chose sides. The result was that Ceren Dondukh in 1731 became khan. He was weak, ineffectual, and a drunkard. Immediately his rivals fought against him; by 1735 he was ousted. Dondukh Ombu, a strong leader, took command of the Kalmyks, but at his death in 1741 the whole divisive succession problem arose again. During all of this time the Kalmyks were attacking and being attacked by the Kazakhs. There was no time for a relaxation of vigilance. The Russians and the Kalmyks remained allied out of necessity in order to fend off their common enemies.

Gradually, Russian control over the Kalmyks became increasingly tighter. Even under capable leaders such as Dondukh Dashi, who ruled from 1757 to 1761, the independence that the Kalmyks were formerly able to exert was being eroded. The final break with the Russians came under Ubashi, Dondukh Dashi's son. The period since the death of Ayuuki was characterized by the Russian government's increased participation in Kalmyk affairs, and it was to end in the return of the majority of the Kalmyks to Dzungaria.

Russian control began with the Russian government appropriating to itself the right to confirm the khan and his deputies. From there it moved to actually appointing the Kalmyk rulers. The Russians then set up a council to further dilute the power of an individual strong leader. All decisions were ultimately subject to the approval of the Russian government. Finally Ubashi and the Kalmyk princes had enough of the Russian interference in their affairs and they decided to migrate back to their former homeland of Dzungaria.

This journey was not to be easy. Even the weather seemed to be against the Kalmyks. In the winter of 1770 the Kalmyks planned to begin their move east; however, the weather was too warm for the Volga to freeze. January came and the group of Kalmyks on the west side of the Volga still could not cross. Fearing that the Russians would discover their plot, the Kalmyks east of the river, 33,000 families, decided that they could wait no longer and began their journey to the east on January 5, 1771.

The migration was to take a tremendous toll on the Kalmyks. They were attacked by the Russians, the Kazakhs, and the Kirghiz. Both cattle and humans came down with several diseases. They had to cross waterless plains, drinking the blood of their cattle to survive. When they finally reached Dzungaria, 70,000 people survived out of the 33,000 families with a population of 169,000, which started the trip.

There were about 13,000 families which had been caught on the wrong side of the Volga, and thus did not have a choice of leaving. As can be imagined, Catherine the Great was not pleased by the actions of the Kalmyks. During the period after 1771, the Russians succeeded in a further integration of the Kalmyks into their empire. The Kalmyks were now, of course, greatly weakened both politically and militarily. To add to their troubles, many of the Kalmyks remaining in Russian territory joined in the Cossack rebellion under the "False Tsar" Pugachev, which swept from the Ukraine to the Urals in 1773.

Catherine the Great, in retaliation, further weakened the Kalmyks. Rule was taken from the Torghuts and given to the Dörbet tribe of Kalmyks. Since the exodus of the majority of Kalmyks in 1771, the title of khan had been abolished by the Tsarina and a deputy khan was the highest ranking Kalmyk. The deputy khan was of course appointed by the Russians. The Kalmyks were subordinated to various Russian ministries, and the Russian administration permeated even to the very lowest levels of the Kalmyk political structure.

Those Kalmyks, who remained after the flight of the majority to Dzungaria, kept for another century their pastoral existence, nomadizing in the pastures between the Don and the Volga. The Kalmyks had almost no agriculture; they remained primarily herders through two-thirds of the 19th century. The Kalmyks were able to trade their horses and the raw pastoral products, such as hides to the Russians. In return they received grain, textiles, metals, and most importantly brick tea, a Kalmyk staple.

By the last third of the 19th century, the Stavropol and Don Kalmyks began to undergo a substantial change in their lifestyle. Agriculture began to be developed and became a major factor in the total economy of the region. Thus the Kalmyks changed to a much more sedentary civilization. Although they still kept to pastoralism, it was now in combination with agriculture. At the same time great areas of land were occupied by Russian peasants, and brought under cultivation and more and more of the Kalmyks also turned to farming. The only type of livestock which was able to hold its own and even increase with an expansion of agriculture was horned cattle. With more and more Kalmyks giving up their traditional nomadic lifestyle, it became easier for them to be Russianized.

The Convention of Dolonnor in 1691 at which the Khalkha khans agreed to come under the power of the Manchus marked the end of Khalkha Mongol independence for more than the next 200

years. It did not, however, mark the end of warfare in Outer
Mongolia. The Oirats continued to control Khalkha territory,
and even after Galdan (the Oirat leader) was defeated in 1696
by the Manchus, the Oirats continued their warfare in Outer
Mongolia. The Khalkha submission to the Manchus did not solve
the problem for which the submission was made. Instead a whole
new set of irritants and problems resulted.

The Manchus did not impose a difficult overlordship on the
Mongols, at least not in the beginning. The Manchus regarded
the Mongols as a very important auxiliary military force and
made great use of them as such, at first against the Oirat, and
later as border guards on the Mongol-Russian frontier. The
Khalkhas also gave service on the relay stations and even on
military posts within the Mongol territory. The Manchus were
entirely in charge of Mongol foreign relations from this time
on.18

The Manchus initiated several actions in order to help
control the Mongols. From 1697 onward there were marriage
alliances between the Ch'ing ruling family and the Khalkhas. In
this way the Manchus hoped to exert some means of control over
the Mongols. Another step in the weakening of the Khalkhas was
the breaking up of the power of the Khalkha khans. There were
three Khalkha khanates when the Manchus gained control. In 1725
a fourth khanate was formed, the Sain Noyon khanate, out of the
Tüshetü khan's realm. By the eighteenth century the Manchus had
further split up the power of the khans by creating a number of
banners, and these held the same power as the khans. In this

way the source of Mongol power was more and more decentralized.

Buddhism, which entered Mongolia from Tibet, had been greatly strengthened in terms of power and prestige among the Khalkhas. This power was centered in one man, the Jebtsundamba Khutukhtu. The first Jebtsundamba Khutukhtu was born in Khalkha in 1635, the son of the Tüshetü khan. The Ondor gegen, as he was known by the Mongols, was looked on as their spiritual leader, but because of his tremendous religious prestige, he also wielded great temporal power as well, especially since he was also a part of Mongol nobility tracing his lineage back to Chinggis. When the second Jebtsundamba Khutukhtu was discovered also to have been reincarnated in the Chinggisid line, the Manchus realized how potentially dangerous the combination of religious prestige and noble Mongol birth could be.[19]

The Ch'ing emperor decreed with the death of the second Jebtsundamba Khutukhtu in 1759 that future incarnations were no longer to be discovered in Mongolia, but confined to the Tibetans. Manchu policy thus strove in yet another way to limit the possibility of any one Khalkha Mongol from being in a position of too much power.

Up until the middle of the 18th century the territory of the Khalkhas had been a battleground. The Oirats had penetrated as far as Erdeni Dzu on several occasions. Even when the Oirats were not invading Khalkha territory, they still were a costly menace to the Khalkhas. The Khalkhas were expected by the Manchus to be the military force to hold back the Oirats. In addition, the Khalkha had to supply the mounts for these armies. A tremendous number of animals were required and the depletion that this caused the Khalkhas would be felt for decades.

In 1691 Galdan of the Oirats was at the height of his power. He had successfully defeated the Khalkha princes, but he had also driven these princes into the arms of the Manchus. At the Convention of Dolonnor the khans and nobles of the Khalkha submitted themselves to Manchu rule. The Oirats now stood alone. They could not rely on any kind of agreement with any of the eastern Mongols. The Inner Mongolians had already submitted to the Manchus in 1634. With no possibility of any other eastern Mongol support, the Oirats were the remaining Mongol power to be reckoned with by the Manchus.

Even when faced with such a formidable opponent as the Ch'ing, the Oirats could not settle their own internal differences, and it was these internal feuds, which were to destroy Galdan and in the end, bring down the independent Oirat empire. Galdan was strong enough to launch a campaign and overrun Khalkha territory in 1695 despite the Khalkha-Manchu alliance. Galdan's loss to the Manchus in 1696 was due more to family insurrection than to the Manchus. Galdan's nephew, Tsewang Rabtan, attacked Galdan from the rear while he engaged in warfare in Khalkha territory. Galdan died in 1697 having been cut off from his source of power on the Ili.[20] A man once in charge of a large empire was now relegated to spending his last year on futile plundering raids.

Neither the defeat of Galdan nor his death put an end to the Oirat empire. It remained a challenge to the Manchus for the next sixty years. Although the Manchus had to be wary of their western frontier, the main confrontation between Oirats and Manchus was shifted to Tibet. The Dzungar Oirats had been intimately involved in Tibet since Gushi khan helped the Fifth Dalai Lama come to power in the 1640s. The Dzungar kept their connection with Tibet throughout the Fifth Dalai Lama's reign and after his death Galdan and the Tibetan regent, Sangs-rgyas rGya-mtsho continued a close relationship.

The Dzungars were the Manchus' strongest Asian enemy at this time. Their need to defeat the Dzungars brought them more and more into Tibetan affairs. The Oirats themselves proved to be their own worst enemies. The Khoshut, another Oirat tribe, who were led by Lha-bzang khan, allied with the Manchu emperor K'ang-Hsi. Backed by the support of the emperor, Lha-bzang marched on Lhasa in 1705 and defeated the regent. Lha-bzang ruled Tibet until 1717, and Tibet was during this period a formal vassal of China. The Tibetans, outraged at Lha-bzang's hostility to the rightful Dalai Lama, could only turn to one possible ally, the Dzungars. Thus Oirat once again was to face Oirat.

Hostilities had continued between Dzungar and Manchu during the opening of the 18th century. Dzungar intervention in Tibet only furthered the spread of the conflict. Tsewang Rabtan viewed the Khoshut-Manchu alliance as a great threat, and in

1715 open warfare broke out once again between the Dzungars and Manchus. The Dzungars first lulled Lha-bzang into letting down his guard by offering a marriage alliance to him. Then they launched an attack which successfully installed them as rulers of Lhasa once again in 1717. The Dzungar conquerors turned into pillagers and looters and by 1720 when the Manchus arrived to retake Lhasa, they were viewed as rescuers by the Tibetans.

The loss of power in Tibet, while a bitter blow for the Dzungars, was not a fatal one. Tsewang Rabtan was able to send troops against the Manchus until his death in 1727. The death of the Dzungar ruler was taken by the Manchus as the proper moment for ending Dzungar strength once and for all. However, leadership of the Dzungars was taken over very capably by Galdan Tsering. The Ch'ing launched several attacks on the Dzungars. However, even though the Ch'ing met with some success, they also sustained significant loses during this time. After their victories the Dzungars launched further devastating raids on the Khalkha territory, and even succeeded as far eastward as Erdeni Dzu in 1732. The Dzungars then overextended themselves and were dealt a severe defeat in 1734.

Galdan Tsering continued his fight with the Manchus with only minor periods of peace until he finally made peace with the Ch'ing just before his death in 1745. His death brought on a struggle for succession, which disrupted the momentary Dzungar-Manchu peace. The Emperor Ch'ien Lung moved strongly to settle this dispute and finally bring control to the Ili and the Dzungars. By 1754 he was able to defeat the Dzungar ruler, and send him fleeing westward.

Amursana rallied the remaining Dzungars to him, but the Manchus finally decisively put an end to Dzungar power. The Ili River region which had been the center of power was occupied from 1757. Soon afterwards Ch'ing control was firmly established over the Tarim Basin right up to the Pamir Mountains. The Ch'ing conquest of the region is reputed to have taken the lives of over a million Oirats. These figures are to be viewed as an exaggeration, but loss of life must certainly have been high.

The Upper Ili was repopulated by some Chinese, but a large portion of the resettlement was with other Oirats. In 1771 the Western Mongols, fleeing increasing pressure from the Russian Tsar, left the Volga steppe, and moved back into their old home territory on the Ili. These Oirats were resettled there by the Ch'ing and they became subjects of the Manchus.

Chapter I - Footnotes

1. History of the Mongolian People's Republic, p. 155

2. Grousset, Empire of the Steppes, p. 503

3. Rossabi, China and Inner Asia, pp. 42-43

4. Serruys, The Tribute System and Diplomatic Missions
    (1400-1600)
    p. 8

5. Grousset, Empire of the Steppes, pp. 505-506

6. Serruys, "Notes on a Few Mongolian Rulers of the 15th
    Century", pp. 82-83

7. Serruys, The Tribute System . . . op cit. p.506

8. Rossabi, op cit. p.34

9. ibid p. 44

10. Serruys, "Notes ...", op cit. p. 84

11. Okada, "Outer Mongolia in the Sixteenth and Seventeenth
    Centuries", p. 73

12. Grousset, op cit. p.512

13. Okada, op cit. p. 79

14. Rossabi, op cit. p. 113

15. Bawden, The Modern History of Mongolia, pp. 63-65

16. ibid. pp. 72-80

17. Howorth, History of the Mongols, Part I, pp. 478-482

18. Rossabi, op cit. pp. 124-132

19. Bawden, op cit. pp.132-134

20. Courant, L'Asie Centrale, pp. 62-63

Chapter II

The Oirat Historical Documents

Due to the importance of the western Mongol peoples to
many areas of world history, it is not surprising that much
material has been written on one or another aspect of their
history. What is surprising is that the native Oirat primary
historical sources have not been fully utilized in studying
Oirat history.

Although much use has been made of indigenous eastern
Mongol sources in dealing with historical problems concerning
the eastern Mongols and the Mongolian People's Republic,
primary sources written by Oirats about their own history have
been less well utilized. In this respect, Oirat sources can be
considered the "poor relations" of Mongolian historical
studies. Professor John R. Krueger summarizes the situation
clearly: "Although Written Oirat literature, with concomitant
study of history, language and culture, ought to form a branch
of Mongolistics nearly as large as sister studies in Written
Mongolian do, it has somehow never received as much attention.
In the first place, it covers a much more limited time span,
and second, has a naturally smaller literature, which to large
degree merely parallels that of standard Mongolian Buddhist
writings. Third, there are fewer study aids and less

accessibility to texts in collections and libraries."[1]

While it is true that there are not as many historical texts in Oirat[2] as in Mongol, it is also true that the historical texts which do exist in Oirat have been much less used than other Mongol historical documents. During the past two decades, scholars in the Mongolian People's Republic have published a number of important Oirat documents, thus making accessible some basic materials for the first time.[3] A number of Mongol scholars have also been actively working in the Oirat field, including the late Prof. Dr. Rinchen, Kh. Luvsanbaldan, and Zh. Tsoloo.[4] Spurred on by the 320th anniversary of the invention of the Oirat script (todo üsüg) in 1968, Kalmyk scholars within the Soviet Union have recently produced a number of new works dealing with Oirat studies and Oirat history.[5]

In terms of Western scholarship, a number of smaller Oirat historical works have been recently translated. These include an article by Professor Joseph Fletcher which surveys Oirat materials,[6] although to a lesser extent than Professor Krueger, and a number of translations dealing with Oirat history by the latter.[7] The larger Oirat historical works, however, have not as yet been studied in the detail needed to give an accurate account of the Oirats from their own sources.

Two of these sources for Oirat history are very traditional. They are not unlike other Mongolian histories in that they stress the genealogies of the various tribes. The oldest of these sources is the Dörbön Oyirodiyin Tööke (History of the Four Oirats) by Emci Ghabang Shes Rab (this text will be abbreviated to GS in further references), written in 1737.[8] Other Oirat works naturally incorporate much information from the GS. This is especially true of the second genealogical-type history, the Xoshuud Noyon Bātur Ubashi Tümeni Tuurbiqsan Dörbön Oyiradiyin Tööke (The History of the Four Oirats Composed by the Khoshuud Prince Batur Ubashi Tümen). This work was written in 1819, and will be abbreviated DO.[9]

Another Oirat source containing valuable historical data but not normally considered an historical document is a collection of Oirat law documents, the Mongolo-oiratskie zakony (this work will be abbreviated MOZ).[10] This work, which was edited by Golstunskii, not only contains the law code of 1640, but those of Ghaldan Khung Tayiji dating to 1678 and of Dondukh Dashi of 1741-1753 as well. The other major Oirat law codes which should be mentioned are the Jinjil decrees of 1822.[11] Since these law codes cover a span of over 180 years, they provide basic materials toward a history of law among the Oirats. More than this, however, they outline the social, political, and religious conditions of the times as well as any strictly historical source could.

Still another work, not strictly a history in the Western sense, but the source for much historical information, is the Biography of Zaya Pandita (hereafter abbreviated ZPB).[12] While biographies of religious personages understandably stress the religious aspects of an individual's life, they also can bring out many historical facts. The Oirat tribe which was to play the largest role in Tibetan affairs during the middle of the 17th century was the Khoshuud. Since Zaya Pandita was born into this tribe in 1599 and lived until 1662, it is not surprising to find that he witnessed the effects of Oirat influences on Tibetan affairs during this time. The biography of Zaya Pandita was written around 1690 and constitutes another early Oirat historical source.[13]

Another type of material dealing with Oirat history is to be found in the Oirat epic Monggholiyin Ubashi Khün Tayijiyin Tuuji Orshiboi (Contained Herein is the History of Ubashi Khün Tayiji of the Mongols, hereafter abbreviated to UBXT),[14] a work also known under the title Dörbön Oyirid Moggholi Daruqsan Touji Kemēkü (The History of the Defeat of the Mongols by the Four Oirats).[15] While this work is epic in nature, it does shed light on certain aspects of history, and it discusses one definite historical event, the battle on the Irtysh, in which the Oirat defeated Ubashi Khün Tayiji.[16]

The last of the sources to be discussed here is the Khalimaq khādiyin tuujiyigi khurāji biciqsen tobci oroshibai (There is contained herein the Concise Written Collection of the History of the Kalmyk Khans, hereafter abbreviated to HKK).[17] This work, which thus far cannot be dated,[18] and whose author is unknown, is the closest of any of the Oirat works to a Western-style history.

As can be seen, a corpus of Oirat historical materials

does indeed exist. Although one might arrive at a different
conclusion when perusing the works of some authors writing on
the subject, C.D. Barkman, in an article which makes good use
of non-Oirat materials, states, "The history of the 'Kalmucks'
or Western Mongols has yet to be written. It is a fascinating
one, but the task of the historican is not made any easier by
the paucity of materials from Mongol sources..."[19] Barkman does
not use any Oirat materials in his work. Even those scholars
who realize the existence of Oirat historical documents have
not made use of these texts. For example, Pelliot, in his _Notes_
critiques _d'histoire_ _kalmouke_, relies almost exclusively on
Chinese sources in a work brought out posthumously. Although
noting the existence of Oirat materials, he ignores them.
Perhaps if Pelliot had lived to publish his work, he might yet
have dealt with these texts differently.[20]

The fact that Oirat sources have not recently been made
use of directly, does not mean that the information contained
therein has not been incorporated in an indirect manner. A
number of early works on the Oirats made use of either oral
recountings of traditional Oirat materials or of the Oirat
texts themselves.[21] These works were then used by succeeding
generations of scholars so that materials from Oirat sources
have, to some extent, been incorporated into Western
scholarship.

Pallas in particular knew the Oirat historical documents.
He mentions specifically the work of Ghabang Shes Rab,[22] and it
is clear from the material which Pallas presents that he made

extensive use of this Oirat work, especially for the genealogical information he records. Pallas knew of other Oirat historical materials, although he did not specifically refer to them.[23] Both Bergmann and Pallas received much of their information from Kalmyks, who in turn drew on their traditional historical sources. Thus two of the works most used by Western scholars include material from Oirat sources, a fact that has gone unnoticed.

Even with this indirect inclusion of some Oirat material, it is obvious that these native sources require greater study. The most interesting of the Oirat texts in terms of Western historiography is the HKK. Two translations of this work exist in Russian.[24] However, the translations of Lytkin, which are over 100 years old, are neither adequate nor reliable. Professor Krueger, in commenting on these translations, states, "Undoubtedly, all of these works are of some use and interest, even if not wholly accurate. Of the two Oirat texts that I have myself at present actually read in whole or part (Zaya Pandita Biography, Tale of Four Oirats), I must state that the translations do not seem very good, in that they skip over the hard phrases, make omissions, or are incorrect."[25] The more recent translation by Bayanova is without annotation. It accepts the sometimes mistaken dating of the HKK.[26]

In the third chapter of this work the author will give a translation of the HKK. The rest of this chapter will be devoted to the study of the position of the HKK in Oirat historiography. As noted above, the HKK is an historical text of great interest, in some ways unique among Oirat histories, as it differs from the traditional Mongol or Oirat historiography. Although it contains genealogical information, this is not the dominant feature in the HKK.

The HKK is closer to being a narrative history in the Western sense than any other Oirat chronicle. The text begins with the migration of the Torghuud to the Volga in 1618 and proceeds in chronological order, with some deviations, through the migration of the Oirats from the Volga to Dzungaria in 1771. It ends in 1775 with these western Mongols happily settled in Dzungaria.

While the text does give a much more straightforward narration of events than do any of the other Oirat historical sources, it should be noted that some traditional elements remain. These will be pointed out later. The text also draws, as we shall see, on earlier Oirat historical material. As noted above,[27] the text of the HKK is to be found in Pozdneyev's chresthomathy. To the author's knowledge, no manuscript of this work is extant. There is a problem of reliability and accuracy when dealing with a text which has been put into print and for which no manuscript exists or is available to check the accuracy of the typeset version. This problem in dealing with texts of Pozdneyev has been noted previously by Professor Krueger: "Unfortunately, printed texts and transcribed texts, if the originals are no longer accessible, can suffer from an enormous flaw, which one may be inclined to forget, namely, that we are at the mercy of the earlier editor. Today in some cases, we have no way of knowing how accurately the editor read or misread. One would expect high standards of Pozdneyev, but it is definitely known that the spellings he employs in his dictionary differ from the original texts, ..."28 In a more recent article Professor Krueger spells out more clearly his views of Pozdneyev's handling of texts: "However, I also feel that Pozdneyev's accuracy can be trusted--he did adjust the spelling in his documents, but he did not restore texts to say something different insofar as I can tell."29

There is one way in which Pozdneyev's work can be checked. In cases where it can be proven that the HKK has relied on an earlier source, and if the prior work is extant, it would be possible to compare the HKK with the earlier source for accuracy. Since the HKK has used a number of sources still available, this methodology is indeed possible. A study of these earlier texts (the MOZ, GS, and DO) can leave no doubt of the overall accuracy of Pozdneyev. Specific examples will be given later in this chapter.

As mentioned earlier, the term Oirat takes in a number of tribes. The number and position of these tribes has been debated.30 However, it is interesting to note that the two traditional Oirat historical sources, the GS and the DO, as well as the HKK, focus their interest on one tribe of the Oirats, the Torghuud. This is not to say that the other tribes receive no attention. They are discussed and sometimes, particularly in the GS and the DO, mentioned extensively. The GS and DO, as we shall see, give genealogoies for the Khoyid,

Choros, Dörböd, Khoshuud, and Dzungars, in addition to the
Torghuud. But more stress is given to the latter, in particular
to Ayuuki Khan of the Torghuud, in the non-genealogical
sections of the GS and DO.

Since the Torghuud were the leading Oirat tribe on the
Volga, and the first tribe to move westward out of Dzungaria,
it should be of no surprise that they are discussed in greater
detail. And since Ayuuki had the longest rule (1670-1722) of
any of the Torghuud, his prominence is also explained. What is
surprising is the relatively minor position which the Dzungars
are accorded by these texts, although they played an important
role on the eastern steppes. This is because these texts are
concerned with the western rather than the eastern end of the
steppe.

This emphasis on the west is particularly striking in the
HKK. By far the greatest part of this text deals with relations
between the Oirats and Russia. There is also, of course, much
information concerning the Oirats and their relations with
other peoples of the western steppes, the Crimea, the Caucasus,
and the Volga regions. It is true that the most dramatic and
well-known event concerning the Torghuud, the immigration from
the Volga to Dzungaria in 1771, ends in Manchu territory.[31] But
the HKK places the emphasis on the events leading up to the
migration and on the flight itself, rather than on life in
Dzungaria. Only about 5 percent of the text deals with the
Oirats under Manchu control. This amounts to approximately 20
lines out of a total of 391 lines of text.

As already mentioned, the HKK employs techniques quite common in Western historiography but not normally found in Oirat histories. None of the Oirat sources except for the HKK makes an attempt to place events in chronological order. Other innovations it contributes to the field of Oirat historiography include evaluative judgements concerning the reigns of a number of khans. The rule of Ayuuki in particular is singled out for evaluation.32

Ayuuki's reign is given high praise and his accomplishments are noted in a long laudatory passage. In addition, he is mentioned in a number of other places as having been able to get the better of the Russians, and as being able to avenge himself on the Russians by outwitting them. The text states: "I am not able to fight with the Tatars of Kuban without orders from the supreme khan.' By this reply [Ayuuki] took in this way his own revenge. The title of khan was not bestowed, but [Ayuuki] acquired it by his own deeds of intellect and virtue."

The Kalmyks considered Ayuuki to be independent of the Russians. This point is stressed, being mentioned not just in the above instance, but also in another passage: "The Dalai Lama Gegen bestowed the title of khan on Ayuuki and presented the seal to him....Ayuuki, although a subject of the Russian tsar, did not inform him and took such a high honor through his own power."33 The pride that the Kalmyks felt for Ayuuki's ability in dealing with the Russians comes through very clearly.

This text, on the other hand, is not very critical of the problems that Ayuuki faced during his reign, such as his major disagreement with his son Phyaqdar Byab in 1701. There was even an assassination attempt on Phyaqdar Byab, who was forced to flee across the Ural river.[34] This incident had major repercussions, since it was this enmity between Ayuuki's sons which helped foster the power struggle that took place just prior to Ayuuki's death. In fact, the HKK says that Ayuuki died sick at heart because of this internecine warfare.[35] Thus Ayuuki's reign was not as successful as the HKK would have us believe.

Ayuuki was not the only khan to receive praise in the HKK. Dondukh Dashi was also treated in a laudatory fashion. He was particularly praised for his law code,[36] a supplement to the code of 1640. The HKK states: "Dondukh Dashi thought that he would make increase literacy and knowledge among his own subjects with a law like that. This is the proof that he had great intelligence and desired the happiness of his subjects."[37]

However, not all of the rulers are praised. For example, Ceren Dondukh is judged particularly harshly. At one point, we read: "Because Ceren Dondukh was an ineffectual man with little strength, he did not resolve the quarrels among the Kalmyks."[38] Later, in discussing Ceren Dondukh's loss of the khanship, the text states: "As for Ceren Dondukh, his subjects and zaisangs complained that he was unable to rule being under the influence of alcohol."39

The HKK shows development over other Oirat texts in that it presents a motivation for an action. The migration from the Volga to Dzungaria is not just described, but the political reasons for this action are stated. The Russians have forced Ubashi to give up much of his power as khan, and this is viewed as leading directly to the movement of the Kalmyks from Russia.40 The other reason hinted at in the text is the fear that the Kalmyks, surrounded by non-believers, might become weakened in their Buddhist belief. This is why the Lamaist community was so agreeable to the move.41 Ubashi acknowledges the importance of the religion in his final thoughts on leaving for Dzungaria. "Besides this, if the Kalmyks arrive healthy in Dzungaria after having prayed to our all-saving Buddha, we shall be dwelling near the most blessed illumined saints and the Tibetan area, the holy sea of religious doctrine which is the basis of happiness in this and future rebirths."42

There are a number of other sections of the text which discuss the motivations for carrying out an action. One concerns the return of Rabjuuri from the Manchu court. The Tülishen mission was viewed by the HKK as trying to ally the Kalmyks with the Manchus against the Dzungars. "Although [the Chinese embassy] said, 'We came seeking [permission] from Tsar Peter...' there were other reasons."43

One other incident concerning the Manchus illustrates the

motivational element exhibited by the HKK. It ascribes the fact
that the Russians made Ceren Dondukh khan directly on their
learning that the Manchus were about to bestow the title on
him. To counteract this Manchu influence, the Russians were
forced to present the title to him.44

Apart from the flight from the Volga, the HKK devotes more
space to the investiture of Dondukh Dashi than to any other
single event. The detailed description given of this episode is
unlike anything found in any other Oirat source. The entire
section covers 60 lines, over 15 percent of the text.45 The
main events of the investiture ceremony take place between
April 28 and May 3, 1757. Nowhere else in the sources is so
much reported about such a short time span. More is written
concerning the migration, but this event goes on for over a
year. The lengthy investiture description, relating the
intricacies of diplomacy, shows a great development, in the
Western sense, in the writing of this historical text.

One aspect which differentiates Oirat historiography from
its Western counterpart is its total ethnocentricity. The HKK
is the first Oirat text to discuss an event which lies in some
way outside Oirat interest. "At that time the great tsar Peter
of Russia, in person, wanted to go to foreign lands, and learn
all the various arts and sciences, and afterwards to instruct
his own subjects."46 Although the tsar's trip abroad had some
repercussions on the Kalmyks, because in his absence Ayuuki was
called upon to defend Russia's southern border, no other Oirat
text would have mentioned Peter's trip. The Oirats, in the HKK,

demonstrate a grasp of historical events outside of their own sphere of interest.

The HKK shows traces of influence of foreign languages, although to a smaller degree than might be expected. Only a few Russian words are found in the text, most of them geographical names or titles such as "warrant officer" and "colonel."[47] There is also one Chinese word in the text, xanza.[48] The number of foreign words in this text is certainly much lower than in the DO.

Besides genealogical material, the older historical texts include legendary material, and a great number of aphorisms or maxims uttered by Oirat leaders. An example, which shows that a ruler should accept the title khan in a humble manner, occurs in the HKK, 4.06-4.07. When Shikür Dayicing is offered the khanship by the Dalai Lama, he gives it back saying, "There are many like me. What kind of khan would I be?" This story can be found in the DO, 33.14-33.15, and in the earlier GS, 82.6-82.9. Both of these texts relate this same incident with almost the same words, an excellent example of how the later HKK made use of material taken from earlier sources.

The DO is the source for the next example of linkage between the HKK and the older sources. The HKK discusses in detail the birth of Tümen Jirghal.[49] It also reports on the reason for selecting this name. Neither Dejid and Ölzöi Oroshixu, the parents of the child, nor the boy himself, are important enough in Oirat history to warrant much mention. In fact, no other birth is given an extensive notice in the HKK. The inclusion of this event and of further episodes in the life of Tümen Jirghal necessitates a digression in the straightforward chronology of events recounted in the HKK. The material about Tümen Jirghal is to be found in the DO,[50] and was incorporated into the HKK. The information was not of primary importance to the events related in the HKK,[51] but since it appeared in another Oirat source it was inserted in the most appropriate place in the HKK.

Another Oirat source from which extensive quotations are taken is the MOZ. As noted earlier in this chapter, the investiture of Dondukh Dashi as khan is thoroughly described. The other major event of this reign, discussed at length in the HKK, is his supplement to the Oirat law codes.[52] The HKK does not merely note the compiling of the new code, nor is it content to describe it. Instead, large passages are quoted directly from the MOZ.[53] These sections from the code are not mentioned in order, but they are presented accurately.

Thus it is clear that even though the HKK is a departure from earlier Oirat historiography, it is still dependent on them. The HKK, while adding much new material, has also utilized much that is found in the older sources. The further chapters of this work will be devoted to a translation of the HKK, and to a discussion of the interrelationships of these early Oirat historical materials.

CHAPTER II - FOOTNOTES

1.   John R. Krueger, "Written Oirat and Kalmyk Studies,"
     Mongolian Studies, Vol. 2, 1975, p. 93. In this article,
     Prof. Krueger discusses the state of Oirat studies and the
     directions in which it should develop. This work brings up
     to date the earlier work of Nikolaus Poppe, "Stand der
     Kalmückenforschung," Wiener Zeitschrift für die Kunde des
     Morgenlandes, Vol. LII, 1955, pp. 346-379.

2.   See John R. Krueger, "Oirat Literary Resources and
     Problems of Oirat Lexicography," American Oriental Society
     Middle West Branch Semi-centennial Volume, pp. 134-157,
     for a listing of Oirat materials.

3.   These works include: Rabjamba caya bandida-yin tughuji
     saran-u gerel kemekü ene metü bolai (Corpus Scriptorum
     Mongolorum, Vol. 5, No. 2, 1959). "Biography of Caya
     Pandita in Oirat Characters," edited by Zh. Tsoloo, who
     has transcribed and indexed the texts (Corpus Scriptorum
     Mongolorum, Vol. 5, Nos. 2-3, 1967). This same volume also
     contains the Dörbön oyirodiyin Töüke, by Emci Ghabang Shes
     Rab and a letter by Davaach Qaan, along with two
     unidentified pages of Oirat. See also Krueger, "Written
     Oirat and Kalmyk Studies," p. 98.

4.   For further information on the works these scholars have
     produced, see Krueger, "Written Oirat and Kalmyk Studies."

5.   Ibid.

6.   Joseph Fletcher, "An Oyirod Letter in the British Museum,"
     Mongolian Studies (ed. L. Ligeti, Budapest, 1970,
     Bibliotheca Orientalis Hungarica), pp. 129-136. See also
     Krueger's remarks on this work in "Written Oirat and
     Kalmyk Studies," p. 95.

7.   These works by John R. Krueger include: "Three
     Oirat-Mongolian Diplomatic documents of 1691," CAJ, 12,
     No. 4, 1969, pp.286-295; "The Ch'ien-lung Inscriptions of
     1755 and 1758 in Oirat-Mongolian," CAJ, 16, No. 1, 1972,
     pp. 59-69; "New Materials on Oirat Law and History," Part
     I, "The Jinjil Decrees," CAJ, No. 3, 1972, pp. 194-205 and
     Part II, "The Origin of the Torgouts," CAJ, 18, No.1,
     1974, pp. 30-42. The above works are all mentioned by
     Krueger in "Written Oirat and Kalmyk Studies," pp.
     106-107. An additional work by Krueger is entitled "Two
     Imperial Decrees to the Kalmyks (1735 and 1828)," UAJ, 47,
     pp. 119-123. A more recent work by Krueger appeared in
     Tractata Altaica: Denis Sinor, sexagenario optime de rebus
     Altaicis merito dedicata, edited by Walther Heissig et
     al., 1976, entitled "A Decree on the Origins of Lamaism
     Among the Kalmyks (1756)," pp. 355-364.

8. For the dating of this text see GS 97.12 and 97.13. The citation for this text is given above in footnote 3.

9. For the dating of this text see DO 24.02-24.15. The DO is found on pages 24-43 of Pozdneyev's Kalmytskaya khrestomatiya. The DO is the second text in this work and has been given the Russian title Skazanie o dörben Oiratakh.

10. The law codes are found in K. Th. Golstunskii, Mongolo-oiratskie zakony 1640 goda ... (St. Petersburg, 1880).

11. See footnote 7 above for Krueger's work on the Jinjil decrees. Valentin A. Riasanovsky gives a translation of sections of some of these law codes in Fundamental Principles of Mongol Law, pp. 92-111 and has an entire section on Kalmyk law in his work Customary Law of the Mongols, pp. 264-287.

12. See footnote 3 above for the citation for this work.

13. For the dating of this biography cf. Ce. Damdisürüng, Mongghol Uran Jokial-un Degeji Jaghun Bilig Orusibai (Ulanbator, 1959), p. 327.

14. This work is found in a supplement to Galsang Gomboyev's edition of the Altan Tobci (St. Petersburg, 1858). The UBXT is given the Russian title: Istoriya Ubashi-khuntaidzhiya i yego voiny s oiratami, pp. 198-212.

15. A manuscript of this work copied by Julg is in Tubingen, see Heissig, Mongolische Handschriften, Blockdrucke, Landkarten (Wiesbaden, 1961), work number 8. For a further reference to the other typeset copies of this text see Krueger, "Oirat literary resources and problems of Oirat lexicography," p. 140.

16. The problems surrounding the dating of this text are fully discussed below, in chapter IV.

17. The text for this work is found in Pozdneyev's Kalmytskaya khrestomatiya, pp. 1-23. There are three editions of this work. They were published in St. Petersburg in 1892, 1907, and 1915. See Krueger, "Written Oirat and Kalmyk Studies," p. 94 for a discussion of the editions of this work. The chrestomathy gives this work the Russian title Kratkaya Istoriya Kalmytskikh Khanov. The edition used here is from the 1892 work.

18. The last date mentioned in the text itself is 1787 (HKK 13.01). However, later in this chapter (notes 50 and 51) material in the HKK will be shown to have been from the DO. Thus the HKK must have been composed after 1819, the composition date for the DO.

19. C.D. Barkman, "The Return of the Torghuts from Russia to China," p. 89.

20. Paul Pelliot, Notes critiques d'histoire Kalmouke. See p. 81 for sources containing Oirat material.

21. The basic works which fall into this category include: Sammlungen historischer Nachrichten über die mongolischen Völkerschaften, by P.S. Pallas, St. Petersburg, Vol. I, 1776, Vol. II, 1801, and Benjamin Bergmann's Nomadische Streifereien unter den Kalmuken in den Jahren 1802 und 1803, Riga, 1804.

22. See Pallas, Sammlungen, Vol. I, p. 56.

23. Op. cit., p. 6

24. Yu. Lytkin translated some of the major Oirat historical works which have been noted above. These include, besides the HKK, the DO, the GS, and the ZPB. These translations were done in the middle of the 19th century, but have recently been reprinted in Kalmytskie istoriko-literaturnye pamyatniki v russkom perevode (Elista, 1969). For further information on this work see Krueger, "Written Oirat and Kalmyk Studies, " pp.95 and 96. A more recent unannotated translation has been published privately in pamphlet form. The translation is by D.N. Bayanova, "Kratkaya istoriya Kalmytskikh Khanov."

25. Krueger, "Written Oirat and Kalmyk Studies," p. 96.

26. See chapter III, footnote 32, below, for the correct dating of the event listed by the HKK as occurring in 1677. Bayanova, "Kratkaya istoriya...," p. 9, uses the 1677 date.

27. See footnote 17 above.

28. John R. Krueger, "Oirat literary resources and problems of Oirat lexicography," p. 147.

29. John R. Krueger, "A Decree on the Origins of Lamaism among the Kalmyks (1756)," p. 356.

30. For the most recent discussion of which tribes are included in the term Oirat, see Haneda Akira, "L'Histoire des Djounghar aux 16e et 17e siecles, Origine des Eleutes," UAJ, XLII, 1970, pp. 119-126, and for a work which sums up the earlier scholarship on the subject, see Pelliot, Notes critiques d'histoire Kalmouke, pp. 3-8.

31. This migration was made famous in the West by Thomas De Quincey in his work The Revolt of the Tartars: or, flight of the Kalmuck khan and his people from the Russian territories to the frontiers of China.

32. See HKK 8.16-9.01.

33. See HKK 4.07-4.08.

34. This incident is described in HKK 5.04-5.08.

35. See HKK 8.15-8.16.

36. A description of this law code is given in HKK 13.13-14.02. The full text of the Dondukh Dashi supplement is to be found in Golstunskii, MOZ 23.04-33.13.

37. See HKK 13.16-13.17.

38. See HKK 9.12-9.13.

39. See HKK 10.10-10.11.

40. For the Russian actions to try to weaken the position of the khan and Ubashi's response see HKK 18.08-18.17.

41. See HKK 18.16-18.17.

42. See HKK 19.03-19.04.

43. See HKK 6.15-6.17.

44. See HKK 9.15-10.01.

45. See HKK 14.04-17.12.

46. See HKK 4.12-4.13.

47. See HKK 16.11-16.12.

48. See HKK 23.11.

49. See HKK 12.09-12.10.

50. See DO 40.05-40.07.

51. For information concerning the reason for interest in Tümen Jirghal see chapter III, note 131.

52. See below chapter III, footnotes 144, 146, and 147 for additional information on the Dondukh Dashi supplement.

53. The passages of the MOZ which are quoted are noted in chapter III. q.v. chapter III below, notes 149, 150, 151, 153, 154, and 155.

Chapter III

A Translation of the History of the Kalmyk Khans

Contained herein is the concise written collection of the history of the Kalmyk khans.

The Kalmyk people, who are at the present time living in the vicinity of the Volga river,[1] are of the Mongol race and also have (share) one language and one religion with these (Mongols). They abandoned their own ancient motherland and settled in the center of Russia. At the time when a conflict arose among the Four Oirats of Dzungaria, Khō Orlȫkh was the tayishi of the Torghuud.[2] He thought to himself that, rather than destroying his own subjects by killing one another, it would be better to go to a distant land and dwell near people of foreign extraction, and war with them and take booty.

In the earth horse year (1618) good men were dispatched in the direction of the Caspian Sea.[3] These [men] learned definitely that uninhabited territory existed there. In the earth dragon year (1628), [Khō Orlȫkh] brought 50,000 households of his own Torghuud and Khoshuud and Dȫrbȫd subjects, and, accompanied by his six sons,[4] he abandoned his own territory of Dzungaria and moved westward.

Prior to their reaching the Ural river,[5] they subdued one

group of Tatars, who were camping beside the Embe river.[6] Crossing over the Ural river they subjugated the Tatars named Noghai, Khatai, Kipchakh and Jiteshen.[7] They arrived at the Volga river in the iron horse year (1630).[8] At that time at both the east and west sides of this river mouth, apart from small numbers of Tatars who were powerless to inflict harm on them, the area was not inhabited. Russian towns were small. In that place fresh grass and last year's grass were plentiful on the steppe. As for Khō Örlökh all the area from Astrakhan to Samara [Kuibyshev], /p.2/ from the Ural river up to the Volga, was made the permanent homeland of his own subjects, and they settled there since it was most suitable. Although this was the territory of the White Khan [Russian Tsar], Khō Örlökh neither informed him that he had taken possession of the territory, nor had he any intention of doing so.

Thus in the iron dragon year,[9] in the year[1640] the Forty and the Four ended their old quarrels and united themselves.[10] In the presence of the Shabayayin Toyin Ecege Inzan Rinbüce and Angshobiye Manjushiri, Amugha Sidhi Manjushri Khutukhtu Gegēn, the kings and princes headed by Erdeni Zasakhtu khan,[11] Tüsetü khan,[12] Güüsi Nomiyin khan,[13] and Erdeni Bātur Khung Tayiji[14] established the great law. Khō Örlökh[15] came and participated in the accomplishment of that joyful great work. [He] brought the established law to his own homeland and ruled his subjects according to it. Then when Khō Örlökh attacked the city of Astrakhan, the Russian people of that city attacked and drove out the Kalmyks. Kho Örlökh was captured in that battle.

During this time, two sons of Khō Orlōkh[16] named Lubzang and Yeldeng,[17] who had previously come from Dzungaria, conquered the Tatars. When the father (Khō Orlōkh) divided the inheritance, at that time, apart from having given his own Torghuud subjects to his own two sons he also gave them these same conquered Tatars. After Khō Orlōkh passed away, his eldest son Shikür Dayicing[18] was made chief tayishi. Through trickery, he took over control of the Nogai Tatars. These Tatars had been the subjects of his own younger brothers. Because of this a quarrel ensued, and Lubzang and Yeldeng lost all their own subjects.[19] Lubzang escaped into Tibet with a small number of people. It was reported that Güüsi khan[20] knew in advance that Yeldeng had lost his subjects.

After this [Shikür] Dayicing became ambitious and great damage was inflicted [by the Kalmyks] who warred on the Russian [territory]. The army which was dispatched from Russian Astrakhan crushed the Kalmyks. Many men were killed, and therefore [Shikür] Dayicing said, "Let us make peace with Russia."[21]

In the wood sheep year (1655) [Shikür Dayicing] sent Dural, Darkhan, and Ceren,[22] as important messengers to the Russian Tsar at Moscow. These messengers went and arrived [before the Tsar] carrying an oath. The Tayishi of the Kalmyks, Shikür Dayicing, together with princes and all the Kalmyk people gave a promise saying, "Let us be faithful subjects of Tsar Alikhsā Mikhalvaci [Aleksei Mikhailovich], let us not attack Astrakhan, let us not plunder anybody." /p.3/

Thereupon the Russian Tsar intended to fight with the Crimean [Tatars] and he asked for auxiliary soldiers from Shikür Dayicing. In the iron ox year (1661) Dayicing went together with his son named Puncokh,[23] and they joined the Russian troops and fought the Crimean [Tatars].

An oath was rendered to Prince Bek'ubci [Bekuvic], governor of Astrakhan, saying, "Let us send to the Russian Tsar whatever booty is taken." Puncokh, in taking the oath, bowed to the Buddha, kissed the object of veneration, the holy book and the relic, licked his own knife, brought the knife to his own throat and swore the oath.[24] Afterwards [Shikür] Dayicing passed on and Puncokh ruled.[25]

In this period Köndölöng Ubashi,[26] the tayishi of the Khoshuud, came from Dzungaria with 3000 households as subjects; settling on the Volga they joined the Kalmyks. At that time Puncokh died in the iron dog year (1670),[27] and immediately his son Ayuuki[28] ruled as tayishi. Dorji Arabtan,[29] a ruler from Dzungaria, came with 1000 subjects and united with his own younger brother [Ubashi Khong Taiji] and strengthened the Kalmyk people. Thereupon Ayuuki proceeded on a campaign to the Kuban. He fought for two months the Nogai Tatars, who had escaped from Russia. His name, because he had repelled them to the Volga, became famous among the people of the right bank.

In the water ox year (1673) Ayuuki, having become subject to the Russian tsar, as had been his own father Puncokh,[30] gave his own allegiance at the river called Shara Ceke.[31] He promised saying, "Let the Kalmyks not attack the Russian cities. Let us not be allied with the Persian emperor, the Turkish sultan, or the king of the Crimean [Tatars]. Let us defend the Russian territory from the enemy," and other things. Meanwhile, in the wood tiger year (1677)[32] the Dörböd Tayishi Sonom Ceren[33] came to the Volga with 4000 households. He became a subject of Ayuuki, which strengthened the latter's might and power. Thereupon, although Ayuuki again presented an oath to become the subject of the Russian tsar before an official named Scherbatov,[34] as soon as a people named the Bashkir fought against the Russians, Ayuuki united with those Bashkir.

In the iron chicken year (1681) [the Kalmyks] entered the provinces of Kazan and Orenburg. They plundered the Russian people and burned many little towns. They captured very many people. After greatly frightening the Russians they pitched camp. Because they acted in this manner, the Russian tsar /p.4/ brought about another conference. The Russian official Prince Andrei Ivanovich Golitsin and Ayuuki met together on the same Shara Cekē river and conferred.[35] By that meeting the Russians stopped the Kalmyk attacks. They [the Russians] sought ways for the Kalmyk princes to not make alliances with foreign kings. After this the Kalmyks stopped their own attacks on the Russian area. The [Kalmyks] campaigned in an easterly direction. As they subjected the Kazakh and Turkmen people they became famous in that territory.[36]

The Dalai Lama Gegen bestowed the title of khan on Ayuuki and presented the seal to him.[37] When the holy saint (Dalai

Lama) proffered the seal and title khan to Shikür Dayicing. Dayicing offered it back saying, "There are many like me. What kind of khan would I be?"[38]

Ayuuki, although a subject of the Russian tsar, did not inform him [the tsar] and took such a high title through his own power.[39] Ayuuki khan did not forget his brother Oirats of Dzungaria. Inasmuch as he was a close relative with them, he gave his own daughter to Cewang Rabtan khan.[40] Immediately he himself proceeded to Dzungaria and brought the remaining Torghuuds to the Volga.

The Oirat people called Khara Kalmyk[41] were constantly warring in Dzungaria, and [therefore] men and creatures could not be peaceful and happy. These Khara Kalmyks came nomadizing to Russia from Dzungaria in the fire tiger year (1686) with their tayishi Caghān Bātur.[42] The Russian tsar settled them on the Akhtuiba river.

At that time the great tsar Peter of Russia, wanted to go, in person, to foreign lands, and learn all the various arts and sciences, and afterwards to instruct his own subjects. When he said he was going to the western people,[43] he [Peter the Great] commissioned Ayuuki khan saying, "Defend the Russian land from our outer enemies in the south." For this reason in the fire ox year (1697), Ayuuki khan met on the same Shara Cekē river with Boris Matveyevich Golitsin, and they had a discussion together.[44] If Ayuuki khan says, "Let us war on Bukhara, Kara Kalpakh, and the Kazakhs, the Russians will give him cannon, twenty pud of gunpowder and ten pud of lead each year. Kalmyks who have fled to Russia are not to wear the cross [become Christians] without orders from the khan; if they wear the cross, charges are levied. If Ayuuki /p.5/ khan desires he can send his own subjects into the Crimea and the Kuban and they are permitted to take booty. If the Kalmyks are defeated, when they take shelter in Russian cities they are not to be expelled, but they are to be assisted." Thus they spoke together.[45] The Russians placated Ayuuki khan in this way.

Thus it was said as a result Ayuuki increased his might and power and his own subjects were made happy. In the iron pig year (1701), the father [Ayuuki] Khan and his son Phyaqdar Byab[46] were quarrelling due to Phyaqdar Byab's wife. The favorite son of Ayuuki named Ghonjib said,[47] "Let me slay my own elder brother." On a dark night [Ghonjib] dispatched to his own elder brother an evil-minded man. That man wounded Phyaqdar Byab, having shot him with two bullets from a gun. Starting from this evil deed there occurred a great quarrel. Ghonjib escaped to the city of Sharatuu [Saratov].[48] Ayuuki khan went to a small Russian city and lived there. Phyaqdar Byab crossed the Ural river together with some of his younger brothers and settled beyond it [the Ural river].

Meanwhile Prince Boris Golitsin, who was dispatched by the Russian tsar, came and made peace between father and son. A son of Ayuuki named Sanjib[49] took 15,000 households as subjects and departed with Phyaqdar Byab. When they went to the Dzungarian homeland, Cevang Rabtan khan made these his subjects. However,

Sanjib himself returned to his family.

As for the Kalmyk people, up until this time [their population] had been gradually increasing, since they had come from Dzungaria. Now it became a time of decreasing [population]. In the fire pig year (1707) Cecens, Kümyks, and Noghais attacked the Russians. At the time Ayuuki did not give the soldiers which he had promised to the Russians.[50] In addition to this, the Bashkirs once more were fighting with the Russians.[51] Mönkö Tömör Tayishi,[52] a subject of Ayuuki, penetrated into the province of Penza and Tambov, burning more than 100 clans. He took very many Russian farmers captive. These were sold in the territories of Persia, Kuban, Khiva, and Bukhara.

In the earth mouse year (1708) there came an official named Peter Matveyevic Aprakhsin.[53] When he asked the cause of this wrong behavior from Ayuuki khan, Ayuuki replied, "Mönkö Temür is the guilty person. I did not know what he was doing." Thereupon they spoke together /p.6/ in conference. Ayuuki khan in addition stated to his own nobles, "You were not dispatched to loot and rob, those [of you] who have crossed to the west side of the Volga."

They agreed saying, "If there is a war, let the Kalmyk aid the nearby Russian nobles. In like manner, let the [Russian] nobles of nearby towns protect the Kalmyks, if the Bashkir or Crimean Tatar or other enemy attack the Kalmyks."

In the iron tiger year (1710) just when Tsar Peter intended to fight with the Turks, the Bashkir again attacked Russia. The tsar and Ayuuki, when they promulgated a written decree, had in mind to oppress them [the Bashkir]. Ayuuki sent off 5,000 soldiers.[54] Besides this, 10,000 troops were sent to the Don river. The great majority of these soldiers were Dörböd. They went in order to pacify the Cossacks, who were thieving and robbing on the Don river.

In the earth tiger year (1698)[55] Ayuuki sent his own nephew[56] Rabjuuri to Tibet telling him, "Do homage to the Dalai Lama, and grant that you may return bringing lamas." Rabjuuri proceeded to Tibet.

On his way back he went and had an audience with the Chinese emperor. The Chinese emperor [K'ang-hsi] by means of a trick held Rabjuuri in Chinese territory. Since ten years had passed and Rabjuuri had not been released, Ayuuki thought that he would get his nephew returned. After making a request from Tsar Peter, an emissary named Samdan was sent to China. In the water dragon year (1712) he arrived at the city of Peking together with a Russian nobleman.[57]

The Chinese emperor met them with the appearance of much happiness. Although they were received with great honor, the Chinese emperor said, "Rabjuuri is not released." They [the Chinese] were afraid, saying, "What if [Rabjuuri] was harmed in the Kazakh territory on the way [home]?"

Immediately the Chinese emperor in turn sent an embassy headed by Tülishen,[58] who detoured through the Russian Siberian province. In the water serpent year (1713) [he] came to the home of Ayuuki in the place called Manu Tokhoi near the city of Tsaritsin [Volgograd]. He had an audience with Ayuuki khan. As for the conversation of the Chinese emissaries, [they] inquired of the health and welfare of Ayuuki khan. Although [the Chinese embassy] said, "We came seeking [permission] from Tsar Peter together with Ayuuki to let [Rabjuuri] return to his own territory via Russian territory," there were other reasons. [The embassy came] to view the territory of the Russian people and moreover to try to perceive the nature and condition of the Russian government. If it were possible [they] would cause a quarrel between Ayuuki /p.7/ and Cewang Rabtan.[59] They had come with such an idea in mind. As for Ayuuki, he was not such a shortsighted man as to abandon his own blood relatives in Dzungaria, and fall into the trap of the foreign Manchus. Bowing, [Ayuuki] accepted the letter of the Manchu ruler. As for the [Chinese] emissaries, they were shown great honor. [Ayuuki stated,] "[I] am very appreciative that the supreme emperor the Huang-ti has troubled himself like this about my nephew. Really, if Rabjuuri comes through Mongol territory, truly there will be many dangers. I shall request the Russian tsar saying, 'On account of this [danger] let him [Rabjuuri] be returned by Siberian territory.' As soon as the order has been issued, I shall inform the emperor." Since [Ayuuki] sent back the emissaries, the emissaries did not attain their own intentions and produced futile results.[60]

In the wood sheep year (1715) the Kuban Sultan Bakhta Girei[61] came fighting on the Volga. He [Bakhta Girei] attacked Ayuuki khan, who was near Astrakhan, and destroyed much territory. When [Bakhta Girei] captured the khan's residence and goods, Ayuuki, together with his queen, escaped. They went to the Russian troops who were exacting reparations in Khiva. The commander of that army, Prince Alexander Bekuvic Cirkaski, stopped the Tatars.[62] As for Ayuuki khan, although he asked that governor, "Shoot down the Tatars!," Bekuvic replied, "I am not able to shoot without orders from the supreme governor telling me to fight with them." The request of [Ayuuki] khan was not accomplished. As for Bakhta Girei, he resettled on the Kuban the Tatars, Jitesēn, and the Tatars known as Jin Buulukh who were the subjects of the Kalmyks.

Thereupon Ayuuki thought to himself, "When war came, the Russians indeed only protected my person. My subjects were not protected according to the agreement. We were food for the enemy; in addition, even my orders were not paid any attention. Let us take revenge!" Meanwhile, Ayuuki heard that Prince Bekuvich was to go as a messenger to Khiva. [Ayuuki] sent also a spy, a Tatar sent to the khan of Khiva. The spy was sent to say, "He is going as the ambassador of the Russians, but his intentions are, 'Let us wage war on you!'" On account of this the people of Khiva set an ambush along the way and killed Bekuvich.[63] Afterwards Ayuuki made peace with Bakhta Girei.

In the fire chicken year (1719) [Ayuuki] gave soldiers to his own son Phyakhdar Byab. He dispatched him to Kuban to give aid to Bakhta Girei.[64] The Kalmyks defeated the Katai, Kharbad, and the Tatars of the great Nogai, /p.8/ who had turned against Bakhta Girei. They [Kalmyqs] forced the return to the Volga of the Jitisēn and Oin Buulukh Tatars.

Immediately, Bakhta Girei entered into the two provinces of Penza and Simbi. He was escorted by 150 Kalmyks. These were supplied by Ayuuki and were led by two [Kalmyk] officials Omba and Bucin. They robbed and captured many people. At that time when the Russian nobles asked for auxiliary forces from Ayuuki, just as Bekuvich had stated previously, Ayuuki replied, "I am not able to fight with the Tatars of Kuban without orders from the supreme khan [the tsar]." By this reply [Ayuuki] took in this way his own revenge. The title of khan was not bestowed, but [Ayuuki] acquired it by his own deeds of intellect and virtue.[65]

In the iron ox year (1721) the eldest son of Ayuuki, Phyakhdar Byab, presented the seal of khan to Dasang,[66] the eldest of his twelve sons, and ordered, "You [other sons] act by his [Dasang's] orders!" Phyakhdar Byab died.[67] At that time Tsar Peter set out in order to fight with the Persians. In the water tiger year (1722) Ayuuki khan, together with his queen Darma Bala[68] and his daughter, came to Tsaritsin [Volgograd]. When they presented themselves to the ruler, Tsar Peter and the queen, were quite pleased.[69] According to Tsar Peter's having wished to obtain soldiers from the Kalmyks, immediately 40,000 Kalmyk [soldiers] campaigned and pacified the Lesgin,[70] who were allied with the Persians.[71]

Tsar Peter proceeded to Astrakhan, and while there, although he issued an order stating, "Let Prince Nazar Dorji become khan of the Kalmyks after Ayuuki khan."[72] Ayuuki's idea was to appoint Ceren Dondukh, his eldest son [as khan].[73] Queen Darma Bala allied with Dondukh Ombu, the son of Ghonjib,[74] saying, "Let us enthrone him as khan." Out of this there again arose a feud.[75] Dasang, the son of Prince Phyakhdar Byab, according to the legitimate manner should become khan.[76] When Dondukh Ombu fought with his younger brothers not only did these [brothers][77] lose all their own subjects but there was also loss of life. Thus in the midst of the quarrel (1722) Ayuuki died sick at heart.[78]

This khan [Ayuuki] ruled for 50 years; during his own time he brought many kinds of good deeds to many people. At the same time, he did not cause a deterioration of his own Kalmyk subjects. Generally, he was respected by those more powerful than himself, and was able to frighten those of equal strength. Although [Ayuuki] was said to be a subject of the Russians, /p.9/ because he accomplished his own desires in all actions, he was the most esteemed khan of the Volga Kalmyk khans.[79] At the death of Ayuuki, Queen Darma Bala ruled.[80] She became the queen of Dondukh Ombu. Because [Darma Bala] said, "Let me make him [Dondukh Ombu] khan," there occurred a great deal of destruction.[81] On account of this Volinski, the governor of Astrakhan, came by the order of the tsar.[82] Although he said, "I am going to make Dorji Nazar khan," that Dorji [Nazar] replied, "If I become khan I will have many enemies. I will not become [khan]. Let one of the two, C[i]ren Dondukh or Dasang, be [khan]!"[83] Ceren Dondukh was appointed deputy khan.[84] Since she had not in this way accomplished her desires, Darma Bala decided on other actions.

There was sent by secret messenger the person named Yeke Abughai to Cewang Rabtan of Dzungaria.[85] He was arranging a marriage for the daughter of Cewang Rabtan,[86] and stated, "I have sent for the betrothal to Ceren Dondukh." Meanwhile, although desirous of returning to Dzungaria, the ancient homeland of the Kalmyks, Ceren Dondukh and Shikür lama and others did not agree.[87]

In the year [1725] the Kalmyks sent 2,000 soldiers to the territory called Turkhai beyond the Volga.[88] They met the daughter of Cewang Rabtan, who was to become the wife of Ceren Dondukh. [They] had been told, "Come and inform us, after [you] have gone to Dzungaria along that way, whether it is possible to reach Tibet."[89] The soldiers returned after four months had passed. They came and delivered the bride into the groom's household, saying, "Up to Turkhai it was a desolate and an uninhabited region, a desert without water. Because Kazakhs usually were living along that way, that road is impossible."

Because Ceren Dondukh was an ineffectual man with little strength, he did not resolve the quarrels amongst the Kalmyks. Dondukh Ombu, although having a wife named Zhan[90] whom he had married from the Kabardinians, was intending to marry his own grandmother.[91] Meanwhile, the Manchu khan wished that Ceren

Dondukh would make war with Dzungaria. The [Manchu khan] sent ambassadors to the Kalmyks. He ordered his own ambassadors saying, "In order for Ceren Dondukh to be persuaded by my words, appoint him khan of the Kalmyks by my authority."[92]

The Russians learned of this. In the year (1731) it [the election] indirectly reached the governor of Astrakhan named Ismayilob.[93] There was brought from the Tsarina the order stating, "Have Ceren Dondukh become the real khan!" [The decree] was presented to Ceren Dondukh before Shikür Lama and other princes and nobles.[94] Thus the Chinese ambassadors returned on their way /p.10/ without accomplishing [their goals]. Ceren Dondukh became khan at once.[95]

Meanwhile after the death of Dasang the eldest son of Phyakhdar Byab, at the time when Tsar Peter proceeded to Astrakhan,[96] the younger brother of Dasang named Peter Tayishi, who was evil-minded, wore the cross [became Christian], and abandoned the religious doctrine of his ancestors.[97] Although [Peter Tayisi] presented a petition to the Tsarina saying, "It is proper that I become khan," on account of not obtaining official approval from above, [he] united with Dondukh Ombu,[98] and attacked Ceren Dondukh and captured his subjects.

Nazariyin Dorji, together with his son named Lübci,[99] and accompanied by many subjects and followers, went and settled on that side of the Ural. In order to suppress that quarrel a Russian official named Buryatingski came with soldiers. Nazariyin Dorji was reconciled with the khan (Ceren Dondukh).

As for Dondukh Ombu,[100] he nomadized on the Kuban with all the princes in his retinue except for Dondukh Dashi[101] and the Torghuud Lawang,[102] and [he] submitted to the power of the Turkish sultan. Peter Tayishi [said], "Let me go with these and hold a discussion." Because he was separated from the Russian soldiers, he escaped and went to the city of Krasnoyarsk. Afterwards Buryatingski captured and imprisoned him. He went to Petersburg by the order of the tsar.

Thereupon although the Russians requested it, Dondukh Ombu did not return from the Kuban. His son Ghaldan Norba[103] broke the peace by attacking the Russians on the Volga and Don rivers. As for Ceren Dondukh, his subjects and zayisangs complained that he was unable to rule because he was under the influence of alcohol.[104] The majority changed their allegiance to Dondukh Ombu. This was thus a time of governmental and religious confusion.[105] The Russian Tsarina in the wood tiger year (1734) sent the leader of the Don Cossacks named Efremov[106] with a letter to remind Dondukh Ombu.[107] She told him, "If you return, I will forget that previous evil that you have committed," Dondukh Ombu replied, "I shall return to my own territory if you make me governor of all the Kalmyks, and make my subjects all who have gone with me now, and if you give to the prince only Christian Kalmyks.[108] The Tsarina approved and he returned.

Immediately Ismailov the governor of Astrakhan came[109] by the order of the Tsarina in the wood rabbit year (1735), and [he] bestowed the rule of the Kalmyks on Dondukh Ombu. Ceren

Dondukh lost the title of khan. By the order of the Tsarina, [Ceren Dondukh] went to [Petersburg]. [Ceren Dondukh] /p.11/ died there. By having become khan Dondukh Ombu fulfilled his own expectations and accomplished his eternal desires. Although he made peace among his subjects and nobles, hatred continued toward Dondukh Dashi, who did not accompany [Dondukh Ombu] at the time of his going to Kuban.[110]

In the fire dragon year (1736) and in the fire snake year (1737) the Kazakhs,[111] who dwelt near the Ural, and who were former enemies of the Kalmyks, attacked and carried off many men and cattle,[112] although at that time the Kalmyks' fame was continuing to spread in other areas.

In the fire dragon year [1736] when the Russians were fighting the Turks,[113] Dondukh Ombu was campaigning with a large army. Because [Dondukh Ombu] governed his own subjects well and because he fought well against the Crimeans, the Tsarina presented [to him] an annual stipend of 200,000 copecks and 1,000 sacks of flour.[114] [She] also presented stipends in turn to his brothers and relatives. Thereupon Dondukh Ombu defeated in their own territory those Kuban Tatars who had united with the Turks. Since [Dondukh Ombu] made 10,000 persons subjects of the Russian Tsarina, the Tsarina Anna Ivanova was greatly pleased. There came especially from Petersburg two court officials of the Tsarina, Peter Soimonov and Efremov,[115] the leader of the Don Cossacks. They gave to him the legal title of khan, presenting to him the banner, sword, sable hat, sable robe, and written order of the Tsarina,

which made Dondukh Ombu khan.[116] In that way Dondukh Ombu was
favored by the Russians.

In his own mind, although he knew when he reported to the
ruler that whatever he desired would materialize, he also was
reporting to the all-venerated Dalai Lama.[117] He said, "Let
there be made khan after me one of my own sons." Those sent to
Tibet did not arrive at the desired place owing to obstacles on
the way. The eldest son of the khan, Ghaldan Norbu, was
thinking, "My father does not want me made khan; he is saying,
'Let me make Randuli, the son of the Khabarda queen Zhan,
khan.'"[118] He [Ghaldan Norbu] incited the Kalmyk people, and
produced a feud which was greatly frightening to the khan. The
tsarina subdued the quarrel, expelling Ghaldan Norbu from the
territory, sending him to the city of Kazan.[119] He died there.

Then in the iron chicken year (1741) when Dondukh Ombu
died, there was a will saying, "Let the ten year old Randuli
become khan."[120] That son [Randuli] and his mother, Zhan for
this reason took a petition to the Tsarina. Without waiting for
a reply, [Queen Zhan] said, "Let me make my own son khan."
[Queen Zhan] had Ubasi,[121] who is the uncle of Bayi, who is the
son of Dorji of Nazar, and the uncle of Ghaldan Danzin,[122] who
is the son of Ayuuki, /p.12/ assassinated. The proper person to
rule, owing to his lineage, was Ghaldan Danzin. Although he had
the strength to take the power of khan from Randuli, for the
sake of the subjects who were dear to him, he was fearful of
doing this.[123] The Tsarina heard of that evil behavior, and
because she said, "Expel from the kingdom the wife and son of

Dondukh Ombu!," the governor of Astrakhan, Tatisciv,[124] came with an army, and mindful of the former good behavior of Dondukh Dashi, the eldest son of Phyakhdar Byab,[125] he was made deputy khan. It was reported to the Tsarina that Dondukh Dashi, on account of his previously unfriendly behavior towards Dondukh Ombu, was settled further down the Samara River in the earth sheep year (1734).[126] At the time he [Dondukh Dashi] became deputy khan he came to Petersburg at the invitation of the Tsarina. When he was ready to return, he had an audience with Tsarina Elizabeth.[127] [She] presented a portrait of herself. As soon as Dondukh Dashi began to rule,[128] a Khoyid prince named Dejīd[129] came from Dzungaria with one group of people. They settled on the Volga.[130] While they were going on the road a son was born to the wife of Dejīd near the city called Tümen of the province of Tobolsk. This son was named Tümen Jirghal [10,000 joys].[131]

After Dejīd had grown old,[132] [his wife] became wife of the Khoshuud, Byamiyang. Although Byamiyang had a previous wife and child, he gave to Tümen Jirghal his own subjects, the Khoyid and Khoshuud, who were united and became the subjects of one prince.[133] In that iron chicken year (1741), there came 3,000 Kazakhs who fought the Kalmyks.[134] Thereupon the Tsarina ordered Tatisciv[135] saying, "Seize Queen Zhan and her children and send them to Kazan." Although Zhan was given a stipend, she did not agree to do that and stopped at Bagha Cōxor.[136] That queen (Zhan) was not able to abandon that which she had once desired.[137] In the water dog year (1742) she went to Kabardinia taking 700 households. She sent her son to the khan of Persia [saying], "Rob the Kalmyks from Dondukh Dashi and give [them] to me." He replied saying, "Let us duly give them to you!" and had inquiries made. When it happened that this was not accomplished, she came to Astrakhan. [She] did not reside peacefully, but acted evilly again. The Tsarina said, "Let her and her children come to Petersburg." They went there [to Petersburg] and donned the cross [became Christians]. She took the family name Princess Dondukov,[138] and the children took the names Peter, Aleksei, Ivan, and Philip.[139] [These] were taught at a military academy. /p.13/As for the descendants of Aleksei Dondukov, in the fire sheep year (1787), they took 1984 Russian subjects to the province called Mogilev.[140] The original subjects of the Erketen and the Bagha Coxor were given to the treasury. Thus the people of Bagha Coxor and Erketen gave up being ruled by their own prince. In this way they first went into the Russian treasury.[141]

In the wood ox year (1745), because the Kalmyks had attacked the Kazakhs, the Russians promulgated an order stating, "Kalmyks and Kazakhs are not to cross the Ural river,"[142] and they sent out a military guard. In the next year [1746] because there was ice on the north shore of the Caspian Sea, the Kazakhs got to the west bank of the Ural. They attacked the Kalmyks, killed 100 persons, and captured some, and acquired a taste [for raiding]. In the next year [1747] when they came that way again the Kalmyks found out and escaped, settling down at a distance [from the Kazakhs]. On account of the danger and the distance involved in pursuing the Kalmyks, the Kazakhs returned empty-handed. The weather grew warm, and because the ice was melting, the Kazakhs said, "Let us return by crossing the Ural." The Ural Kazakhs, seeing them, fought them. Some fell through the ice and died. Others were killed [by fighting]. Many were confused and turned back.

As for the previous great law code of the Forty and Four,[143] although it had been suitable for the living conditions of the Mongols and Oirats, the Kalmyks had now been separated from them and many years have passed, customs have changed. On account of moral qualities emerging that had not existed previously, there was a necessity for a new law code.[144] A new law code was also needed because the Kalmyks were living in the midst of many foreign peoples and interacting with them.[145] Dondukh Dashi khan wrote the new statute, and supplemented the old law.[146]

As for what was ordered in that statute, it was as follows:[147] "A clergyman who held vows, having performed actions which were unsuitable, was severely punished. A common man, who takes vows,[148] is also punished harshly if he misses his readings and three monthly fasts.[149] Respect and honor the clergy who have acquired good knowledge![150] Now boys up until 15 years of age must learn Mongol writing. If they are not taught take a fine from their own father and give [the fine] to their teachers and have them taught."[151]

Dondukh Dashi thought that he would increase literacy and knowledge among his own subjects with a law like that. This is the proof that he had great intelligence and desired the happiness of his subjects.[152] He forbade people to enter into the gurum rite.[153] He was thinking, "As for princes /p.14/ they are not to punish commoners who are guiltless; do not act in haughty and arrogant ways. Let one be on guard against actions which are not suitable to his own person."[154] [The law] said, "If nobles are investigating a person or if there is a sudden quarrel or a man is hit while relay horses are stolen there is no punishment."[155] Besides this he caused to make very clear [by] supplementing all the old laws, the old regulation of thefts and actions.[156]

In the fire ox year (1757) Tsarina Elizabeth[157] reflected on the good manner in which the realm of the Kalmyks of Dondukh Dashi was ruled.[158] [She] decreed an order stating, "Let him [Dondukh Dashi] become lawful khan and his son Ubashi become deputy khan."[159] The governor of Astrakhan named Z'ilin, came and made him [Dondukh Dashi] the legal khan. This is how Z'ilin wrote that he presented the title of khan. The governor of Astrakhan sent an official named Bak'ūnin and a letter stating, "Let us meet on the river named Shara Cekē!"[160] This was negotiated with Dondukh Dashi.[161]

On the 23rd of April they [the Russians] set out from Astrakhan in order to fight [protect themselves from] the Kazakhs and Mangghads;[162] they took officers of the army, one company of grenadiers, the army band and three cannons. Meanwhile Dondukh Dashi advanced in the direction of that same place [Shara Cekē].

On the 28th day of April when that governor had arrived in the territory,[163] the khan at that time dispatched two important zayisangs. When these zayisangs had reached their destination, they inquired immediately of everyone's health. They settled down [within] a verst from the tent of the governor. At that time the official Bak'ūnin, who was a privy counselor, informed the khan saying, "You go and meet the governor," and when that was approved, in the afternoon the governor sent his own carriage to the khan by an official. The khan straight away brought the portrait which was bestowed upon him previously by the Tsarina [Elizabeth].[164]

As for the son [of Dondukh Dashi, Ubashi], he followed with about 5,000 closely allied Kalmyks on saddled horses. As the khan drew near to the tent of the governor, the guards, due to the importance of these officials, halted in the manner of a military maneuver stopping near the governor. An army officer met the khan at the governor's gate. At the entering [of the khan] the governor rose from his seat, and seated the khan at his own left side, and had the son [Ubashi] sit beside his own father. Thereupon the governor had the zayisangs and Russian officials who were in attendance go out. When the order bestowed by the Tsarina, and /p. 15/ the document to be heard by the subjects, and the documents to be sworn to by the khan father and son were presented, the khan with his son got up, took their hats, and read [the document]. After having read [the decree] the khan with his son said, "We believe the supreme ruler's tent is in the east direction." They demonstrated their own appreciation to the great ruler by bowing in the eastern direction. They made the promise to always give tribute to this great ruler, and bowed thrice in that direction.[165]

On the 29th day of April the governor went to have an audience with the khan. There proceeded beside him four soldiers and civil servants. On both sides of his wagon were three or four unarmed soldiers having only swords. In front there were six soldiers with one leader, and there were more than 100 Tatars and Cossacks accompanying [him].[166] In front of the green canopy that was erected in front of the tent the zayisangs met the governor. Near the door the khan himself met the governor. The [khan] showed respect by making the [governor] enter [the tent] first. When they entered the wife and son of the khan and the wives of the officials rose. As for the khan, he seated the governor on his right side on a throne with a back rest. The princes and zayisangs were sitting cross-legged on rugs according to their own custom. The khan and governor agreed to conduct the next day all the ceremonies for the investiture of a khan.[167]

At noon on the 30th day of April the son of the governor and one army officer and six soldiers brought the carriage of the governor to the khan,[168] sending to the queen the carriage of Bak'ūn. Also, since Ayuuki's own queen was invited, that queen [Darma Bala] said she was sick and did not come.[169] The khan and his wife came by the carriage which was sent, and the son by saddled horse. The others, the Dörböd prince Ghalden Ceren,[170] Nimgen Ubashi[171] of the Torghuud, Byamyang[172] of the

Khoshuud and the bannermen[173] leading the multitude of lamas and ordinary zayisangs and commoners also came. As for the nobles, they were wearing yellow silk robes. When these had arrived, the soldiers stood and presented arms in their honor. The soldiers and civil officials were met beyond the tent; at the door the governor himself met and had [them] enter. The [governor] received and greeted the khan in the great felt ten-panelled yurt which had been received from the khan. The [governor] seated the khan father and the son on the seats which were prepared on the west side. As for the queen and nobles, lamas, and officials, they sat, having unrolled rugs according to their own custom.[174]

Thereupon /p.16/ the governor stated thus to the khan, "The great ruler has bestowed her order on me, to proclaim that the all-compassionate, supreme power-holder of all Russia, the great Tsarina Elizabeth Petrovna, considering that Dondukh Dashi has performed faithful service for many years, by her great grace is making him khan of the Kalmyks, and is making the son Ubashi deputy khan. By announcing this to these two the Tsarina also shows her compassion to the Kalmyk people." As for the translator, when he was interpreting these words into the Kalmyk language, the khan, together with his son, knelt in the eastern direction showing their own appreciation to the Tsarina. Thereupon as a result of the governor having made this known, the oath of allegiance was given before the shrine of Shakyamuni Buddha, the khan of all. Afterwards the son holding the shrine over the crown of his head swore an oath. After that, placing their own right hands on the written oath of fealty, they affixed the seal.[175] After that, by order of the governor one civil servant announced for all to hear the written decree [for Dondukh Dashi] to become khan. The Kalmyk interpreter repeated the announcement. Immediately the khan, together with his son and also all the princes and zayisangs, showed their appreciation to the Tsarina by bowing to the east. The governor handed the written decree to the khan.

Meanwhile the decree to be heard by the subjects was read from the governor's tent to the four directions. The gifts presented to the khan were thus accepted by the khan. Assessor Bak'ūnin hung the sword [on the khan]. Porudcikh [the warrant officer],[176] who was the son of the governor, dressed [the khan] in the robe. The Junker[177] Colonel[178] placed the hat [on the khan]. The nephew of the governor, Vasili Kinviyekov (Kindyakov) presented the unfurled flag. Afterwards the officials took [the flag] and erected it in front of the yurt.[179]

Besides this the khan had the zayisangs carry these same robe, hat, and sword to the front of the yurt and displayed these to his subjects. The khan gave his oath of allegiance and the decree was read. As soon as he took these gifts the governor and the other officials conveyed their congratulations to the khan. The soldiers standing outside presented their weapons, the drums were beaten and music played, and three cannons were fired in his honor. Thereupon while the food was prepared, the khan and queen and princes and officials came out from the yurt and they were again honored as before.

The food was served as follows: the khan with his son, the governor, Junker, Bak'ūnin, princes and some zayisangs sat at the first table [head table]. The queen, lamas, and zayisangs sat on the front seats. /p.17/ The food was prepared in two yurts for the wives of these [above] and other officials. At the time when a toast was proposed which said, "Grant peace to the Tsarina and her imperial family!," the wine was drunk and the cannon was fired. For the common subjects there was arranged and set out six cooked oxen and nine entire sheep and portions of cow, sheep, grain, liquor, and mead.[180]

The khan in his own reply extended an invitation stating, "Tomorrow come to my yurt and eat."[181] He [the khan] rode off with the banner presented by the Tsarina in front. On the second day of May, the governor came to the khan's [yurt]. When he had provided food, a toast for the good health and peace of the Tsarina and the imperial family was made. When the liquor was drunk the soldiers fired their weapons and played music. The Tatars and Cossacks who accompanied the governor were entertained in a separate yurt. After the repast was served, there was Kalmyk-style wrestling and fireworks.[182] The khan and all of his subjects watched and were greatly pleased. At the departure of the governor, the khan with his son accompanied [the governor] as far as his carriage.[183]

On the third day of the Russian month of May, [the governor] came and was received in an audience at which he offered his regards towards the khan. They returned in the evening from there. Indicating a high hill, [the khan] said, "I have the idea to erect a stone monument on top of this [hill], inscribing in the Russian and Kalmyk languages a memorial about that which was bestowed by the Tsarina.[184] The commissioner of Yangkhal [Chernyi Yar][185] was ordered to preserve it. Then that city's mayor said, "Let me be helped!" The governor spoke to that mayor, and went to Astrakhan. The khan travelled to his own palatial tent. Thus Dondukh Dashi made his own subjects happy ruling for four or five years. In the iron snake year (1761) he died.[186]

The son Ubashi, who had previously acted as deputy khan, became khan without any contest whatsoever. In the wood pig year (1755) the Chinese defeated Amursana khan[187] of the Dzungars. [The Chinese] drove into Russian territory [Amursana] himself and massacred all the Oirat people. At that fearful time, an Oirat prince named Ceren Taishi[188] came heading towards the Volga leading 10,000 households of Khoshuud, Dörböd, and Khoyid. [Ceren Taishi] arrived, just as Ubashi ruled as khan.[189] Dondukh Ombu quarrelled with [his] father. As for Cebekh Dorji,[190] the son of Ghaldan Norbu who had died in Kazan, he was saying, "I am surely the truly legal person to become khan. /p.18/ I am senior to Ubashi;[191] I will not become subject of [this] khan." He [Cebekh Dorji] went proceeding to the Don with sixty men.[192]

Thereupon by the order of the Tsarina he went to Petersburg. Although thinking equally evil toward both Russia and Ubashi, he was hiding [this] within himself, saying, "Let me go by the khan's order!" He came back. Thus he was not able to accomplish his intended evilly conceived deed.[193] [Cebekh Dorji] thought, "If the Russians are aware that evil is done to Ubashi, I will certainly become khan."[194] [Cebekh Dorji] said, "Let us abandon Russian territory and go to our own former territory of Dzungaria,"[195] and he rose up. In addition to this, Ceren Tayishi stopped desiring to live in Russian territory and also wanted to return saying, "Let us return [to Dzungaria]." To Ubashi he said, "As we had come from there just a little earlier we know very well the good pastures and the way to go." [Ceren Tayishi] was saying, "[You] come and follow me, if you want to arrive there hale and hearty. Now in that place there is no ruler, and we are without a khan to rule over ourselves. You will become special khan." He rose up.[196]

Besides this prior to the coming to rule of Ubashi, all of the officials of the council were usually chosen from among the Torghuuds, the khan's personal servants. As for the order bestowed by Tsarina Catherine to confirm the making of Ubashi deputy khan, when she said, "On the khan's council let there be three magistrates and one lama, only one from the subject Torghuuds. One zayisang from the subject Torghuud who are descendants of Dondukh Ombu. One zayisang from the Dörböd. Not to mention one zayisang from the Khoshuuds. These are named magistrates. The princes supervise their election. If the magistrates do not approve, the khan is not to make a decision on any matter whatever." This was ordered [by the Tsarina].[197]

As for the magistrates, prior to this, they were not a

people who jointly decided on an action with the khan. They were subjects who carried out the orders and [gave] assistance to him [the khan]. Now because the court had authority they were examining and making decisions just like a khan. The khan must comply with the words [decisions] of his subject people. When subjects contended with him, it decreased the power and the might of the khan. The supreme high title was weakened. Ubashi khan had considered all of this saying, "It is indeed best to go."[198] He approved what was reported by Cebekh Dorji and Ceren Tayishi. The Lamaist community, the princes and officials assembled, and when they learned of the proper truth they all approved. It was unnecessary for the common subjects to learn [of the decision].[199] /p.19/

He [Ubashi] thought, "The Kalmyk people will proceed happily if they think Dzungaria is a fine country and is richer than the Volga steppe. From olden times up until now the Mongol and Oirat people have not deviated from the orders of the supremely ordained khan. Besides this, if the Kalmyks arrive healthy in Dzungaria, after having prayed to our all-saving Buddha, we shall be dwelling near the most blessed illumined saints and the Tibetan area, the holy sea of religious doctrine which is the basis of happiness in this and future rebirths,[200] and [dwelling near] our ancient brother Mongols with whom is shared one language and one religion. [We] shall settle over the hearths of the Oirats who had been slaughtered by evil enemies; we will go in the happiness and suffering of our own ancestors."

All things were prepared for the making of the distant journey. In order to protect [themselves], 20,000 troops were assembled.[201] On account of the dwelling of many Kalmyks on the west side of the Volga, [the Kalmyks] stayed and waited saying, "When it becomes winter and the Volga freezes, let us travel going out on the east side [of the Volga] over the ice.

Although the Russians did not know very well what occurred in the Kalmyk territory, since there was great confusion, some [Russians] became aware [of the situation]. Although they notified their own superiors, the official named Kisangski,[202] who was in charge of the actions of the Kalmyks paid no heed, and was saying [these reports were] false. Unfortunately in that year the winter was warm [mild]. Up until the Russian new year the water did not freeze. The Kalmyks were unable to wait for it to become cold. Beketov, the governor of Astrakhan, was informed that the Kalmyks were intending to go.[203] Because he left to inform the Tsarina, Ubashi panicked and abandoned his own comrades who dwelt on the west side of the Volga on the 5th day of the first Russian month in the iron rabbit year (1771).[204]

[Ubashi] set out heading towards Dzungaria, his own homeland, having worshipped the Buddha in order to have a peaceful and healthy journey. Cebekh Dorji and Ceren Tayishi, together with the other nobles whom they were leading, were accompanied by their own women and children and 33,000[205] of their own subject families. These were driving all their own cattle having taken their own possessions and having brought their own Buddha image. They prostrated themselves before the Buddha[206] to have a peaceful and healthy journey, and set out intending to go to Dzungaria, their own ancient homeland.

When they left their own territory, they killed the Russians who had been living there. Immediately, on account of having proceeded to rob from many merchants, goods, wines, etc., they were going happily being without a shortage of things. Having crossed the Ural river, happiness passed. The time was approaching [for the Kalmyks] to encounter many enemies and to suffer.·

The governor of Orenburg,[207] who heard of the movement of the Kalmyks, ordered Nurali khan[208] of the Kazakhs, /p.20/ "Wage war on the Kalmyks, taking any booty for your own selves and return these Kalmyks to Russian territory!" The governor of Siberia jointly gave an order like that to Ablai Sultan[209] and many other sultans dwelling in the vicinity of their own territory. Immediately an order came from the Tsarina. Indeed an order such as that was unnecessary. The ones called Kazakhs since time immemorial were indeed mortal enemies of the Kalmyks. Learning that such a deed had happened, they were incomparably happy. The time had come to acquire booty and take revenge. All the khans and sultans were preparing armies and were awaiting the coming of the Kalmyks.

Although the Ural Cossacks from among all of the Russian troops had the power to pursue and halt the Kalmyks, fatefully they quarrelled and did not obey the orders of their superiors.[210] Therefore the Cossacks of Orenburg came alone.[211] Although these [Cossacks] joined with Nurali khan, because there was no fodder in that place to which they were to go, the horses became emaciated and lagged behind Nurali and [the Cossacks] returned [to Orenburg]. The army, which was to set out to these places, made preparations for going, and time passed. On the 12th day of the fourth Russian month [the army] left from the fortress named Orsk. They arrived at the Irgiz river,[212] which was in the territory of the Kazakh, and joined with the Nurali khan. The Kalmyks were far ahead, having reached the Turkhai river which flows one verst beyond that river.[213] There the Russian army joined up with the armies of Nurali khan and Kiyibi khan.[214] They pursued and went near the mountain named Takh.[215] The army soldiers were suffering from impure water and hunger, and were swollen with sickness. The horses also became greatly emaciated. In the meantime, the Kalmyks were gradually going further, and as they could not be overtaken, Traubenberg, the head of the Russian forces, withdrew, bringing his own army back.[216]

The Kazakhs were not able to capture the Kalmyks. Therefore they said, "Let us only attack and take plunder."[217] Having crossed the Ural river, Ubashi with his subjects subsequently entered into that robber territory and suffered endlessly. Starting from this river up until Dzungaria this was entirely Kazakh territory. As for this territory the water was scarce, without wells; it was a boundless desert and on account of an abundance of sand, in the heat of the summertime it was unbearable. /p.21/ Due to this the Kalmyk cattle and people, suffered from swelling and from all kinds of other illness. In addition those who were so ill were a burden on their own comrades and obstructed their progress.[218]

Because it was not suitable for all the people and animals to travel by only one roadway, they went separately each in his own group. The Kazakhs, who are greedy as devils, and who are not fearful to interrupt life [to kill],[219] and who are greedy for goods, as soon as they saw the Kalmyks bringing all their cattle and their own jewelled treasure, attacked from four directions. The Kazakhs were residing on their own territory, and since both the horseman and their mounts were in good shape, although they were only a few who came and attacked the Kalmyks, they drove off the Kalmyk people and their cattle, and with each meeting between them the [Kalmyks] were certainly gradually becoming fewer. In general the attacks of the Kazakhs were innumerable. If one were to speak of the khans and sultans who attacked and looted with many soldiers, [the following would be mentioned]. The sultan named Ayicuvakh[220] slaughtered one group of Kalmyks on the Sikis [Sagiz] river.[221] Nurali khan looted there between the Mughucar mountain and the Or river.[222] The sultan named Ablai attacked frequently and came out looting the silver. All of these, thus, were endlessly robbing many people, cattle, and possessions.[223]

Having endured such sorrows, the Kalmyks approached the eastern boundary of the Kazakh territory. When they arrived at the territory of the Kazakh sultan named Irnali, he caused more harm through evil treachery than all of the other

Kazakhs.[224] When Irnali heard that the Kalmyks had come near to his own territory, he sent a person to Ablai. [Irnali] ordered [Ablai] saying, "Attack the Kalmyks from the rear!" Others of his own allies attacked [the Kalmyks] from the flanks. [Irnali] taking 10,000 of his own soldiers rode out to meet [the Kalmyks]. [Irnali] had hidden away in a safe and distant place his own blood relatives and the women, children, and old people of his subjects and their own goods and valuables.[225] Ablai, on account of having heard the words of the sultan, did not proceed. [Irnali] was left by himself. [Irnali], since he did not have sufficient force, was afraid of attacking the Kalmyks. [He] carried out evil trickery. [Irnali] spoke a report as if thinking, "Let us halt the Kalmyks and return them to Russia!" Since Ubashi was unaware of the number of Kazakhs with their allies, he feared to proceed forward, and halted, and said, "Let us deliberate!"[226] What with their conferring together, by the time they came to an agreement, the first half of a month had passed. In the meantime /p.22/ Irnali had assembled many men by various means. Ubashi saw that the soldiers of the Kazakhs had become very many. [Ubashi] was thinking, "Let us avoid the spilling of blood again!" He dispatched a man to Irnali and when he said, "Let us make peace!" Irnali pretended that he approved. The Kalmyks were unaware of the evil thoughts of Irnali. [The Kalmyks] having proceeded a little way further encamped. While the Kalmyks were overnighting Irnali entered among them, attacking suddenly in the dark of night. They were chopped to pieces, the people who travelled during the day and were exhausted, and who were sleeping peacefully. The [Kazakhs] went taking and stealing very great amounts of booty.[227]

Thereupon while they escaped from one danger, they arrived in the territory of the Burad [Kirghiz tribe], and they fought together with the enemy. Those called Burad have a language like the Kazakhs and the Tatars. They raise cattle and usually dwell in felt tents, and are poor, and are tenacious, unmerciful even with their own lives. They are a people who are heroic in war, loving robbery and desirous of booty. The Burad, as soon as they heard that the Kalmyks had come rejoiced as if it were a day of joyful triumph, and assembled 100,000 soldiers.[228]

Ubashi khan said, "We will avoid this territory." They entered onto a plain without grass and water at a distance of 550 versts north of Lake Balkash.[229] Because travelling there caused them to become very hot, the men were thirsty. Because they drank the blood of their horses and cattle, there arose an epidemic. Again a great many people died. Of the cattle which had set out from the Volga, not even one-third remained. When they emerged having trekked in that gobi for ten days, now they were met beyond the gobi by the ones named Burad. From both front and rear, day and night the [Burad] went following and attacking. They robbed men, animals, and possessions, taking even more than all of the Kazakhs.[230]

A year had expired since they had set out from the Volga. In the spring of the water dragon year [1772] they reached the territory called Tamagha near Dzungaria.[231] Out of the 33,000 families with a population of 169,000 who had left Russia,

there remained 70,000 people.[232] At their drawing near to
Dzungaria, the governor-general of the Chinese army sent an
adjutant to Ubashi khan asking, "With what intention have you
arrived?" Ubashi khan deliberated with his Lamas and nobles for
seven days and nights. Although they said they would not become
subjects of the Manchu Emperor, /p.23/ as there were no other
means of taking Dzungaria from the Chinese but warfare, they
notified [the Manchus] saying, "We came in order to become
subjects of the Manchu Emperor."[233] The Chinese were very happy
at the coming of such new subjects. Correspondingly Ubashi in
the meeting with the general of that place bestowed on him the
Russian jade imperial seal and other presents.[234]

In the autumn of that same year [1772] Ubashi khan and the
other princes went to the Manchu emperor and had an audience
with him. The Manchu emperor named Törö Nayiraltu [Ch'ien-Lung]
was very happy and honored [the Kalmyks].[235] To Ubashi khan he
presented the title Zoriltu Khan, and gave titles to the other
princes by ranks. They were appointed in the manner of Mongol
khans and princes. The Chinese nation, having conquered
Dzungaria, divided it into five aimaqs. These places were
named: Ili, Bar Kol, Urumci, Khara Usun, and Tarbaghatai.
Soldiers were garrisoned there.

The Manchu emperor divided the Kalmyks making banners as
the Mongol [banners]. Three clans of Torghuuds were residing in
the Tarbaghatai and Khara Usun aimakh. Ubashi Khan with four
groups of Torghuuds as well as princes of the Khoshuud resided
on the good land by the banks of the two rivers, the Yeke

Yuldus [great star] and the Bagha Yuldus [little star], within the territories of Kongkoi and Khoton. Other princes settled in the aimakh of Ili.[236]

Because of the many things which were needed by these people, who had arrived having been robbed of all their own goods, while going on this distant journey, the Emperor bestowed 1,125,000 horses, cows, and sheep, 20,000 canisters[237] of brick tea, 20,000 sacks of rice, and 51,000 sheep skins, 51,000 [pieces] of cloth, 1,500 puds of cotton, 400 felt yurts, and 400 puds of silver.[238]

After this when the Russian Tsarina asked the Chinese Emperor saying, "Give back the Kalmyks!," the Chinese replied, "Previously when [we] sought Ceren Tayisi who had gone to your territory from Dzungaria, [he] was not given by you.[239] Likewise now I am not giving to you." Thereupon in the wood sheep year (1775) when Ubashi Khan died his son Cevang Dorji Namjyal became khan.[240] The Kalmyks in that manner entered the middle of Russia from the [time of] Khō Orlȫkh, and during the [next] 140 years, while they stayed becoming a strong and populous people, Ubashi left and went to the Altai. The Kalmyks who remained, not having gone with him [Ubashi] now are being ruled according to their own custom by their own princes. They are residing happily.[241]

CHAPTER 3 - FOOTNOTES

1. The Oirat name for the Volga is Ijil, cf. Ramstedt, Kalmückisches Wörterbuch, p. 205b.

2. Khō Orlŏkh„is listed in the GS and the DO as the Son of Zulzaghan Orlŏkh (GS 74.15, DO 30.01). Zulzaghan Örlŏkh was the eldest of six sons „of Boyigho Örŏlŏkh (GS 74.12; DO 29.17 gives Buyigho Orŏlŏkh).

3. The Oirat spelling for this Caspian Sea as found in HKK 1.08 is K'aspu.

4. Khō Orlŏkh had six sons and six daughters (GS 74.15, DO 30.01). The eldest son was Khudai Shŭkŭr Dayicang (GS 74.16, 74.17; DO 30.01, 30.02), the second (eldest) was Yendeng (DO 30.02 has Ghŭmbŭ Yeldeng, HKK 2.08 and 2.12 also give Yeldeng). The third eldest son was Kiresen (GS 74.17, DO 30.02). The fourth eldest was Sajin (GS74.17; listed as Sanjin in DO 30.02). The fifth eldest was Blo Bzhang (GS 74.18; listed as Luuzang in DO 30.02 and as Lubzang in HKK 2.08, 2.11, and 2.12). The sixth son was Shŭngkei (GS 74.18; listed as Sŏngkŏ in DO 30.02). The DO does not give designations as to the order of age of the above sons except to state that Khudai Shŭkŭr Dayicang was the eldest. Chapter 101 of the Piao Chuan, Pelliot, Notes..., p. 26, gives a partial genealogy for the family of Khō Orlŏkh. "Juljaghan-örlăk eut un fils, Kho-örlăk, qui est l'ancetre des anciens Turghut...Khoörlăk eut 6 fils. L'ainé s'appelait Shŭkŭr-daicing; il y avait ensuite Yăldăng-noyan, puis Lubjang-noyan; aucun des autres n'a eu de descendants, et c'est pourquoi il n'en est pas fait mention." Pelliot on page 33 of this same work discussed the problem of the genealogy and origin of the Torghuud. He also mentioned the difference between the Pallas Sammlungen and the Piao Chuan genealogies. The Chinese text gives nine descendants from Wang khan to Khō Orlŏkh; Pallas gives only seven. It has not, however, been noted by Pelliot that Pallas used the Ghaban Shes Rab text as the source of his information; Pallas, Sammlungen, Vol. I, p. 56, transcribes the name of the author of the work as Gabung Scharrap. Pallas had already established in a footnote on page 6 that the Kalmyks had several histories. It is evident from the content of his work that Pallas made extensive use of these histories in the Sammlungen.

5. The Oirat name for the Ural river is Zai, cf. Ramstedt, Kalmückisches Wörterbuch p. 407b.

6. HKK 1.12 gives Embe as the transcription for the name of this river.

7. These are all Turkic tribes.

8. The date for the arrival of the Oirats on the Volga is not definite in Chinese sources. "Le text chinois dit seulement 'sous Tch'ong-tcheng' (1628-1644)." Pelliot, Notes, p. 81, footnote 204 discusses the various dates given for the Oirat arrival on the Volga.

9. The text of the law code identifies the date more exactly: Bātur Tömör glu kemekü jiliyin namuriyin dundadu sarayin tabun sinedü sayin ödör tu: MOZ 1.12-2.01.

10. The law code of 1640 gives a much longer list of who participated in this meeting: Shakyayin Toyin Ecige Inzan Rinbuce kiged Anggshobhya Manjushiri Amugha Sihdi Manjushiri ghurban khutukhtuyin gegeni ömönö...Batur tömör glu kemekü jiliyin namuriyin dundadu_ sarayin tabun sinedu sayin ödör tü : Erdeni Zasakhtu xan ekilen Tüshetü khan : Ubashi Dalai Noyon : Dalai Khung : Khung Noyon : Cecen Noyon : Dayicing Khung Tayiji : Yeldeng Noyon : Mergen Noyon : Erdeni Khung Tayiji : Dayibung Khung Tayiji : Tenggeri Toyin : Ayoushi Khatun Batur : Erdeni Batur Khung Tayiji : Köndölöng Ubushi : Guusi Nomiyin khan : Örlökh : Shükür Dayicing : Yeldeng : Dayicing Khoshuuci : Ocirtu Tayiji : Mergen_ Dayicing : Cöü Ker : Cecen Tayiji : Medeci Tayisi : Bo Yeldeng : Mergen_ Noyon : Damarin : döcin dörbön khoyoriyin noyod yeke cāji ekilen bicibe :
    Even though the detail is greater in the law code, the three religious personages are the same in both works.

11. Serruys, Genealogical Tables of the Descendants of Dayan-qan, p. 156, informs us that the descendants of Asikhai-darkhan khung-tayiji became rulers of Zasakhtu-khan of Outer Mongolia. The Zasakhtu khan was one of the major Khalkha khans. The title itself was originally self-assumed. There had been a close relationship between the Oirats and the Zasakhtu-khan as can be seen by the fact that Zaya Pandita of the Oirats was given this title by Zasakhtu khan. Erdeni Zasakhtu khan died in 1661. For further information, see Bawden, History of Modern Mongolia, pp. 5, 26, 34, and 63.

12. Abatai was the progenitor of the Tüshetü khans. This khanate was separated from Sain Noyon khanate by the Orkhon. The area of the Tüshetü khanate included the basin of the Tula, the region known as Urga (Ulan Bator), see Grousset, Empire of the Steppes, p. 512. The line of Tüshetü descended originally from Dayan. The Tüshetü khan in 1640 at the creation of the law code was Gombodorji. His son in 1650 at the age of fifteen became the first Jebtsundamba Khutukhtu, see Bawden, History of Modern Mongolia, pp. 25 and 33.

13. Khan of the Oirats according to DO 32.16. DO 33.02 explains how he was given the title Nomiyin khan. He is leader of the Khoshuud, see Bawden, History of Modern Mongolia, p. 50.

14. Title given to Kharakhula by the fifth Dalai Lama in 1635. Kharakhula was the ruler of the Dzungar tribe of the Oirats, and as such expanded and consolidated their power from Western Mongolia to Turkestan in the first part of the seventeenth century. He died about 1665. cf. Bawden, History of Modern Mongolia, p. 50.

15. The Oirat Mongol Law Code of 1640 gives one person named Orlŏq as having attended this meeting. It is not known whether this is meant to be Kho Ŏrlŏkh.

16. Lubzang, the fifth son of Khō Ŏrlŏkh according the GS 74.18, where the name is listed as Blo bzhang. The GS is the only text which indicates a chronology for the sons.

17. Yeldeng was the second eldest son of Khō Ŏrlŏkh according the GS 74.17, which lists the name as Yendeng. See Footnote 4, above.

18. Shikür Dayicing, the eldest son of Khō Ŏrlŏkh according to GS 74.16, which lists the name as Khudai Shükür Dayicang. See Footnote 4, above.

19. GS 85.01 and DO 35.13 report on the destruction of Yeldeng by Shikür Dayicing.

20. For a thorough history of Güüsi see Ahmed, SinoTibetan Relations in the Seventeenth Century, pp. 118-162.

21. Pelliot, Notes, p. 27, only gives information on Chinese-Kalmyk relations, the Chinese text makes no mention of the fact that a Kalmyk mission was sent to the Russian tsar. It is interesting to note, however, that the Kalmyks make no note of the mission to the Chinese emperor which takes place at the same time as the mission to the Russian Tsar. Pelliot, Notes, p. 27, "La 12ᵉ annee, etc., " Golstunskii discusses the envoy's arrival in Moscow. Here Shikür Dayicing, through his envoys, became the first of the Kalmyk chiefs to take an oath of perpetual allegiance to Russia. See also Golstunskii p. 102, Mongolo-oiratskie zakony 1640 goda...

22. The messengers Dural, Darxan, and Ceren are not mentioned in the other Oirat sources.

23. Although the HKK does not give further genealogical information concerning the line of Khudai Shikür Dayicing, the other Oirat sources are not so reticent. Khudai Shikür Dayicing, according to the DO, 30.02-30.03, has four sons, the eldest being Rgyalbo. The other sons are Nima Sereng, Puncokh, and Rbyal Cang. The GS, 74.18 and 75.01, also lists Khudai Shikür Dayicing as having four sons. Although the reading of the text is not without problems, I would offer the following translation. He has no sons by Güre, but by

Dayougha he has Rgyalbu, Nama Sereng, Puncukh, and Gyamcub. Pelliot provides us with additional information. Unfortunately, this information does not match with the genealogies as given in the Oirat sources. "Arabjur était un Turghut. Son aieul à la 5e génération s'appelait Shükür-daicing, lequel eut 4 fils. L'ainé s'appelait Guru, le 2e Dashi, tous deux morts sans postérité; le 3e s'appelait Ponsuk; le 4e Nam-Cärän." Notes, p. 29.

24.   Baddeley, Russia, Mongolia, China, Vol. 2, p. 49, gives the following description of Puncokh's oath taking: "Punzuk, chief of the Torguts and father of Ayuka Khan, when taking the oath of allegiance to Alexei Mikhailovich in 1661, said, "I bow to and kiss the image of my God (i.e. Buddha), book of prayers, riding-whip, and rosary, and I lick my knife and put it to my throat."

25.   Although no other information is given as to precisely how Puncokh came to power, DO 36.16 discusses the division of the inheritance of Khudai Shükür Dayicing. Three of the sons are given a portion: Rkyalbu, Nima Sereng, and Puncokh. Puncokh takes the largest share for himself.

26.   According to Pallas, Sammlungen, Vol. I, p. 29, Köndölöng Ubashi did not enter Russian territory. The HKK apparently has confused Köndölöng Ubashi with his son Ubashi Khün Tayiji. For the internal evidence for this mistake see Footnote 25. The full name of Köndölöng Ubashi is given by Pallas, Sammlungen, Vol. I, p. 29, as Tümmedä Uosang Kündelüng Düürgatschi Ubascha. The DO 26.17 lists this as two separate men Tümedi Köndölöng and Düürgeci Ubashi. See also Ocherki istorii Kalmyckoi ASSR, p. 110.

27.   Details of his death are given in GS 84.02-84.03 and DO 35.07. Puncokh was seized and killed by Mergen Tayiji.

28.   The Oirat sources, which are usually so complete in listing the names of all of the sons of an important political figure, are lacking with regard to the names of the sons of Puncokh. The GS 75.01 simply states that Puncokh had three sons. Two were without descendants. The eldest son was Ayuuki khan. DO 30.03 says even less about the sons of Puncokh: "Puncokh had three sons, the eldest was Ayuuki khan." The only other bit of genealogical information on this matter in Oirat sources is found in GS 75.06: "There were produced 32 descendants in the Puncokh line from the six sons of Orlökh."

29.   Although problems still remain with the genealogies of Köndölöng Ubashi, it is clear that he is the father of both Ubashi Khung Tayiji and Dorji Tayiji (Dorji Arabtan). Cf. Do 27.02 and the Pallas genealogical chart opposite p. 30. Therefore the brother of Dorji

Arabtan spoken about in the HKK text could not be Köndölöng Ubashi but the father presumably is Ubashi Khung Tayiji the brother.

30. The oath that Puncokh swore is mentioned above in Footnote 24.

31. Shara Cekē is listed in Pallas as the Sarpa river. This river is located between the Don and the Volga. The oath which Ayuuki took is also quoted there. Cf. Pallas, Sammlungen, Vol. 1, pp. 60-61.

32. The date 1677 in the HKK is in error. The wood tiger year is 1674, not 1677.

33. GS 91.15 and DO 29.04 give the name as Solon Ceren Tayishi. The DO is the only source which gives further genealogical information. Dalai Tayishi is listed as the father of thirteen sons including Ceren Tayishi. Two other sons are also mentioned: Toyin and Dayicing Xoshuuci. DO 36.10, in discussing the disposal of the inheritance of Dalai Tayishi, states that portions of his estate were given to three sons. Only Dayicing Xoshuuci is mentioned by name. Presumably the other recipients are Toyin and Solon Ceren Tayishi. Pallas gives the name as Solom Zeren. Cf. Pallas, Sammlungen, Vol 1, p. 63.

34. This event is not mentioned by other Oirat sources nor is the following meeting. Cf. Footnote 35.

35. No other Oirat sources discuss this meeting. A.I. Golitsin was governor of Astrakhan; on his meeting with Ayuuki cf. Ocherki istorii Kalmyckoi ASSR. Dooktyabr'skii period. (Moscow, 1967), pp. 142-143.

36. This is the only Oirat text which gives precise information about the fighting between Ayuuki and the Turkic peoples. The only other place which even mentions in any way these battles is GS 86.14-15; this is also picked up in DO 36.07. There one catches a brief glimpse of religious intolerance. The Kipchakh and Khatai are described as "wrong-doctrined." The other rationale for fighting is the need to nourish the Oirat people with the booty of these raids. Sarkisyanz, Geschichte der orientalischen Völker Russlands bis 1917, pp. 253-254 gives a concise description of the warfare occurring at this time.

37. Although mention is made in the Chinese sources of Ayuuki receiving the title of khan, there is no mention that Ayuuki received this title from the Dalai Lama. Cf. Pelliot, Notes, p. 27, for references to these Chinese sources. For a discussion of titles among the Oirats cf. Krader, Social Organization, p. 129; Pallas, Sammlungen, Vol. 1, pp. 187-188; and Koehne, "Das Recht der Kalmüken," pp. 445-475. A limited, more recent discussion of Mongol titles can be found in Hangin,

Köke Sudur, p. 19.

38. The GS and DO relate this same incident in almost the same language. This section constitutes a good sample of the more narrative history of the HKK which can be traced to an earlier, more traditional type of Oirat historiography. Cf. GS 82.6-9 and DO 33.14-15.

39. Although Ayuuki had been ruling as tayishi since 1670, there is no exact date given for the taking of the title khan by Ayuuki. Pallas, Sammlungen, Vol.1, p. 68, simply states that by 1700 Ayuuki is using the title khan. Cf. also Howorth, History of the Mongols, Vol. 1, p. 567.

40. Pallas, Sammlungen, Vol. 1, p. 68, states that it was Ayuuki's oldest daughter Sederdshap who married Cewang Rabtan Khan.

41. Cf. Pelliot, Notes, p. 82, for this term.

42. This name is not mentioned in any Oirat historical text, nor have I discovered any mention of it in the secondary literature.

43. Peter I's trip to western Europe ("Great Embassy") took place in 1697-1699. Cf. Richard Pipes, Russia Under the Old Regime, p. 338.

44. This meeting is not mentioned in other Oirat sources nor have I discovered a mention of it in the secondary literature.

45. During the entire twenty-year period from 1673 to 1693 Ayuuki is continually switching his allegiance with the Russians. Cf. Pallas, Sammlungen, Vol. 1, pp. 61-66, and also Ocherki istorii Kalmyckoi ASSR, pp. 136-162.

46. GS 75.03 lists the sons of Ayuuki as Phyakhdar skyab, Mgün skyab, Ceren Dorub, and Ghaldan Danjin. DO 30.03 gives the same set of sons. Pallas, Sammlungen, Vol. 1, pp. 49, 69, mentions Phyakh dar skyab as the son of Ayuuki. The Chinese source used by Pelliot, p. 29, claims that Ayuuki had eight sons. The only sons who are said to have produced descendants are Sahdur jab and Günjab. This Chinese transcription of the names is of course closer to their pronounciation than those given above which more accurately transcribe the Tibetan spelling of the names. Pelliot, Notes, p. 29, lists Shakdurjab as having thirteen sons. However, he lists only four by name: Dondob-rashi, Batu, Dorji-rashi, and Busurmun. The DO 30.05 and 06 is the only Oirat source which mentions Phyakhdar sphyab's offspring. This source gives the names of 12 sons: Batu, Dacang, Bakhsadai, Donrob Rashi, Danjin Dorji, Nikhtar, Göncöb Byab, Bodong, Solom Dobcin, Dorji Arshi, Yadakh, and Busuruman Tayiji.

47. Mgün skyab according to GS 75.03.

48. These events are related in Pallas, Sammlungen, Vol. 1, pp. 68-69. GS 85.05 mentions that Phyakhdar Byab was forced out by his father Ayuuki.

49. Sanjib is not mentioned in any of the other Oirat sources to which I have had access. It should be pointed out that Pallas, Sammlungen, Vol. 1, p. 69, and Pelliot, Notes, p. 29, are at odds with the other Oirat sources over the number of offspring that Ayuuki had. Cf. Gaston Cahen, History of the Relations of Russia and China under Peter the Great 1689-1730, p. 52.

50. Cahen, ibid.

51. For details of the Russian-Bashkir struggle between 1705-1711, cf. Alton S. Donnelly, The Russian Conquest of Bashkiria 1552-1740, pp. 45-50.

52. A Dörböd, the son of Sonom Ceren Tayishi. Cf. Footnote 33 above.

53. A treaty was signed on the banks of the Akhtuiba by Aprakhsin and Ayuuki, by which the latter undertook for himself and all his people to become forever the loyal subjects of the Russian sovereign and to pursue and attack the Tchetchens and Nogais. See Baddeley, The Rugged Flanks of Caucasus, Vol. 1, p. 82. See also Ocherki istorii Kalmyckoi ASSR, p. 157. This work gives Aprakhsin the initials F.M.

54. Donnelly, p. 48, quotes the following letter from Ayuuki reporting his actions: "Boyar Peter Matveevich Apraksin brought Your Sovereign decree, informing us that the Bashkir brigands are loose and for us to send an army to destroy the Bashkir bandits. According to Your Sovereign decree I sent Nazarov, the son of Darzha, and four other leaders and 4,000 good military men with him who...attacked and drove off men, women, children, and cattle and horses, and seized Bashkir lands."

55. The year 1678 is printed in the Oirat text. The events related actually occurred in 1698, the earth tiger year. The text has simply misprinted 78 for 98.

56. The term aci is ambiguous, meaning either "grandson" or "nephew." The genealogy given in DO, p. 30 states that Nima Sereng and Puncokh are sons of Khudai Shikur Dayicing. Ayuuki is the son of Puncokh, and Nazar is the son of Nima Sereng. Rabgyur is the son of Nazar. Thus Rabgyur (Rabjuuri in HKK) is the nephew of Ayuuki.

57. This incident is detailed in Pelliot, Notes, p. 28, and Cahen, History of the Relations of Russia and China, pp. 52, 53.

58. Neither of the envoys, Samdan or Tulishen, are
     mentioned in any of the other Oirat chronicles, nor are
     these events discussed. Tulishen wrote an account of
     his mission to the Oirats entitled I-yü-lu, printed in
     1723. Sir George Thomas Staunton translated this work
     into English in 1821 under the title Narrative of the
     Chinese Embassy to the Khan of the Tourgouth Tartars,
     in the Years 1712, 13, 14, & 15; by the Chinese
     Ambassador, and Published by the Emperor's Authority at
     Pekin. Samdan is mentioned as Sāmōtan by Staunton, p. 9
     and Rabjuuri is transcribed as ōlāpu-chu-eur, p. 8. For
     a further reference to Samdan cf. Imanishi, Tulishen's
     I-yü-lu, Revised and Annotated, p. 58.

59. The imperial edict of K'ang-hsi issued to instruct
     Tulishen concerning his manner of behavior toward
     Ayuuki and Cewang Rabtan is totally at odds with this
     position. "Should he (ayu-kee) express to you a wish
     for our assistance in any hostile operation against
     Tse-vang-Rabdan, you are by no means to make any
     promises...but are thus to reply...The affair you
     propose is one of great magnitude, and one in which it
     would not be proper for us to concur. You may, indeed,
     if you choose, lay the matter before his Sacred
     Eminence, but it is our opinion that our Emperor
     desiring nothing more than that all nations under
     heaven should enjoy peace and tranquility, has no
     intention whatever of occasioning to Tse-vang-Rabdan
     any disturbance. Indeed, we can pledge ourselves that
     this is the case." Staunton translation, History of the
     Relations of Russia and China, pp. 10 and 11; Imanishi,
     Tulisen's I-yü-lu, p. 59.

60. Both Cahen, History of the Relations of Russia and
     China, pp. 54-59, and Pelliot, Notes, pp. 29 and 83-85,
     treat this event extensively. See also Eminent Chinese
     of the Ch'ing Period, edited by Arthur W. Hummel, pp.
     784-787.

61. For a general discussion of the Girei family see The
     Encyclopaedia of Islam, Vol. II, pp. 1112-1114. Cf.
     Ocherki istorii Kalmyckoi ASSR, p. 211, for Bakhta
     Girei, Sultan of Kuban.

62. Donnelly, The Russian Conquest of Bashkiria, p. 41. V.
     Illeritskii, "Ekspeditsiia Kniazia Cherkasskogo v
     Khivu," Istoricheskii zhurnal, No. 7, 1940, pp. 40-51
     gives an account of the Bekovich-Cherasskii (Devlet
     Girey Bekovich) mission to Khiva.

63. B.H. Sumner, Peter the Great and the Emergence of
     Russia, p. 174, gives no indication that the Kalmyks
     had a hand in this defeat, nor does Donnelly, The
     Russian Conquest of Bashkiria, p. 41. John F. Baddeley,
     The Russian Conquest of the Caucasus, p. 10, gives a
     vivid description of the death of Bekovich-Cherkasskii.

64. Ayuuki had decreed in 1713 that his son Phyakhdar Byab

would succeed him. Pallas, Sammlungen, Vol. 1, p. 70.

65. Although this statement might strike the reader as boastful, and possibly not accurate, it seems that this was indeed the case. This would explain Howorth's statement: "About this time he seems to have been granted the title of Khan by the Russian Emperor for after the year 1700 he is so styled in official documents, and is no longer called Taishi." History of the Mongols, Vol. 1, p. 567. See also Pallas, Sammlungen, Vol. 1, p. 68.

66. No other Oirat document mentions Dasang.

67. According to Pallas, Sammlungen, Vol. 1, p. 70, and Howorth, History of the Mongols, vol. 1, p. 568, Phyakhdar Byab's death ended the chance for Dasang to take over the leadership of the Kalmyks. However, this seems not the only reason for Dasang's not ruling. See below, Footnote 96.

68. The HKK is the only Oirat text to mention Darma bala.

69. John Bell of Antermony, in his Travels from St. Petersburg in Russia, to diverse parts of Asia, Vol. II, pp. 331-333, gives a very good description of this meeting. The HKK does not detail the ceremonies which accompanied such a diplomatic meeting. The Tsar entertained Ayuuki and Darma Bala on his ship.

70. In August, 1721, Lezghian tribesmen attacked the town of Shemakha, causing much loss to Russian merchants and providing Peter with a pretext for military intervention. Hunczak, Russian Imperialism, p. 244.

71. John Bell reports in Travels from St. Petersburg, p. 333, that the Tsar "intimated to Ayuka Chan that he would be desirous of ten thousand troops to accompany him into Persia. The King of the Kalmucks replied, that ten thousand were at the Emperor's service, but that he thought one half of that number would be more than sufficient to answer all his purposes; and immediately gave orders for five thousand to march directly and join the Emperor at Terky."

72. This must be Rdo rje Mgün po, the son of Nazar mentioned in both GS 75.05 and DO 30.04. Both Nazar and Ayuuki trace their lineage to Khudai Shükür Dayicing, the eldest son of Khō Orlökh, Nazar through Nima Sereng, and Ayuuki through Puncokh.

73. Actually his eldest living son, now that Phyakhdar Byab was dead. It should also be noted that even though Ayuuki did not agree with the tsar's ideas on who should be the next khan, he fulfilled his troop commitment to Peter. This is noted by John Bell, Travels from St. Petersburg, Vol. II, p. 340, "... and also the five thousand Kalmycks sent by the AyukaChan,

according to agreement as formerly mentioned. They were all well mounted, and had many spare horses, which were of great use."

74.   Dondukh Ombu is a grandson of Ayuuki through his father Ghonjib (GS 75.03 Mgün Skyab; DO 30.03 Mg'un Sphyabs), who is a son of Ayuuki. Ghonjib and Phyakhdar Byab are the only sons of Ayuuki to produce offspring, Pelliot, Notes, p. 29. Ghonjib has two sons listed as Donrob Wangbo and Boqsorogho. GS 75.04 and DO 30.06 Dondukh Wangbo and Bokhsorgh. According to DO 30.07 Dondukh Wangbo had five sons, Ghaldan Norbo, Rangdol, Dodbi, Asarai, and Yobsar. The DO is the only Oirat source which gives this genealogical information. Pallas, Sammlungen, Vol. 1, p. 81, has Zhan being the mother of Randul, Dodbin, Assarai, and Dshoubuksar.

75.   According to both the GS 87.13 and DO 36.17, Ghonjib was to be given leadership of the Torghuud by Ayuuki. Evidently he must have died before he could rule, although his death is not recorded in any other Oirat texts. The only other explanation for his not taking over would be that he fell from favor but there is no indication in any of the sources that this was the case. Pallas, Sammlungen...vol. I, p. 69, and Howorth, History of the Mongols...vol.I, p. 567, state that soon after 1704 Ghonjib died. Howorth gives no definite date for this death.

76.   Dasang, however, died c. 1722; see below footnote 96.

77.   HKK 8.14 uses the plural ending -ner on döü, younger brother, but the genealogies list him as having only one brother. See footnote 74.

78.   Pallas, Sammlungen...vol. I, p. 70, gives 1624 as the date of Ayuuki's death. The 16 is an obvious misprint for 17, but whether or not Pallas is stating 1724 as the death of Ayuuki is not clear. Pallas gives Ayuuki's age as 83. Sarkisyanz, Geschichte der orientalischen Völker Russlands bis 1917, p. 253 lists 1724 as the date of Ayuuki's death.

79.   This praise for the long and good rule of Ayuuki is certainly well deserved. The Torghuud had remained strong and basically unified up until this time. It is interesting that none of the secondary sources reflect this praise. It is very striking glorification by the Oirats of one of their great leaders.

80.   Pelliot, Notes...p. 29, claims that Dharma Bala is the mother of Phyakhdar Byab.

81.   This had been Dharma Bala's plan even before Ayuuki's death.

82.   Pallas, Sammlungen...vol. I, p. 71, see also Ocherki istorii Kalmyckoi ASSR, p. 187.

83.   Howorth, <u>History of the Mongols</u>...vol.1, p. 568, adds
       that Dorji turned down the title of khan because he was
       unwilling to give his sons as hostages to the Russians.

84.   Ceren Dondukh is listed as the son of Ayuuki in GS
       75.03 and DO 30.03. No other information is given about
       Ceren Dondukh in these texts. Ceren Dondob is mentioned
       by Tulishen, cf. Imanishi, <u>Tulishen's</u>...p.153.

85.   Although Cewang Rabtan as khan of the Dzungars is very
       significant in Oirat history, and in relations between
       the Manchus, Tibetans, and eastern Mongols, it is
       important to note that neither the GS nor the DO even
       mention him. These histories do not accord the Dzungars
       a major role.

86.   The marriage of Ayuuki's daughter to Cewang Rabtan has
       previously been mentioned, cf. footnote 35. Courant
       also mentions this marriage, <u>L'Asie</u> <u>centrale</u>...p. 44,
       as does Baddeley, <u>Russia, Mongolia, China</u>...Vol. 2, p.
       439. This is a well-known and well-documented event.
       However, the marriage between a daughter of Cewang
       Rabtan and Ceren Dondukh is not mentioned in any other
       sources that I have seen. This second marriage alliance
       between Torghuud and Dzungars certainly demonstrates
       their continued close contacts.

87.   Thus Ceren Dondukh did not go to meet his future bride.

88.   This region is in Kazakhstan in the area of the Turgay
       river. <u>Atlas of the Soviet Union</u>, Moscow, 1969. See
       also Violet Conolly, <u>Beyond the Urals</u>, p. 23.

89.   The idea of scouting a way to Tibet was not a frivolous
       gesture on the part of Ceren Dondukh. In October, 1731,
       another group of Torghuud composed of about 300 men
       reached   Lhasa.   They   came   by   way   of
       Siberia-Kiakhta-Mongolia-Western China. A mission of
       investiture was sent in response to this group in 1735
       by the Dalai Lama to Ceren Dondukh: Petech, pp. 148,
       160.

90.   Zhan became the mother of Randuli by Dondukh Ombu, HKK
       11.13. For the sons of Dondukh Ombu see footnote number
       74.

91.   HKK 9.02 has already stated that Darma Bala became the
       wife of Dondukh Ombu. His own grandmother mentioned in
       the text here, is Darma Bala.

92.   The Ch'ing emperor was Yung Cheng from 1723-1736. I
       have not found a reference to this mission in Oirat
       sources. Neither Pallas nor Howorth, who give a long
       description of the investiture of Ceren Dondukh, make
       any   reference   to   a   Manchu   mission.   Pallas,
       <u>Sammlungen</u>...vol. I, p. 73-76, Howorth, <u>History of the</u>
       <u>Mongols</u>...,pp. 568-570. However, Cahen, in "Deux

ambassades chinoises en Russie au commencement du XVIIIe siecle," Revue Historique CXXXIII, 1920, pp. 85-89, discusses this mission.

93. The meeting between I. Ismayilov and Ceren Dondukh is noted in Ocherki istorii Kalmyckoi ASSR, p. 189.

94. The Shikür lama as the highest official of the Buddhist Church officiated: Pallas, Sammlungen...,vol. I, p. 75.

95. The text makes it seem that the investiture took place in 1731; actually it did not take place until September 10, 1735: Howorth, History of the Mongols..., vol. I, p. 568. It seems strange that there is no mention in the HKK of the patent sent by the Dalai Lama, which played a major part in the ceremony: see footnote 89, and also Pallas, Sammlungen..., vol. I, pp. 73-76, and Howorth, History of the Mongols..., vol. I, pp. 568-570.

96. Phyakhdar Byab had twelve sons according to DO 30.05 and 06. The GS does not give this genealogy. The DO lists Batu, Dacang, Bakhsadai, Donrob Rashi, Danzin Dorji, Ikhtar, Goncob Byab, Bodong, Solom Dobcin, Dorji Arshi, Yandakh and Busuruman as Phyakhdar Byab's sons. Dacang in the DO text is Dasang in the HKK. Dasang must have died in 1722, the date of Tsar Peter's trip to Astrakhan. See also footnote 67, Pelliot, Notes..., p. 29, quoting the Chinese text chapter 103, says that Phyakhdar Byab has thirteen sons; Dondobrashi, Batu, Dorji Rashi, Busurumun are the only sons mentioned by name. Dasang is not mentioned. Bergman, Nomadische...vol.I, pp. 145, 146 mentions Dasang's relationships.

97. Obviously when Peter became a Christian he also changed his name. It is not possible at this time to determine what Peter's original Mongol name was.

98. Both Peter and Dondukh Ombu are grandsons of Ayuuki. Dondukh Ombu ruled 1735-1741.

99. Dorji, the son of Nazar, is listed as having three sons, Lob kya, Bai, and Danzin, in GS 75.06. The names of the sons are spelled Lubphye, Bai, and Danzin in DO 30.04 and 05.

100. These actions are detailed by Pallas, Sammlungen..., vol. I, p. 78 and Howorth, History of the Mongols...Vol. I, p. 568.

101. Dondukh Dashi is mentioned in the genealogy in footnote 96.

102. For Lawang's actions see Pallas, Sammlungen...vol. I pp 50-51.

103. Ghaldan Norbu is one of five sons of Dondukh Ombu

according to DO 30.07. The other sons are Rangdol Dodbi, Asarai, and Yobsar. GS gives no genealogy for Dondukh Ombu.

104.   The HKK views Ceren Dondukh's attempts at rule in a very poor light. Even though he had the backing of the Russians, Manchus, and the Dalai Lama, he could not end the continual internecine feuding which eventually caused his downfall.

105.   There was religious confusion because some of the Kalmyk groups began switching religious beliefs from Buddhist to Christian.

106.   The HKK 10.13 spells this name Yeperebem, cf. Ocherki istorii Kalmyckoi ASSR, p. 191.

107.   This is Tsarina Anna who ruled 1730-1740. See Mina Curtiss, A Forgotten Empress: Anna Ivanovna and Her Era 1730-1740.

108.   This is another indication of the religious conflict which existed at the time among the Kalmyks.

109.   Ismailov's career in the Tsar's service is traced by Cahen in chapter IX of History of the Relations of Russia and China Under Peter the Great. He died in 1738. See Cahen, p. 77.

110.   See HKK 10.09 and 10.

111.   The Kazakhs had been pushed westward by the Dzungars in the beginning of the 18th century. They were then in the position of being attacked by the Bashkir, Russians and Kalmyks, as well as the Dzungars. The Kazakhs in the 1720s sought protection in an alliance with the Russians. The Russians pressured the Kazakhs into stopping their attacks on the Kalmyks, but this pressure was certainly not totally successful.

112.   Donnelly, The Russian Conquest of Bashkiria...p. 115 mentions a war between the Kalmyks and the Kazakhs in 1738.

113.   This is the Russo-Turkish war of 1736, whereby the Russians occupied the Crimea.

114.   Pallas, Sammlungen...vol. I, p.78 gives a different stipend for Dondukh Ombo. For his help in the Kuban, Dondukh Ombo is given 3,000 rubles in gold and 2,000 sacks of flour.

115.   See footnote 106. The spelling in HKK 11.09 is Yepremob.

116.   Dondukh Ombo had previously been given the power to rule (HKK 10.16 and 10.17), but had not officially been invested as khan. Howorth's statement in History of the

Mongols...vol.I, p. 570, "...Donduk Ombo was accordingly, in 1735, invested with the khanate by Ismailof, the governor of Astrakhan, an authority which he held till his death in 1741.", is wrong. Pallas does not mention this making of Dondukh Ombo khan after 1736. Because Howorth is dependent on Pallas as his source for this information, and since Pallas does not mention the actual investiture, Howorth has been misled. Courant, L'Asie centrale...p. 131 states that Dondukh Ombo was made khan at the death of the khan (Ceren Dondukh) who had returned to St. Petersburg (my translation). This is in full agreement with HKK 10.17 and 11.01. Courant, however, makes the same mistake as Howorth, claiming Dondukh Ombo was invested with the title by the governor of Astrakhan.

117. Cf. Petech, China and Tibet...p. 161.

118. Cf. Pallas, Sammlungen...vol.I, p. 79 and Howorth, History of the Mongols...vol.I, p. 571. Howorth misspells the name Randuli as Kandul, misreading the German "R" for a "K." See also Geiger, Peoples and Languages of the Caucasus, pp. 18-19, for a discussion of the Circassians.

119. GS 96.06 mentions Ghaldan Norbu's fighting in 1737.

120. Cf. Courant, L'Asie centrale...p.131.

121. Ubashi was one of the three sons of Nazar: see GS 75.05 and DO 30.04. GS lists rDo rje mgun bo, Rab gbyur and Ubasha, while the DO has four sons, mistakenly separating Dorji and G'ombo as two separate names and also listing Rabphyur and Ubashi. See also footnote 72.

122. See footnote 46.

123. Pallas, Sammlungen...vol. I, p.78 states that Ghaldan Danzin was assassinated. But the further explanation given by the HKK makes it clear that Ubashi was the person slain.

124. Donnelly, The Russian Conquest of Bashkiria...chapter 8 pp. 96-122, discusses Tatishchev's career.

125. Footnote 96 lists the sons of Phyakhdar Byab, but this is the only mention that Dondukh Dashi is his eldest son.

126. HKK 10.06 and 07.

127. Pallas, Sammlungen...vol. I p. 81 states this was in 1742 at the coronation of Elizabeth in Moscow. For a description of the coronation see Longworth, The Three Empresses, pp. 178-180.

128. Dondukh Dashi ruled 1741-1761.

129. Dejīd is the son of Bata Noyon of the clan of Yoboghon Mergen. See DO 27.16 and DO 39.15: both give the same genealogy.

130. DO 40.13 also documents this movement to the Volga.

131. The DO 40.10-13 gives a detailed description of the birth of this child. No other child's birth is given such an account in any other Oirat chronicle. However, the explanation for this emphasis is not a mystery. Tümen Jirghal is the father of Batur Ubashi, the author of the DO. Thus Batur Ubashi is stressing his own genealogy. The HKK has merely taken the material from this earlier source.

132. DO 40.15-16 gives more detail in stating that Dejīd died when Tümen Jirghal was three years old.

133. Once again because this is of such interest to the author of the DO, he relates these events in much more detail. The wife of Dejīd is given by name in DO 40.03 as Olzöi Orosikhu. Dondukh Dashi gives his approval for the marriage between Olzöi Orosixu and Byamiyang, DO 41.05. HKK 12.07-11 is a digression from the rather straight narrative history of the Torghuud. This material is of interest to the Khoyid and Khoshuud, but is out of place in this narrative. Obviously the material has been taken from the DO, as noted above in footnote 131.

134. The Lesser Horde of the Kazakhs under Abu'l-Khayr khan visited St. Petersburg and accepted Russian suzerainty. The Middle Horde accepted Russian protection in 1740. Cf. The Cambridge History of Islam, vol. I, p. 506. Thus by 1741 Russia had a very real role in keeping peace between Kalmyk and Kazakh. For the structure of the Kazakh hordes see Krader, Social Organization of the Mongol-Turkic Pastoral Nomads, pp. 192-209.

135. For Tatishchev see footnote 124 above. This line in the text HKK 12.12 is a restatement of HKK 12.03.

136. Pallas, Sammlungen..., vol. I, p. 81, Howorth, History of the Mongols..., vol. I, p. 571.

137. Her desire was rule over the Torghuud. This section is just a restatement of her ambition as seen in HKK 11.16-17.

138. This is a Slavicization of the name Dondukh. Pelliot, Notes..., p. 69, gives an explanation of the name Dondukh.

139. Pallas, Sammlungen..., vol. I, p. 81, states that the Princess took the name Wiera (=Vera) and does not mention anything about taking the family name of Dondukov. Pallas also lists the names of two daughters of Zhan: these are Nadezhda and Lyubov.

140.   Although Pallas, Sammlungen..., vol. I., p. 81,
         discusses the career of Aleksei, he does not mention
         this incident. Mogilev is in White Russia.

141.   According to Howorth, History of the Mongols..., vol.
         I, p. 571, prior to this Russian takeover Randuli had
         taken over the Bagha Coxor, which was the ulus of his
         father.

142.   The Ural river was the border for both the Kalmyks and
         Kazakhs. The river served as the eastern border for the
         Kalmyks and the western border for the Kazakhs.

143.   This is the law code of 1640. For the text of this code
         see K. F. Golstunskii, Mongolo-oiratskie zakony 1640
         goda..., St. Petersburg, 1880.

144.   This was not the first change in the law code of 1640.
         The first change occurred in 1678 with the supplement
         of Ghaldan Xung Tayiji. For a discussion of the code of
         1640 in general, and in particular the amendment after
         the Dondukh Dashi addition to the code see Krueger,
         "New Materials on Oirat Law and History Part One: The
         Jinjil Decrees," CAJ, vol. XVI no. 3, 1972, pp.
         194-205.

145.   There are a number of references to the various foreign
         peoples with whom the Kalmyks were now interacting in
         the Dondukh Dashi supplement. See for example MOZ
         27.03-04 and MOZ 33.01-02.

146.   The text of the new statute of Dondukh Dashi is given
         in Golstunskii, MOZ 23.04-33.13. MOZ 23.12 gives a
         Tibetan   spelling to the name: Don Grob bKra shis.

147.   It should be noted that, although this supplement
         purports to contain changes due to the new conditions
         under which the Kalmyks are now living, the greatest
         portion of the code is made up of regulations which
         certainly could fit either a Kalmyk of the mid 17th or
         mid 18th century. The text itself opens with a long
         Buddhist invocation. As can be seen by the statutes
         which are described in HKK 13.13-14.02, these laws deal
         with the everyday events in the life of a Kalmyk and
         are not very different from the original code in 1640
         or the Ghaldan Khung Tayiji supplement of 1678.

148.   The first section of the code deals with the laws of
         faith and religion.

149.   MOZ 24.09-10.

150.   MOZ 24.08.

151.   MOZ 25.01, 02, 03.

152.   This is high praise indeed for Dondukh Dashi. He was

not, however, the only person who was interested in the teaching of the Mongol language. The Jinjil decrees of 1822 contain right at the outset an advocacy of literacy: "Let any layman of the world read and study Mongolian. If the sons of nobles and zayisangs are not attentive to reading and writing Mongolian, the fine is a three year old camel from the father. Turn over his son to a teacher and teach [him]." The text continues for four more paragraphs. See Krueger, "New Materials on Oirat Law and History Part One: The Jinjil Decrees," P. 200 for complete translation.

153. MOZ 24.06, Tibetan form for gürüm or gurim = sKu rim. See Lessing, Mongolian English Dictionary, p. 392, Das, A Tibetan-English Dictionary, p. 91.

154. MOZ 24.01-02.

155. MOZ 25.11-12.

156. For a general discussion of Mongol and Oirat laws see Riasanovsky, Fundamental Principles of Mongol Law.

157. Footnote 127 has already recounted the meeting between Dondukh Dashi and Elizabeth in Moscow.

158. There were certainly other more pressing reasons for the Tsarina's interest in making Dondukh Dashi a khan. She hoped that this would keep his loyalty and thus he would stay an ally of Russia. 1756 had been a difficult year: it marked Russia's participation in the war against Prussia on the side of Austria, the Seven Years' War. This was also the year that the Ch'ing dynasty attacked the Dzungars. Russia thus had to worry about actions in the east. Earlier, in 1754-1755, a rebellion by the Bashkirs had to be put down. Thus Russia needed a stable ally in the form of the Torghuud. For an overall view of Russian foreign policy during this time see Vernadsky, Political and Diplomatic History of Russia.

159. Up until this time Dondukh Dashi had been serving as deputy khan. The Torghuud were without a khan. Neither the DO nor the GS gives any genealogical information about Ubashi.

160. See footnote 31. Ayuuki had also taken the oath of allegiance at this river. Pallas, Sammlungen...vol. I, p. 82 mentions both Z'ilin, the governor of Astrakhan and Bakunin, who is titled "Assessor."

161. According to Pallas, Sammlungen... vol.I, p. 82, the request by Dondukh Dashi was to make his son Ubashi deputy khan. Because Dondukh Dashi did not go to the Dalai Lama for investiture, the Russians were pleased. On March 21st of 1757 the request was granted and a pension of 500 rubles given. The actual investiture ceremony took place in April, 1758.

162. For Mangghad see Mankatten, Pallas, Sammlungen... vol. I, p. 79.

163. Ibid. p. 82.

164. See HKK 12.06-07.

165. Pallas, Sammlungen... vol.I, 83, gives a very similar description of this event. There is a feeling of great emotion on the part of Dondukh Dashi and Ubashi which does not come out in the HKK. During the bowing, for instance, Pallas claims they did so with tears in their eyes and the bow is described as a full kowtow. They touched their heads to the ground.

166. The numbers of soldiers accompanying the governor are different in Pallas, Sammlungen...vol. I, p. 83. The six dragoons and the 100 Tatars and Cossacks are mentioned, but a definite number (24) of grenadiers is also noted.

167. All of the ceremonies which had taken place thus far were only a prelude to the actual investiture ceremony.

168. Pallas, Sammlungen...vol. I, p. 84 gives the rank of lieutenant to the governor's son.

169. Pallas, ibid.; Darma Bala had of course been at the meeting between Ayuuki and Tsar Peter in 1722, forty-five years before. From Bell's account Darma Bala must have been quite old by this time. "The Queen was about fifty years old..." Travels from St. Petersburg...vol. 2, p. 332.

170. Galdan Ceren is mentioned because he is a descendant of Solom Ceren Tayishi. In 1677, Solom Ceren Tayishi, a Dörböd, brought 4,000 households from Dzungaria and placed himself under Ayuuki. HKK 3.13. Ghaldan Ceren is descended from Solom Ceren Tayishi. The linkage is as follows: Solom Ceren Tayishi's son was Möngkö Tömör, whose son was Citer, whose son was Lhabang Dorub, whose son was Ghaldan Ceren. See DO 29.04-05.

171. There is no other mention of Nimgen Ubashi in the Oirat texts.

172. Byamyang is the ruler of the Khoshuud. See HKK 12.09-10.

173. Pallas, Sammlungen...vol. I, p. 84 lists the term tuqci as a proper name. Tuqci is a "standard bearer" or "bannerman." See Krueger, Materials for an Oirat-Mongolian to English Citation Dictionary, Part 3, p. 524, 1984.

174. Pallas, Sammlungen...vol. I, p. 84 gives us our only knowledge of the name of Dondukh Dashi's wife; her name

is Tscheren Dshall.

175.   The role of Buddhism can clearly be seen in this
        oath-taking ceremony. The ceremony is reported by
        Pallas, Sammlungen...vol. I, p. 84.

176.   It is interesting to note the use of Russian words in
        the HKK, such as Porudcikh ("warrant officer"). The
        very end of the DO text also includes some Russian
        words. None of the other Oirat texts include Russian
        words.

177.   The German title Junker is transcribed Yüngker in HKK
        16.12.

178.   Polk'obaniq = "colonel" in Russian.

179.   Also in Pallas, Sammlungen...vol. I, p. 85.

180.   Ibid.

181.   For a discussion of Kalmyk hospitality see Rubel, The
        Kalmyk Mongols...pp. 38 and 39.

182.   Rubel, The Kalmyk Mongols...p. 40, discusses Kalmyk
        leisure activities.

183.   Pallas, Sammlungen...vol. I, p.86.

184.   Pallas, Sammlungen...vol. I, p. 86, says the place for
        this memorial was not far from Solanoi Sanmistsche.
        This is on the Volga just south of Chernyi Yar and
        north of Nikol'skoe. See Atlas Astrakhanskoi Oblasti,
        Glavnoe upravlenie geodezii i kartografii. Moscow,
        1968.

185.   Yangkhal is the city of Chernyi Yar, cf. Ramstedt,
        Kalmückisches Wörterbuch p. 215b.

186.   Pallas, Sammlungen...vol. I, p. 86, gives his death as
        January 21, 1761, as does Bergmann, Nomadische...vol.
        I, p. 146.

187.   For a full account of Amursana and his defeat, see
        Bawden, The Modern History of Mongolia, pp. 110-134.
        See also Krueger, "The Ch'ien-lung Inscriptions of 1755
        and 1758 in Oirat Mongolian," CAJ vol. XVI no. 1, for a
        translation of two inscriptions erected in honor of the
        Manchu victory over the Dzungars. For information on
        the repopulation of Dzungaria see Bawden, "A Mongol
        Document of 1764 Concerning the Repopulation of Ili,"
        ZAS, vol. 5.

188.   No genealogy for Ceren Tayishi is given in the other
        Oirat sources. It is strange that the only other source
        which discusses the importance of Ceren Tayishi in this
        period of Kalmyk history is Courant, L'Asie
        centrale...p.130. Pallas, Sammlungen...vol. 1, p. 91

only mentions Ceren after the migration back to China is complete.

189. Ubashi takes over after his father's death in 1761. He does not, however, have the title of khan. He is ruling under the title of deputy khan since he has not been given the title by the Russians. Pallas gives more information about the family history of Ubashi than do any of the other Oirat sources. According to Pallas, Sammlungen...vol. I, p. 86, Ubashi is only 17 years old when he takes over as ruler. Ubashi has married the daughter of the Khoshuud ruler Aerranpall. Aerranpall is listed by Pallas, Sammlungen...vol. I, p. 92, as taking his ulus on the flight out of Russia.

190. Cebekh Dorji is one of the three sons of Ghaldan Norbu, the other two sons are Kiyirib and Akh Sakhal, DO 30.08. For Ghaldan Norbu's genealogy see footnote 91. Ghaldan Norbu's line which included Cebekh Dorji were still embittered over the switch which allowed Dondukh Dashi's line to begin their rule. See also Bergmann, Nomadische...vol. I, pp. 147 and 148.

191. Ubashi is only 17 as mentioned in footnote 189.

192. This was a rebellion by Cebekh Dorji to show his dislike for the idea of having Ubashi rule. See Pallas, Sammlungen...vol. I, p. 86.

193. Cebekh Dorji could not be made khan of the Kalmyks, however the Russians were happy to try to split up the power of the khan and thus gave Cebekh Dorji the position of power on the newly formed council which was to act as overseer of the khan. See Pallas, Sammlungen...vol. I, p. 87, and Bergmann, Nomadische...vol. I, pp. 150-153.

194. Cebekh Dorji felt that he was next in line and would become khan if Ubashi was ousted.

195. It seems difficult to reconcile this statement with the one directly preceding it. Cebekh Dorji must have become disenchanted with the Russians. See also Barkman, "The Return of the Torghuts from Russia to China," p.96.

196. One can see clearly in HKK 18.05-18.08 the important role that Ceren plays in the migration of the Torghuud. This role is not brought out in other sources.

197. These stringent restrictions on the khan's power were conditions of his ruling as deputy khan.

198. It is very clear from the HKK that the primary reason for Ubashi's decision to leave the Volga region was the restrictions on his power imposed by the Russians. He also of course realized that a power vacuum existed in Dzungaria since the overthrow of Amursana. This power

vacuum is hinted at in the speech of Ceren Tayishi, see HKK 18.05-18.08. For a discussion of the other motives for the migration, see Howorth, History of the Mongols...vol. I, pp. 573-574 and Barkman, "The Return..." pp. 97 and 98.

199. This statement clearly shows the lack of input into decisions that the common subjects had.

200. One other motive in the desire to leave the Volga was religious. The Kalmyks with only few exceptions had remained loyal followers of the Buddha. However, on the Volga they were surrounded by Christians and Moslems, and cut off from their religious leaders in Tibet. The religious aspect is certainly not played up in the HKK but in this passage it comes through very clearly. Pallas, Sammlungen...vol. I, pp. 88-89, discusses the role of the chief lama of the Torghuud Mongols, Loosang Dshalzan Arantschimba the son of Bambar, in the movement of the Kalmyks. Neither Bambar nor Loosang are mentioned in any of the Oirat sources. The Buddhist Church might have begun to fear a loss of faith among the Kalmyks. In fact some 14,000 Kalmyks living in the vicinity of Stavropol were converted to Christianity in 1771. Krader, Social Organization...p. 119.

201. It must be remembered that Russia during this time was fighting wars on a number of fronts against Poland and Turkey. Ubashi aided the Russians cause in 1769 and 1770 by marching against the Kuban, see Bergmann, Nomadische...vol. I, pp. 167 and 168, and Weigh, RussoChinese Diplomacy 1689-1924, p. 27. Besides these external pressures, domestic troubles broke out. In 1771 the plague visited Moscow. There were riots in the city which were suppressed only with difficulty. Vernadsky, Political and Diplomatic History of Russia, p. 265.

202. Bergmann, Nomadische...vol. I, pp. 168-169.

203. Ibid.

204. Several sources have the statement that January 5, 1771 was set in advance as a propitious day for the start of the migration. Rubel, The Kalmyk Mongols...p. 14, goes so far as to state that it was set by the Dalai Lama. There is no reference given for this fact and I have not found another source to corroborate the Dalai Lama's involvement. Howorth, The History of the Mongols...vol. I, p. 575, quotes De Hell, "It was on the fifth of January, 1771, the day appointed by the high priests..." It is true as Rubel points out on p. 22 that not all the Kalmyks wanted to leave, the HKK is quite straight forward in stating that Ubashi panicked and fled.

205. There has been an enormous range of figures given for the number of families which took part in this

migration. See Baddeley, Russia, Mongolia, China, vol. II, pp. 439-440 for the various figures. A more recent work by Weigh gives the incredibly high figure of 700,000 families taking part in the migration, Russo-Chinese Diplomacy, p. 27. See also footnote 232 below.

206. The importance of their religious belief is once again brought out with this statement.

207. The governor of Orenburg at this time was General Ivan Andreevich Reinsdorp, see Alexander, Autocratic Politics in a National Crisis, p. 7.

208. Cf. Courant, L'Asie centrale...p. 136. For information on Nurali, leader of the Little Horde, see Alexander, Emperor of the Cossacks.

209. Ablai Sultan is head of the Middle Horde, see p. 136 of Courant, L'Asie centrale... and Hambly, Central Asia, p. 147.

210. At this time there was great discontent among some of the Yaik Cossacks. Alexander in Emperor of the Cossacks states on p. 35; "In a further gesture of defiance the 'disobedient' Cossacks refused to take part in the pursuit of the Volga Kalmyks, who had abruptly cast off Russian suzerainty in 1771 and fled across the Orenburg-Yaik border on the way to China. Indeed, 200 Yaik Cossacks joined the nomads in their change of residence and citizenship."

211. Courant, L'Asie centrale...p. 13, states that Traubenberg is the commander of the Russian army. This agrees with the HKK 20.14. For additional information on General von Traubenberg see Alexander, Emperor of the Cossacks, pp. 36-38.

212. The HKK 20.09 has Ercis as the name of the river. Ercis normally refers to the Irtysh. See Ramstedt, KWB p. 127a. Although I have not found a reference for Ercis meaning the Irgiz river, it is obvious from the context of this passage that it is the Irgiz and not the Irtysh which is meant.

213. The Turkhai river is near the Irgiz not the Irtysh. See footnote 212 above, see also Bergmann, Nomadische...pp. 201-204.

214. No mention of Kiyibi khan has been found in any of the sources dealing with the migration of the Kalmyks.

215. Takh is one form of Turkish for mountain. Since many mountains have takh in their name I have been unable to determine the location of this mountain.

216. See footnote 211.

217.　The original orders had been to capture the Kalmyks and bring them back to their territory on the west bank of the Volga. Now that the Kazakhs are free of Russian supervision they can attack the Kalmyks for their own profit.

218.　This passage summarizes the natural difficulties of the trek from the Volga to Dzungaria.

219.　The Kalmyk feelings toward the Kazakhs are certainly made plain by this portion of the text. The Kazakhs had their chance at revenge.

220.　Ayicuvakh is sultan of the Little Horde, cf. Apollova, Ekonomicheskie i Politicheskie Svyazi Kazakhstana s Rossiej v XVIII - Nachale XIX v. p. 264.

221.　The Sagiz river is west of the Embe river.

222.　The Mugodzar Mountains are south east of the Or river (the Or is a tributary of the Ural) and west of the Irgiz river.

223.　Ablai and Nurali linked up on one occasion and fought the Torghuud at the Sirin-silik river. The Kazakhs were driven off on this occasion. See Barkman, "The Return of the Torghuts..." p. 101.

224.　Irnali is discussed in the Hsi-yü wen-chien lu, chuan 6, pp. 17ā23a, see Barkman, "The Return of the Torghuts..." p. 97.

225.　See Barkman, "The Return of the Torghuts..." p. 102.

226.　Ibid.

227.　The HKK gives a much fuller account than that found in Barkman, "The Return of the Torghuts..." pp. 102-103.

228.　These are the same type of remarks that are found in the Chinese sources. See Barkman, "The Return of the Torghuts..." p. 103.

229.　De Mailla, Histoire Générale de la Chine...vol. XI, p. 583. Barkman, "The Return of the Torghuts..." p. 103.

230.　Barkman, "The Return of the Torghuts..." p.103, gives a translation from the Chinese which is very similar to the HKK. "The people drank the blood of horses and cows, and epidemics claimed many victims. The dead numbered three hundred thousand [Barkman claims this is highly exaggerated] while only thirty to forty per cent of the cattle were preserved. Only after more than ten days did they escape, destitute and disorganized, from the desert, but then the Buruts, who had been waiting outside the Gobi for a long time, pursued and killed, plundered and robbed them, day and night, now in the front, now in the rear, either with their whole forces or in scattered groups, and the number of men, women, children, cattle, and goods that was stolen from them, was several times as high as what the Kazakhs had robbed."

231. This is T'āmu ha mountain, see Barkman, "The Return of the Torghuts..." p. 103.

232. This figure of 33,000 families leaving Russia with a population of 169,000 and arriving in China with 70,000 people should settle the question of how many Kalmyks migrated. Bergmann, Nomadische...vol. I, p. 219, first mentions the discrepancy in the Russian and Chinese figures and Howorth, History of the Mongols...vol. I, p. 579, tries to reach a conclusion lacking information from Chinese and Oirat sources. Barkman, "The Return of the Torghuts..." pp. 106-107, discusses the problem adding information from Chinese sources. His conclusion that, "approximately 85,000, but in any case less than 100,000 people" arrived in China matches the HKK figures closely. See also footnote 205.

233. It became obvious to the Kalmyks that they would not be able to just settle into territory in Dzungaria without contending in some way with the Manchus, and they were certainly in no position to fight with them.

234. The Manchu court was not unanimous in its acceptance of the Kalmyks. Some feared a plot, especially since Ceren who had fled Dzungaria after the Amursana debacle now returned. Ceren also feared Manchu reprisals. See Barkman, "The Return of the Torghuts..." pp. 104-105. The general mentioned is Shu-hōte, see Hummel, Eminent Chinese of the Ch'ing...pp. 659-661.

235. For Ch'ien-lung's attitude at the return of the Torghuud, see Mish, "The Return of the Torgut," JAH vol. 4, 1970, p. 8.

236. Barkman, "The Return of the Torghut..." pp. 108-109, discusses the ranks given to the Kalmyks as well as their new territories. See also Hummel, Eminent Chinese of the Ch'ing...p. 660.

237. Khanza, see Mathews' Chinese-English Dictionary no. 3574, kuan: a tea canister.

238. The figures of what was received by the Kalmyks from the Manchus upon entering Dzungaria differ enormously in other sources. The number of cattle received is much lower in other texts. Mish, "The Return of the Torgut" p. 81, states 185,000 head of cattle including horses and sheep were presented. Barkman, "The Return of the Torghuuts..." p. 106, states, "The Torghuts received therefore over two hundred thousand head of cattle and horses."

239. Ceren Tayishi migrated to the Volga after Amursana's

defeat, see footnote 188. The treaty of Kiakhta does provide for the return or execution of fugitives, cf. Mancall, Russia and China: Their Diplomatic Relations to 1728, p. 309.

240.   This is the only mention of Cevang Dorji Namjyal in the Oirat sources.

241.   This optimism about the happiness of the Kalmyks remaining in Russia is not born out by the other sources. Many of them took part in the Pugachev rebellion, see pp. 97-99 of Emperor of the Cossacks by Alexander. Autocratic Politics in a National Crisis by Alexander also mentions Kalmyk involvement. See also Barkman's remarks on pp. 109-110 of "The Return of the Torghuts..." concerning the Russians preventing further movement of the Kalmyks.

I. Краткая исторія Калмыцкихъ хановъ.

ᠲᠡᠷᠡ ᠪᠦᠬᠦᠨ ᠢ ᠪᠢᠴᠢᠭᠰᠡᠨ ᠪᠠ 1640 1655

[Mongolian script text]

[Mongolian script text in traditional vertical Mongolian writing, arranged in columns read left to right. The text contains the following year markers embedded within the columns: 1681, 1677, 1670, 1673, 1661.]

ᠪᠣᠯᠵᠣ ᠰᠠᠷᠠᠭᠤᠯᠵᠠᠨ ᠪᠣᠯᠵᠣᠷᠠᠨ ᠣᠴᠢᠷᠠᠨ ᠭᠡᠵᠦ ᠪᠠᠶᠢᠨᠠ ᠂᠂

1701

1708

ᠳᠠᠷᠠᠭᠠ ᠪᠠᠷ

ᠮᠠᠨᠵᠤ ᠪᠤᠰᠤ ᠠᠬᠠᠮᠠᠳ ᠳᠤᠮᠳᠠᠳᠤ ᠪᠠᠭ᠎ᠠ᠃
ᠪᠠᠶᠠᠨ ᠪᠤᠰᠤ ᠡᠮᠦᠨ᠎ᠡ ᠳᠤᠮᠳᠠᠳᠤ ᠪᠠᠭ᠎ᠠ᠃
ᠮᠠᠨᠵᠤᠤᠳ ᠡᠨᠡ ᠬᠥᠮᠦᠨ ᠪᠠᠶᠢᠨ᠎ᠠ᠃

1719

1715

ᠮᠣᠩᠭᠣᠯ ᠪᠢᠴᠢᠭ

1731

1725

1*

1734

1735

1741

1737

1736

ᠮᠣᠩᠭᠣᠯ ᠪᠢᠴᠢᠭ

1784

3000

1742

15

1787

1745

1984

ᠮᠠᠨᠤᠰᠢᠶᠠᠯ ᠂ ᠣᠶᠣᠨ ᠠᠳᠠ ᠰᠠᠨᠠᠭᠤᠯ ᠨᠤᠨᠤ ᠲᠡᠷᠡᠭᠦᠨ ᠣᠨᠤᠰᠠᠰᠠᠯᠲᠠᠢ ᠪᠠᠷᠢᠭ ᠰᠠᠶᠢᠲᠤᠷᠠᠨᠲᠤᠩ ᠨᠡᠶᠢᠭᠦᠯ ᠂ ᠠᠮᠠᠨ ᠦᠶᠢᠰᠤᠲᠢᠶᠢᠰᠠᠨ ᠬᠡᠲᠦᠷᠡᠨ ᠬᠡᠯᠡᠭᠡ

ᠨᠢ ᠠᠲᠤᠶᠢᠮᠠᠨ ᠤᠰᠤᠭᠤᠨᠤᠨᠤ ᠨᠤᠨᠤ ᠲᠠᠰᠤᠨᠤᠶᠢᠰᠤ ᠂ ᠡᠷᠢᠨ ᠠᠲᠤᠨᠤ ᠭᠦᠷᠦᠨᠤ ᠲᠤᠲᠤᠶᠢᠰᠤᠨ ᠬᠡᠲᠦᠷᠦᠭ ᠲᠡᠷᠡᠭᠦᠨᠵᠢ

ᠮᠠᠨᠤᠶᠢᠰᠤᠨ ᠨᠢ ᠨᠠᠰᠤᠶᠢᠰᠤᠨ ᠨᠤᠨᠤ ᠨᠠᠰᠤᠨᠤ ᠶᠠᠮᠠᠨ ᠤᠰᠤᠶᠢᠰᠤ ᠂ ᠲᠠᠰᠤᠨᠤᠶᠢᠰᠤ ᠬᠡᠲᠦᠷ ᠤᠰᠤᠶᠢᠰᠤᠨ ᠶᠠᠮᠠᠨ

ᠨᠠᠶᠢᠮᠠᠨ ᠤᠶᠢᠨᠤ ᠲᠠᠰᠤᠶᠢᠰᠤᠨ ᠨᠠᠰᠤᠨ ᠤᠶᠢᠰᠤᠨ ᠨᠤᠨᠤ ᠲᠠᠰᠤᠶᠢᠰᠤᠨ ᠲᠠᠰᠤ ᠨᠠᠶᠢᠮᠠᠨ ᠲᠠᠰᠤᠨᠤᠶᠢᠰᠤ ᠂ ᠤᠰᠤᠶᠢᠰᠤᠨᠤ

ᠮᠠᠰᠤᠶᠢᠰᠤᠨ ᠠᠲᠠ ᠲᠠᠰᠤᠶᠢᠰᠤ ᠨᠤᠨᠤ ᠨᠠᠰᠤᠶᠢᠰᠤᠶᠢᠰᠤᠶᠢᠰᠤᠨ ᠨᠢ ᠠᠲᠠ ᠰᠠᠶᠢᠰᠤᠶᠢᠰᠤᠶᠢᠰᠤ ᠂ (ᠲᠠᠰᠤᠨᠤᠶᠢᠰᠤ

ᠨᠠᠶᠢᠮᠠᠨᠵᠢ ᠂ ᠲᠠᠰ ᠲᠠᠰᠤᠶᠢᠰᠤᠶᠢᠰᠤᠨ ᠨᠤᠨᠤ ᠰᠠᠶᠢᠰᠤᠶᠢᠰᠤᠶᠢᠰᠤᠨ ᠲᠠᠰᠤ ᠂ ᠨᠠᠰᠤ ᠲᠠᠰ ᠲᠠᠰ ᠲᠠᠰᠤᠶᠢᠰᠤᠶᠢ

ᠨᠠᠶᠢᠮᠠ ᠯᠢ ᠲᠠᠰᠤᠶᠢᠰᠤᠶᠢᠰᠤᠶᠢᠰᠤ ᠲᠠᠰᠤᠨ ᠲᠠᠰᠤ ᠂ ᠰᠠᠶᠢᠰᠤᠶᠢᠰᠤᠶᠢᠰᠤ ᠲᠠᠰᠤᠯ ᠂ ᠨᠠᠰᠤᠶᠢᠰᠤᠶᠢᠰᠤᠶᠢᠰᠤ ᠲᠠᠰᠤᠶᠢ

ᠨᠠᠶᠢᠮᠠᠨ ᠯᠢ ᠲᠠᠰᠤ ᠰᠠᠶᠢᠰᠤᠶᠢᠰᠤᠶᠢᠰᠤ ᠨᠠᠰᠤᠶᠢᠰᠤᠶᠢ ᠨᠢ ᠮᠠᠰᠤ ᠲᠠᠰᠤᠶᠢᠰᠤᠨᠤ ᠨᠢᠷᠤ ᠂ ᠨᠢᠷᠤ ᠯᠢᠯᠢ ᠮᠠᠰᠤᠨᠤᠨᠤ

ᠨᠠᠶᠢᠮᠠᠨ ᠂ 1757 ᠲᠠᠰᠤᠶᠢᠰᠤᠶᠢᠰᠤᠶᠢᠰᠤ ᠲᠠᠰᠤᠶᠢᠰᠤᠶᠢᠰᠤ ᠂ ᠯᠢ ᠲᠠᠰᠤᠶᠢᠰᠤ ᠨᠢ ᠮᠠᠰᠤᠶᠢᠰᠤ ᠲᠠᠰᠤᠶᠢᠰᠤ ᠲᠠᠰᠤᠶᠢᠰᠤᠶᠢ

ᠨᠠᠰᠤᠶᠢᠰᠤᠶᠢᠰᠤ ᠲᠠᠰᠤᠶᠢᠰᠤ ᠮᠠᠰᠤᠨ ᠲᠠᠰᠤᠶᠢᠰᠤ ᠲᠠᠰᠤᠶᠢᠰᠤᠶᠢᠰᠤᠶᠢᠰᠤ ᠲᠠᠰ ᠂ ᠲᠠᠰ ᠲᠠᠰ ᠲᠠᠰᠤ ᠨᠢᠷᠤ ᠲᠠᠰᠤᠶᠢᠰᠤᠶᠢ

ᠮᠠᠰᠤᠶᠢᠰᠤᠶᠢᠰᠤ ᠨᠠᠰᠤᠶᠢ ᠰᠠᠶᠢᠰᠤᠶᠢᠰᠤ ᠲᠠᠰᠤ ᠲᠠᠰᠤᠶᠢᠰᠤᠨ ᠨᠢᠷᠤ ᠲᠠᠰᠤᠶᠢᠰᠤ ᠂ ᠲᠠᠰᠤᠶᠢᠰᠤᠶᠢᠰᠤ ᠲᠠᠰᠤ ᠮᠠᠰᠤᠶᠢᠰᠤᠶᠢᠰᠤ

ᠨᠠᠶᠢᠮᠠᠨ ᠯᠢᠯᠢ ᠲᠠᠰᠤ ᠲᠠᠰᠤᠶᠢᠰᠤ ᠨᠢ ᠮᠠᠰᠤᠶᠢᠰᠤ ᠂ ᠯᠢ ᠲᠠᠰᠤ ᠲᠠᠰᠤᠶᠢ ᠨᠠᠰᠤ ᠲᠠᠰᠤᠶᠢᠰᠤ ᠲᠠᠰ ᠲᠠᠰᠤᠶᠢᠰᠤ

ᠨᠠᠶᠢᠮᠠ ᠂ ᠯᠢᠯᠢ ᠮᠠᠰᠤᠶᠢᠰᠤ ᠲᠠᠰᠤ ᠲᠠᠰ ᠰᠠᠶᠢᠰᠤᠨ ᠲᠠᠰᠤᠶᠢᠰᠤ ᠲᠠᠰᠤᠶᠢᠰᠤᠶᠢ ᠨᠢᠷᠤ ᠰᠠᠶᠢᠰᠤᠶᠢᠰᠤ ᠂ ᠨᠠᠰᠤᠶᠢᠰᠤ

ᠨᠠᠶᠢᠮᠠᠨ ᠬᠠᠰᠤᠶᠢᠰᠤ ᠲᠠᠰ ᠬᠠᠰᠤᠶᠢᠰᠤᠨ ᠨᠢ ᠨᠠᠰᠤᠶᠢᠰᠤ ᠬᠠᠰᠤᠨᠤ ᠯᠢ ᠨᠠᠰᠤᠶᠢᠰᠤ ᠂᠂ ᠯᠢᠯᠢ ᠲᠠᠰᠤᠶᠢᠰᠤᠶᠢᠰᠤ

ᠨᠠᠰᠤᠶᠢᠰᠤᠨ ᠨᠢᠷᠤ ᠬᠠᠰᠤᠶᠢᠰᠤᠶᠢᠰᠤᠶᠢᠰᠤ ᠨᠠᠰᠤᠶᠢᠰᠤ ᠯᠢ ᠂ ᠰᠠᠶᠢᠰᠤᠶᠢ (ᠨᠠᠰᠤ) ᠲᠠᠰᠤᠨᠤᠶᠢᠰᠤ ᠨᠢᠷᠤᠶᠢᠰᠤᠶᠢ

ᠨᠢ ᠲᠠᠰᠤᠶᠢᠰᠤᠶᠢ ᠨᠠᠰᠤᠶᠢᠰᠤᠨᠤ ᠯᠢ ᠂᠂ ᠯᠢᠯᠢ ᠲᠠᠰᠤᠶᠢᠰᠤᠶᠢᠰᠤᠶᠢᠰᠤ ᠲᠠᠰᠤᠶᠢᠰᠤᠶᠢᠰᠤᠶᠢᠰᠤ ᠲᠠᠰᠤᠶᠢᠰᠤᠨᠤ ᠨᠠᠰᠤᠶᠢᠰᠤ

ᠨᠠᠶᠢᠮᠠ ᠨᠢᠷᠤ ᠬᠠᠰᠤ ᠲᠠᠰᠤᠶᠢᠰᠤᠨᠤ ᠬᠠᠰᠤᠶᠢᠰᠤ ᠯᠢᠯᠢᠯᠢ ᠬᠠᠰᠤᠶᠢᠰᠤᠶᠢᠰᠤᠶᠢ ᠲᠠᠰ ᠲᠠᠰᠤᠶᠢᠰᠤᠶᠢᠰᠤᠶᠢᠰᠤ ᠲᠠᠰᠤᠶᠢᠰᠤᠶᠢ

ᠨᠢ ᠲᠠᠰᠤᠶᠢᠰᠤᠨᠤ ᠲᠠᠰᠤᠶᠢᠰᠤ ᠲᠠᠰᠤᠶᠢᠰᠤᠶᠢᠰᠤ ᠂᠂ ᠲᠠᠰᠤᠶᠢᠰᠤᠶᠢᠰᠤᠶᠢᠰᠤᠶᠢᠰᠤ ᠲᠠᠰᠤᠶᠢᠰᠤ ᠨᠢ ᠨᠠᠰᠤ ᠲᠠᠰᠤᠶᠢᠰᠤᠶᠢᠰᠤᠶᠢ ᠂᠂

ᠬᠠᠶᠢᠷᠠᠬᠠᠨ ᠬᠥᠮᠦᠨ ᠤᠨ ᠲᠥᠷᠥᠯ ᠭᠡᠭᠴᠢ ᠃ ᠠᠴᠠ ᠲᠥᠷᠥᠭᠰᠡᠨ ᠮᠠᠨᠢ ᠃ ᠬᠠᠷᠢᠨ ᠰᠠᠭᠤᠵᠠᠢ ᠃ ᠡᠨᠡᠬᠦ ᠤᠳᠠᠭᠠ ᠬᠠᠷᠢᠨ ᠃ ᠲᠡᠮᠳᠡᠭᠯᠡᠭᠰᠡᠨ ᠂ ᠡᠨᠡ ᠨᠢ ᠲᠡᠭᠦᠰ ᠬᠦᠷᠲᠡᠵᠦ ᠂

ᠰᠠᠨ ᠠᠵᠤ ᠪᠠᠷ ᠪᠠᠢᠭᠤᠯᠬᠤ ᠶᠢᠨ ᠲᠤᠯᠠᠳᠠ ᠃ ᠨᠢᠭᠡᠨ ᠠᠷᠭᠠᠳᠠᠵᠤ ᠃ ᠪᠠᠷᠠᠭ᠎ᠠ ᠬᠦᠯᠢᠶᠡᠭᠰᠡᠨ ᠃ ᠲᠡᠳᠡᠨ ᠴᠤ ᠃ ᠭᠡᠭᠴᠢ ᠲᠤᠰᠤ ᠰᠠᠢᠬᠠᠨ ᠃

ᠭᠡᠵᠦ ᠬᠦ ᠬᠥᠭᠵᠢᠯ ᠤᠨ ᠤᠷᠤᠭᠰᠢᠳᠠ ᠃ ᠡᠨᠡ ᠨᠢ ᠤᠳᠤᠬᠠᠨ ᠳᠤ ᠃ ᠵᠠᠩᠭᠢᠯᠠᠭ᠎ᠠ ᠃ ᠪᠣᠯ ᠲᠤᠰᠤᠨ ᠤ ᠃ ᠡᠳᠦᠷ ᠪᠤᠷᠢ ᠬᠠᠷᠢᠨ ᠃

ᠲᠠᠭᠤᠷᠢᠶᠠᠯ ᠲᠡᠭᠦᠨ ᠤ ᠲᠤᠬᠠᠢ ᠃ ᠡᠳᠦᠷ ᠪᠦᠷᠢ ᠃ ᠤᠯᠠᠮ ᠬᠥᠭᠵᠢᠭᠡᠳ ᠃ ᠲᠡᠷᠡ ᠨᠢ ᠃ ᠨᠢᠭᠡᠨᠲᠡ ᠠᠳᠠᠯᠢ ᠃

ᠬᠠᠷᠢᠨ ᠡᠨᠡ ᠨᠢ ᠬᠡᠷᠡᠭᠯᠡᠬᠦ ᠃ ᠲᠤᠰᠤ ᠨᠢᠭᠡᠨ ᠪᠦᠯᠦᠭ ᠃ ᠰᠠᠭᠤᠷᠢ ᠨᠢ ᠃ ᠮᠥᠨ ᠴᠤ ᠃ ᠪᠣᠯᠤᠭᠰᠠᠨ ᠢᠶᠠᠷ ᠃

ᠬᠥᠮᠦᠨ ᠲᠥᠷᠥᠯᠬᠢᠲᠡᠨ ᠤ ᠃ ᠠᠵᠤ ᠠᠬᠤᠢ ᠬᠥᠭᠵᠢᠯ ᠤᠨ ᠃ ᠠᠴᠠ ᠲᠥᠷᠥᠭᠰᠡᠨ ᠃ ᠲᠤᠰᠤ ᠪᠣᠯ ᠃ ᠬᠠᠷᠢᠨ ᠃

ᠮᠠᠨ ᠤ ᠤᠯᠤᠰ ᠤᠨ ᠃ ᠡᠳ᠋ ᠤᠨ ᠵᠠᠰᠠᠭ ᠤᠨ ᠃ ᠨᠡᠩ ᠴᠤ ᠃ ᠬᠥᠮᠦᠨ ᠲᠥᠷᠥᠯᠬᠢᠲᠡᠨ ᠤ ᠃ ᠲᠤᠰᠤᠨ ᠤ ᠃

ᠰᠠᠭᠤᠷᠢ ᠪᠣᠯᠤᠭᠰᠠᠨ ᠃ ᠪᠠᠷᠢᠯᠭ᠎ᠠ ᠶᠢᠨ ᠃ ᠡᠳᠦᠷ ᠪᠦᠷᠢ ᠃ ᠬᠡᠷᠡᠭᠴᠡᠭᠡ ᠃ ᠲᠤᠬᠠᠢ ᠃

ᠲᠤᠰᠤ ᠬᠡᠷᠡᠭᠯᠡᠬᠦ ᠳᠤ ᠃ ᠠᠵᠤ ᠠᠬᠤᠢ ᠶᠢᠨ ᠃ ᠲᠤᠰᠤᠨ ᠤ ᠬᠡᠷᠡᠭᠴᠡᠭᠡ ᠃ ᠬᠠᠷᠢᠨ ᠃ ᠡᠳᠦᠷ ᠪᠦᠷᠢ ᠃

ᠲᠤᠬᠠᠢ ᠃ ᠠᠵᠤ ᠠᠬᠤᠢ ᠶᠢᠨ ᠃ ᠪᠠᠷᠢᠯᠭ᠎ᠠ ᠶᠢᠨ ᠃ ᠲᠤᠰᠤ ᠃ ᠲᠤᠰᠤ ᠃

ᠰᠠᠭᠤᠷᠢ ᠪᠣᠯᠤᠭᠰᠠᠨ ᠃ ᠲᠤᠰᠤᠨ ᠤ ᠃ ᠬᠡᠷᠡᠭᠴᠡᠭᠡ ᠃ ᠬᠠᠷᠢᠨ ᠃ ᠬᠡᠷᠡᠭᠴᠡᠭᠡ ᠃

1755

1761

2

ᠪᠢᠴᠢᠭᠡᠰᠦ ᠪᠤ᠂ ᠲᠡᠷᠢᠭᠦᠨ ᠴᠠᠭᠠᠷᠢᠭ ᠤᠨ ᠤᠳᠤᠷᠢᠳᠤᠯᠭᠠ ᠵᠢ᠂ ᠨᠡᠷ᠎ᠡ ᠨᠢ ᠬᠦᠬᠦᠯᠦᠭᠰᠡᠨ ᠤᠴᠢᠷ ᠲᠤ ᠳᠡᠪᠡᠯ ᠳᠡᠬᠡᠭᠡᠨ ᠬᠥᠬᠡᠲᠡᠢ᠂ ᠨᠥᠬᠡᠷ ᠬᠥᠮᠦᠨ ᠵᠠᠯᠠᠭᠤ ᠨᠠᠰᠤᠨ ᠤ ᠲᠡᠷᠢᠭᠦᠨ ᠵᠡᠷᠭᠡ ᠵᠢ᠂ ᠨᠡᠷ᠎ᠡ ᠨᠢ ᠴᠦ ᠦᠭᠡᠢ ᠤᠷᠤᠭᠤ᠂ ᠳᠡᠭᠡᠷ᠎ᠡ ᠡᠴᠡ ᠤᠷᠤᠭᠤ᠂ ᠵᠠᠷᠢᠮ ᠬᠥᠮᠦᠨ ᠤ ᠳᠡᠷᠭᠡᠳᠡ ᠬᠥᠮᠦᠨ ᠤ ᠬᠦᠦ ᠪᠤᠶᠤ ᠬᠠᠳᠠᠮ ᠡᠴᠢᠭᠡ᠂ ᠡᠭᠡᠴᠢ ᠳᠡᠭᠦᠦ ᠨᠡᠷ ᠦᠨ ᠬᠤᠭᠤᠷᠤᠨᠳᠤ᠂ ᠦᠨᠳᠦᠰᠦᠲᠡᠨ ᠦ ᠴᠢᠨᠠᠷᠲᠠᠢ ᠬᠦᠴᠦᠨ ᠤ ᠤᠴᠢᠷ ᠢᠶᠠᠷ ᠬᠡᠯᠡᠭᠳᠡᠬᠦ ᠦᠭᠡᠢ᠂ ᠨᠡᠷ᠎ᠡ ᠲᠡᠢ ᠪᠤᠯᠬᠤ ᠡᠷᠬᠡ ᠲᠡᠢ᠂ ᠨᠡᠷ᠎ᠡ ᠲᠡᠢ ᠬᠥᠮᠦᠨ ᠤ ᠲᠤᠬᠠᠢ ᠶᠠᠷᠢᠬᠤ ᠳᠤ᠂ ᠬᠥᠮᠦᠨ ᠤ ᠨᠡᠷ᠎ᠡ ᠶᠢᠨ ᠤᠳᠬ᠎ᠠ ᠶᠢ ᠲᠠᠶᠢᠯᠪᠤᠷᠢᠯᠠᠬᠤ ᠳᠤ᠂ ᠤᠯᠠᠨ ᠵᠦᠢᠯ ᠦᠨ ᠰᠠᠨᠠᠭ᠎ᠠ ᠪᠠᠷ ᠨᠡᠷ᠎ᠡ ᠥᠭᠴᠦ ᠪᠠᠶᠢᠭᠰᠠᠨ ᠶᠤᠮ᠃

1771

5

33000

ᠳᠤᠷ ᠃ ᠮᠥᠩᠭᠡᠵᠢᠨ ᠬᠠᠯᠵᠠᠨ ᠬᠥᠪᠡᠭᠦᠨ ᠨᠢᠭᠡᠨ ᠡᠳᠦᠷ ᠃ ᠠᠳᠤᠭᠤ ᠬᠠᠷᠢᠭᠤᠯᠵᠤ
ᠶᠠᠪᠤᠬᠤ ᠳᠤᠷ᠃ ᠮᠤᠷᠢᠨ ᠤ ᠪᠠᠨ ᠳᠡᠭᠡᠷ᠎ᠡ ᠤᠨᠲᠠᠵᠤ ᠃ ᠨᠢᠭᠡᠨ ᠵᠡᠭᠦᠳᠦᠨ
ᠦᠵᠡᠪᠡᠢ ᠃ ᠵᠡᠭᠦᠳᠦᠨ ᠳᠡᠭᠡᠨ ᠃ ᠲᠡᠭᠷᠢ ᠡᠴᠡ ᠨᠢᠭᠡᠨ ᠬᠥᠪᠡᠭᠦᠨ ᠪᠠᠭᠤᠵᠤ
ᠢᠷᠡᠭᠡᠳ ᠂ ᠴᠢ ᠮᠢᠨᠦ ᠦᠭᠡ ᠶᠢ ᠰᠤᠨᠤᠰ ᠃ ᠴᠢᠮ᠎ᠠ ᠶᠢ ᠪᠢ ᠠᠪᠴᠤ
ᠲᠡᠭᠷᠢ ᠶᠢᠨ ᠤᠷᠤᠨ ᠳᠤᠷ ᠤᠷᠤᠭᠤᠯᠤᠶᠠ ᠃ ᠭᠡᠰᠡᠨ ᠳᠦᠷ ᠃ ᠬᠥᠪᠡᠭᠦᠨ
ᠬᠡᠯᠡᠷᠦᠨ ᠃ ᠪᠢ ᠡᠵᠢ ᠠᠪᠤ ᠪᠠᠨ ᠣᠷᠬᠢᠵᠤ ᠃ ᠬᠠᠮᠢᠭᠠᠰᠢ
ᠶᠠᠪᠤᠬᠤ ᠪᠤᠢ ᠃ ᠦᠯᠦ ᠶᠠᠪᠤᠶ᠎ᠠ ᠭᠡᠪᠡᠢ ᠃ ᠲᠡᠷᠡ ᠬᠥᠪᠡᠭᠦᠨ
ᠡᠷᠭᠢᠵᠦ ᠤᠳᠠᠯ ᠦᠭᠡᠢ ᠃ ᠬᠠᠷᠢᠭᠠᠳ ᠬᠥᠮᠦᠨ ᠤ ᠳᠦᠷᠢ
ᠪᠡᠷ ᠃ ᠬᠥᠪᠡᠭᠦᠨ ᠤ ᠡᠮᠦᠨ᠎ᠡ ᠵᠤᠭᠰᠤᠭᠠᠳ ᠃ ᠨᠠᠳᠠ ᠲᠠᠢ
ᠬᠠᠮᠲᠤ ᠶᠠᠪᠤ ᠭᠡᠪᠡᠢ ᠃ ᠡᠨᠡ ᠬᠥᠪᠡᠭᠦᠨ ᠠᠷᠭ᠎ᠠ ᠦᠭᠡᠢ
ᠳᠠᠭᠠᠵᠤ ᠶᠠᠪᠤᠪᠠᠢ ᠃ ᠨᠢᠭᠡᠨ ᠠᠭᠤᠯᠠ ᠶᠢᠨ ᠤᠷᠤᠢ ᠳᠤᠷ
ᠬᠦᠷᠦᠭᠡᠳ ᠃ ᠲᠡᠷᠡ ᠬᠥᠪᠡᠭᠦᠨ ᠬᠡᠯᠡᠷᠦᠨ ᠃ ᠡᠨᠳᠡ ᠴᠢ
ᠵᠤᠭᠰᠤ ᠃ ᠪᠢ ᠲᠡᠭᠷᠢ ᠳᠦᠷ ᠭᠠᠷᠴᠤ ᠃ ᠡᠨᠡ ᠶᠠᠪᠤᠳᠠᠯ ᠢ
ᠮᠡᠳᠡᠭᠦᠯᠵᠦ ᠢᠷᠡᠶ᠎ᠡ ᠭᠡᠭᠡᠳ ᠃ ᠲᠡᠭᠷᠢ ᠳᠦᠷ ᠭᠠᠷᠴᠤ
ᠤᠳᠠᠯ ᠦᠭᠡᠢ ᠃ ᠬᠠᠷᠢᠭᠠᠳ ᠢᠷᠡᠵᠦ ᠬᠡᠯᠡᠷᠦᠨ ᠃ ᠲᠡᠭᠷᠢ
ᠡᠴᠡ ᠵᠠᠷᠯᠢᠭ ᠪᠤᠯᠤᠷᠤᠨ ᠃ ᠲᠡᠷᠡ ᠬᠥᠪᠡᠭᠦᠨ ᠢ
ᠠᠪᠴᠤ ᠢᠷ᠎ᠡ ᠭᠡᠪᠡ ᠃ ᠡᠳᠦᠭᠡ ᠴᠢ ᠨᠠᠳᠠ ᠲᠠᠢ
ᠬᠠᠮᠲᠤ ᠶᠠᠪᠤ ᠭᠡᠭᠡᠳ ᠃ ᠬᠥᠪᠡᠭᠦᠨ ᠢ ᠳᠠᠭᠠᠭᠤᠯᠵᠤ
ᠲᠡᠭᠷᠢ ᠳᠦᠷ ᠭᠠᠷᠪᠠᠢ ᠃ ᠲᠡᠭᠷᠢ ᠶᠢᠨ ᠡᠵᠡᠨ ᠲᠡᠷᠡ
ᠬᠥᠪᠡᠭᠦᠨ ᠢ ᠦᠵᠡᠭᠡᠳ ᠃ ᠮᠠᠰᠢ ᠪᠠᠶᠠᠷᠯᠠᠵᠤ ᠃
ᠡᠨᠡ ᠬᠥᠪᠡᠭᠦᠨ ᠢ ᠮᠢᠨᠦ ᠳᠡᠷᠭᠡᠳᠡ ᠰᠠᠭᠤᠯᠭ᠎ᠠ
ᠭᠡᠭᠡᠳ ᠃ ᠠᠯᠲᠠᠨ ᠰᠢᠷᠡᠭᠡᠨ ᠳᠡᠭᠡᠷ᠎ᠡ ᠰᠠᠭᠤᠯᠭᠠᠪᠠᠢ ᠃

ᠠᠯᠢᠪᠠ ᠬᠡᠷᠡᠭᠳᠡᠢ ᠶᠢᠨ ᠲᠤᠬᠠᠢ ᠦᠯᠡᠳᠡᠨ ᠴᠦ ᠠᠮᠠᠷ ᠦᠭᠡᠢ ᠪᠠᠶᠢᠨ᠎ᠠ ᠁

ᠮᠠᠨᠳᠤᠯ᠎ᠠ ᠭᠡᠰᠡᠨ ᠬᠡᠯᠡᠯᠴᠡᠭᠰᠡᠨ ᠪᠤᠯᠤ᠃ ᠳᠠᠷᠠᠭ᠎ᠠ ᠨᠢ ᠮᠢᠨᠢ ᠬᠡᠯᠡᠯᠴᠡᠨ᠂ ᠪᠢᠷᠠᠨᠴᠠᠷ ᠬᠦᠨᠳᠦᠳᠬᠡᠨ᠂ ᠳᠠᠬᠢᠨ ᠰᠦᠨᠢ ᠪᠤᠯᠤᠨ᠃

Chapter V

A Study of the Relationships
between the Oirat Texts

The Oirat historical sources that are available for study are quite varied. But at the same time, they have much in common, and much which might connect them with each other. In the present work, with the exception of the HKK, these materials have only been mentioned briefly in Chapter II.[1] They will now be discussed in more detail, with particular attention to how they relate to one another. It has already been demonstrated that the most recent of the histories, the HKK, has been dependent on earlier sources. Is there also a connection among the earlier sources themselves? This chapter will attempt to discover if such a connection exists.

The UBXT in many respects is unique among Oirat as well as among Mongol sources. It describes the invasion of the Khalkha Mongols, under the leadership of Ubashi Khůn Tayiji, against the Khoshuud, led by Bayibaghas Bātur. This, however, is not what sets off this historical work from any other Oirat or Mongol work. The UBXT revolves around one single event. This event is the defeat of Ubashi Khůn Tayiji. The hero of the story is not a warrior on the Oirat side, but a seven year old boy. The events which unfold in this work are not reported by this seven year old hero, nor by the Oirats, but in a unique twist, by the villains of the story, the eastern Mongols.

This is the only Oirat text of which I am aware that describes events through the eyes of an adversary. Even the title of the work hints at a change from the normal. As noted in Chapter II, page 4, two titles have been given to this work: <u>Monggholiyin</u> <u>Ubashi</u> <u>Khūn</u> <u>Tayijiyin</u> <u>Tuuji</u> <u>Orshibui</u> (Contained Herein Is the History of Ubashi Khūn Tayiji of the Mongols), <u>Dörbön</u> <u>Oyirid</u> <u>Monggholi</u> <u>Daruqsan</u> <u>Touji</u> <u>Kemēkū</u> (The History of the Defeat of the Mongols by the Four Oirats).[2] In these titles, the emphasis is placed very explicitly on either Ubashi Khūn Tayiji or the Mongols, and not on the Oirats.

Normally, if one had an Oirat text with the title of <u>The History of Ubashi Khūn Tayiji,</u> one would expect Ubashi to be both the hero of the story and an Oirat. As noted above, this is not true in this instance. Ubashi is the leader of the rival eastern Mongols. The entire text is structured around the actions of Ubashi and the Mongols. The tactics and strategy for defeating the Oirats are described in detail, and the number and deployment of their forces are treated.

The author of this text is unknown, but from the detailed descriptions given it is possible that someone within Ubashi's camp was responsible for keeping the story alive. This person would not have to be an Oirat, or even know the Oirat script. He could have simply related the very moving story about the seven year old boy's bravery and shrewdness after the battle was ended. This seems a more acceptable explanation for the

development of this story than believing that an Oirat author
would have created the tale with the focus on Ubashi and the
Mongols.

If the author of the text was an Oirat, and if he did set
down a story whose central character was Ubashi, a Mongol, then
that author would have set a precedent in Oirat literature.
Because there is no literary evidence that points to any
earlier Oirat work having this feature, nor does any later
Oirat chronicle make use of this technique, the viewing of
events through the eyes of an adversary should not be
considered the beginning of a new literary trend. If indeed an
Oirat originally wrote the story, then this technique ceased
after this one story, for no evidence exists that this
experiment was repeated, and thus no development takes place.
However, if the story was told or set down by an eastern
Mongol, then the story teller was only applying the traditional
modes of relating the tale. No new development in literature
would have been made in that case.

Besides the problems connected with the authorship of the
text, there is the question of the dating of the text. At first
glance there would seem to be no problem, for the text ends,
"Oyiridiyin sak'uusun dolon nasutai köbüün dü Khubilji mongghol
du caling orkiqsen tereni ghal ghakhai jil bilii geqsen,"[3]
thus the last lines of the text give as the date the fire pig
year. The fire pig year occurred in 1587 and 1647, but neither
of these years can be correct for the events mentioned in the
UBXT.

The date for the UBXT usually has been given as 1587.[4]
This date has been called into question by Okada,[5] who
believes that a mistake occurred in the writing of one of the
elements in the sixty year cycle. Instead of the fire pig year,
the correct date, is the water pig year (1623). But this is not
a date that can fit into the historical events of the period.

In order to try to arrive at a solution to this dating
problem, it is first necessary to make an historical study of
the period. The first problem to be encountered is with the
name of Ubashi Khün Tayji.[6] There are a number of persons,
who have either the name or title of Ubashi Khün Tayiji and it
is easy to perceive that confusion might arise in discovering
the proper historic position for each of these individuals.

The UBXT reports that Ubashi is killed in the fight
against the Oirats.[7] Given this information, it might be
possible to obtain the proper date for this event, and also for
this defeat of the Mongols by the Oirats. The only Oirat source
which mentions any of the events which take place in the UBXT
is the DO. Surprisingly, this source even lists a date for
Ubashi Khün Tayiji. Unfortunately, this date is different from
any thus far mentioned. The DO states: "From the time of Ubashi
Khün Tayiji until now, the earth rabbit year, one hundred and
eighty years have passed."[8] The DO was written in the earth
rabbit year, which was 1819. One hundred and eighty years
earlier would set the date for Ubashi as 1639. This was, as we
shall see, impossible.

Ubashi Khün Tayiji, known as "Altan khan," had been in contact with the Russians since 1616.[9] In 1633, Ubashi sent another mission to the Russians. However, by 1634, when a Russian mission arrived, Ubashi's son Yeldeng was ruling as Altan khan.[10] Thus it would seem that Ubashi died in 1633 or 1634. We are left with a discrepancy in the date for Ubashi's death in a number of sources.

There is one other Oirat text, the MOZ, which presents indirect evidence concerning the date for the death of Ubashi. The law code of 1640, as has already been pointed out, includes a list of participants.[11] Although all important Mongol and Oirat leaders are mentioned in the text, there is no reference to Ubashi Khün Tayiji but only to his son Yeldeng. This would indicate that by 1640, Ubashi was no longer ruling and was probably dead.

No source other than the UBXT mentions exactly how Ubashi died. Assuming that the DO gives the correct date for Ubashi's death, the only sources dating his death are Oirat sources. However, the two texts disagree as to the date of his death, and other evidence shows that the dates listed by the DO and UBXT have to be incorrect. The date of 1639 in the DO cannot be correct if Ubashi's son is in command and ruling as Altan khan in 1634. In the same fashion, neither 1587 nor 1647 can be considered possible dates. The 1647 date is shown to be incorrect by the same facts which refute the 1639 date. As for 1587, if he was defeated and killed in that year, he was not likely to be negotiating with the Russians in 1616 and 1633. For the same reason the date of 1623, proposed by Okada, must also be dismissed. In fact, in that same year Ubashi was victorious in battle over the Oirats.[12]

From the information available there seems to be no way to reconcile with historical reality, the dates given in the two Oirat sources. They are obviously wrong. Could the events given in UBXT also be incorrect? This would be highly unlikely. Neither the Oirat nor the Mongol sources normally deliberately falsify information concerning deaths or defeat in battle. The differing dates present a problem which cannot be resolved at this time.

A dilemma regarding the UBXT was mentioned in passing earlier in this chapter. It concerns the actual authorship of the UBXT. It is necessary to understand that the normally accepted date for the invention of the Oirat "clear script" (todo üsüg) has been 1648. Recently, this date has been questioned mildly by Rinchen and Lubsanbaldan,[13] although no one has yet seriously proposed an alternative. If this date of 1648 for the creation of the Oirat script is true, it would either mean that an oral tradition for the UBXT was necessary, or that the text was first taken down in written Mongol. Because in the text the Mongols are described in a poor light, the possibility that it was written by an eastern Mongolian seems remote. It could, however, have been written into Mongolian by a western Mongol, who knew the Mongolian script. Professor Krueger has uncovered internal evidence that the UBXT was transmitted orally for a long period of time: "Finally, we may describe a third level of Oirat writing, the Written Colloquial,...These would be relatively recent compositions completely under the influence of the spoken language, written by persons probably knowing no Written Mongolian at all, who in effect transcribed as they spoke, with an occasional bow towards the conventions of representing sounds as at the middle level. An example of this level is... the Dörbön oyirid mongxoli darugsan touji kemekü (The Story of the Four Oirats Defeating the Mongols)."[14] From this evidence it is possible to conclude that the UBXT had a history of oral recitation prior to its being written down. It is possible that the original date was changed during this process of oral recitation.

The DO is the only Oirat source which discusses directly any of the events related in the UBXT, but it does not include any of the legendary elements found therein. The seven year old boy hero of the UBXT is not mentioned in the DO, nor are his actions. According to the UBXT, this child is captured by Mongol spies[15] and questioned by Ubashi concerning the disposition of the Oirat troops. The young boy proves to be too clever for the Mongols. With seeming innocence he relates information about each group of the Oirats, but describes every group mentioned as incredibly fierce, with large numbers of warriors and horses.[16] The Mongols lose more and more confidence as they listen to the heroic deeds of the Oirat warriors.

Eventually Ubashi Khün Tayiji realized that this seven year old had demoralized his men, and therefore decided to kill the boy. When the child found out that he would be killed for having obeyed Ubashi's orders to present information about the Oirats, he cursed Ubashi and the Mongols. This curse predicted the defeat of Ubashi and his death, and was viewed as an omen.[17] The curse is carried out when the Mongols are defeated and Ubashi is killed.[18]

These events are not mentioned in the DO. The DO does state that Ubashi Khün Tayiji attacked the Oirats in 1636.[19] It also describes very briefly the fight between the Mongols and the Oirats, and the eventual capturing and slaying of Ubashi Khün Tayiji. These events in the life of Ubashi took place on the Irtysh.[20] Although the DO treated in a slight way the subject matter found in the UBXT, the materials cannot be considered to be related to one another. There seems to be no connection in terms of borrowing of materials between the two texts.

Not even the basic events of this struggle between Ubashi of the Mongols and the Oirat are mentioned in the other Oirat historical texts. It is only in a very vague and general way that any mention of this struggle is made. The HKK, for example, hints at earlier trouble between the Oirats and Mongols as the reason for the law code of 1640: "Thus in the iron dragon year, in the year [1640] the Forty and the Four having ended their old quarrel united their own thoughts."[21]

The UBXT is thus a unique text from a number of standpoints, both in a literary sense and also in an historical way. The UBXT holds a position apart from the other Oirat historical documents. It neither accepted material from these other sources, nor was any attempt made to adopt the text of the UBXT into other sources.

The MOZ is the next historical text to be discussed. As noted in Chapter II, it contains a number of law codes. The time span that is covered by these texts range from 1640 to the middle of the 18th century, and, if the Jinjil decrees are added, until 1822.[22] These law codes are not strictly historical texts, but because they were written over a period of almost two hundred years, they can serve as an important source in considering the legal history of the Oirats. The main code and its three supplements also display the Oirat legal structure under four different regimes.

Certainly, it is not possible to write a legal history of the Oirats by using only the MOZ. This fact has been very well stated by Krader: "We have an anomalous situation in the Kalmuk law of having an abundance of materials, but little that can serve in furthering the study of the actual application of Kalmuk law. There exist a number of excellent works on Kalmuk law codes with ample commentaries in a number of languages, but few case materials."[23] But if actual case studies are missing, much other information is included in this source. Although the information found in the UBXT text was not directly incorporated into other Oirat sources, the material of the MOZ is utilized by the remaining Oirat historical texts. The MOZ, in the Dondukh Dashi supplement, also incorporated a portion of an earlier Oirat work. This will be discussed later in this chapter.

The law code of 1640 has been translated on a number of occasions. By the beginning of the 18th century, the Russian government had secured a copy of the text in Oirat script, which was translated by Bakunin into Russian around 1724.[24] This translation reached V.N. Tatishchev, the Director of Kalmyk Affairs, in 1742.[25] Later translations were published by Pallas, Leontovitch, and Golstunskii. The work of Golstunskii contains both the text and translation.[26] Later Pozdneyev included a portion of the MOZ in his chrestomathy. The sections presented by Pozdneyev made up approximately one half of the MOZ. These passages were MOZ 2.6 to 10.4; 21.8 to 23.2; and 25.1 to 33.5.[27]

A partial translation from Russian into English of the Oirat law codes is given by Riasanovsky.[28] Although these translations exist, the translations of the Oirat material are not adequate. The language found in the law codes is very terse, and it thus sometimes creates great difficulty in arriving at an accurate rendering of the text. Therefore, a definitive translation of the law codes has yet to be made.[29]

Because of the importance of these law codes to the Oirats, it is not surprising that passages from the MOZ are found in other Oirat historical texts. The GS and the DO

discussed in general terms the law code of the Oirats. The GS
mentioned some goals that the law code was to achieve.[30] This
portion of the text from GS 79.02 to GS 79.07 does not quote
any single passage of the MOZ, but rather summarizes ideas
found in many different sections. This portion of the GS text
later is used in the DO text. The section DO 34.04-34.07
repeats the GS with some distortion and the dropping of
words.[31] Thus the DO has incorporated the MOZ material by
means of the GS text.

A more direct link between the MOZ and an Oirat historical
document can be found in a number of incidents related in HKK.
For example it records the fact that an important meeting took
place in 1640: "Thus in the iron dragon year, in the year
[1640] the Forty and the Four having ended their old quarrels
united their own thoughts."[32] The HKK also gives a greatly
condensed version of the list of participants who attended the
creation of the law code: "...the kings and princes headed by
Erdeni Zasakhtu khan, Tüsetü khan, Güüsi Nomiyin khan, and
Erdeni Bātur Khung Tayiji established the great law."[33] This
partial listing is taken from the complete list of participants
given in MOZ 2.01-2.05. None of the actual laws of the 1640
code are repeated in the HKK, nor is the supplement of Ghaldan
Khung Tayiji written in 1678 included. The text of this
supplement is to be found in the MOZ between 20.08 and 23.02.[34]

There is one supplement of the law code which has been
preserved in the HKK in much more detail than any other part of
the law code. This is the supplement of Dondukh Dashi found in

Golstunskii, MOZ 23.04-33.13.[35] The HKK first states a reason
for needing a new supplement. It should be noted that only the
1640 law code is mentioned in this opening statement. There is
nothing written in the HKK about the Ghaldan Khung Tayiji
supplement. The HKK states: "As for the previous great law code
of the Forty and Four, although it was very suitable for the
living conditions of the Mongols and the Oirats, because the
Kalmyks have been separated from them and many years have
passed, customs have changed. On account of moral qualities
being born which had not existed previously, there was
necessity for a new law code. A new law code was also needed
because the Kalmyks were living in the midst of many foreign
peoples and interacting with them. Dondukh Dashi khan wrote the
new statute, and supplemented the old law."[36]

The HKK next quotes portions of the actual supplemental
code of Dondukh Dashi: "As for what was ordered in that
statute, it was as follows: 'A clergyman who held vows, having
performed actions which were unsuitable, was severely punished.
A common man, who takes vows, is also punished harshly if he
misses his readings and three monthly fasts. Respect and honor
the clergy who have acquired good knowledge! Now boys up until
15 years of age must learn Mongol writing. If they were not
taught, take a fine from their own father and give [the fine]
to their teachers and have them taught.'"[37]

After several sentences which praise Dondukh Dashi for
increasing literacy, the HKK resumes cataloguing some of the
laws as follows: "He forbade people to enter into the gurum

rite. He was thinking, 'As for princes, they are not to punish commoners who are quiltless; do not act in haughty and arrogant ways. Let no one be on guard against actions which are not suitable to his own person.' [The law] said, 'If nobles are investigating a person or if there is a sudden quarrel or a man is hit while relay horses are stolen there is no punishment.'"[38]

In these instances the HKK quoted directly from the MOZ, and specifically from the Dondukh Dashi supplement of the MOZ. The MOZ has been previously seen to have been used by the GS and through this text to the DO. However, the MOZ is not only a source for other Oirat texts, in its turn the MOZ has also in at least one instance been dependent on an additional Oirat source. The introduction to the Dondukh Dashi supplement had previously been used in the opening remarks of the Biography of Zaya Pandita. The two texts are exactly the same, except for a number of distortions in the MOZ, which include minor changes in spelling and the deletions of some case endings.[39] The MOZ is thus a link in Oirat historiography for the earlier ZPB, which was written around 1690, and the later traditional histories. The GS was written in 1737, and the DO was composed in 1819.[40]

The Mongol-Oirat law code of 1640 pre-dates the creation of the Oirat script. In studying the MOZ, one is faced with the same problem of transmission of the text as is found with the UBXT. This problem has been discussed earlier in this chapter. The problem of whether there was at first a written Mongol version of this text, or if the dating of the Oirat script is incorrect, has been previously mentioned by Professor Krueger.[41]

If, as pointed out by Krader, the Oirat law sources are lacking in case materials, they cannot be found wanting in other areas. They cover almost every aspect of Oirat life. There are rules for religous or sexual behavior, education, grazing of cattle, hunting procedures, etc. These texts still have much to reveal about the society and culture of the Oirats, and are a valuable historical source.

Within the law codes themselves, from the 1640 code through the Jinjil decrees, one can witness the dependence of the later legal structure on the earlier one. Laws first promulgated in 1640 are carried through the various supplements, and are noted again in 1822. The importance of Buddhism and of the clergy is brought out by all of the codes. The practice of having separate fines and punishments for the different social ranks is also stable throughout all of the law codes.

Thus far in this chapter, two entirely different types of Oirat literature, both of which have important material for the historian, have been viewed. There is another Oirat source, written from a third viewpoint, which also contains material of historical importance. This work is the Biography of Zaya Pandita.[42] During the past two decades, interest in Zaya Pandita and his literary and historical importance has incrased. In 1959, Rinchen published a written Mongol version of the biography,[43] dependent on the Oirat text. The Oirat text, with a transcription and index of proper names, was edited by Tsoloo in 1967.[44]

The ZPB is not a biography in the modern sense. It was written for a religious purpose, and thus it is only natural that the religious events in the life of Zaya Pandita are stressed. The biography traces the religious life of Zaya Pandita.[45] Each major religious event is discussed, every important religious ceremony at which Zaya Pandita was in attendance is noted. This does not mean that the ZPB is without interest to the historian. As Tucci states: "All the rest is a shadow, but those who are capable of investigating can find in these shadows allusions, hints, names, sometimes even dates, which, being put together and throwing light one upon the other, illuminate the dark and still uncertain horizon of Tibetan history. These biographies become still more useful when they insert into ther narrative fragments of chronicles, myths or pedigrees, lists of masters, itineraries, dates of the foundation of temples and monasteri[e]s. To recognize this is to admit that an historian cannot ignore the rnam t'ar."[46]

What Tucci says about the use of the rnam t'ar in Tibetan history is also true concerning the religous biography in Mongol or Oirat history. The ZPB is especially detailed in terms of the itinerary of Zaya Pandita. This biography is also exceptional in regards to other types of historical information, both direct and indirect. This will be shown in later examples.

Zaya Pandita was a member of the Khoshuud tribe, who among the Oirats were to play the largest role in Tibetan affairs during the middle of the 17th century. Zaya Pandita was born in 1599 and died in 1662. As he lived during this important period of Khoshuud history, it is only natural that his biography contains much of interest for the historian. There have been a number of important misconceptions about the genealogy and name of Zaya Pandita.

Some chroniclers following Baddeley,[47] have claimed that Zaya Pandita had been adopted by Baibagas, who was at that time a childless prince. The ZPB gives a very clear and precise genealogy for Zaya Pandita. It states that he was the fifth of eight sons of Bābakhan.[48] The close similarity in the names of the two Oirat princes, Baibagas and Bābakhan, must have occasioned this error on the part of earlier historians.

This confusion over names extends even to the name of Zaya Pandita himself. Zaya Pandita is, of course, a title. This title was conferred on him by Zasakhtu khan of the Khalkhas in 1642. Nam mk'ai rgya mc'o was his actual name. As recently as 1969, Siegbert Hummel,[49] and earlier Vostrikov[50] and Pozdneyev,[51] along with many others, have called the Oirat Zaya Pandita Blo bzan 'p'rin las. In fact, there was good reason for this confusion, as during the lifetime of the Oirat Zaya Pandita there was an eastern Mongol lama with the same title of Zaya Pandita. This eastern Mongol lama had the name Blo bzan 'p'rin las, and even though he was not born until 1642, a confusion of names occurred. The Mongols themselves, however, have never confused these two individuals. Professor Rinchen, in his introduction to the written Mongolian biography of the Oirat Zaya Pandita published in the MPR in 1959, gave the correct name of the Nam mk'ai rgya mc'o.[52]

Zaya Pandita was born at a time when the Oirats were becoming increasingly attracted to Buddhism. Babakhan, as well as many other princes of the Oirats, was already filled with enough religious fervor to wish that at least one of his sons would enter the Buddhist clergy. Zaya Pandita was chosen to become a monk, and in 1616 became a bandi (novice). That same year he arrived in Tibet.[53] For the next twenty-two years, Zaya Pandita studied and practiced Buddhism in Tibet. During this time he was made a gelung by the Panchen lama, and spent time studying under the Panchen lama.[54] In 1638, Zaya Pandita left Tibet to carry out the directives of the Panchen lama, who told him to preach to and translate for the Mongol speakers.[55] The desires of the Panchen lama were certainly to be fulfilled.

The next few years were to involve the Khoshuud in major historical events. Although some historians have tried to bestow an important political role on Zaya Pandita during this period, and Dr. Bawden for one even claims that Zaya Pandita was as much as anyone responsible for the entente between the western Mongols and Tibet.[56] The sources themselves give no concrete evidence for this role.

In 1638, the Khoshuud prince Guushi khan entered Tibet to defend the Fifth Dalai Lama against the ruler of gTsang, who favored the Red Hat, or Karmapa, sect. By 1642, Guushi khan controlled all of dbUs and gTsang, the central provinces of Tibet; however, he handed them over to the Dalai Lama as a gift, and from then on the Dalai Lama was the temporal as well as spiritual ruler of Tibet, and the theocratic state was now definitely established in Tibet. Thus an Oirat tribe played a major role in bringing the Yellow Hat sect of Buddhism into control of Tibet.

Zaya Pandita does not seem to have played a significant role in this event. The first mention of any contact between Zaya Pandita and Guushi khan in the ZPB was not until 1652, when Zaya Pandita met with the Dalai Lama and Guushi khan at Drepung monastery in Tibet.[57] Thus during the period when Guushi khan was gaining control of Tibet and turning it over to the Dalai Lama there was no mention of any contact with Zaya Pandita.

The second important political event during the period of Zaya Pandita's life was the meeting of the independent Mongol tribes of both the east and west in 1640 at which a common legal code was adopted, in an attempt to establish some sort of unity among the Mongols and Oirats. Historians once again without having the necessary evidence have deduced that, because of his later fame, Zaya Pandita must have played a role at this conference.[58] Zaya Pandita's name, however, is absent from the list of thirty-three major personages at the conference. This list, which precedes the law code, is found in the MOZ.[59] It must be remembered that at this time Zaya Pandita had been back from Tibet only one year, and had not yet received the title of Zaya Pandita. Thus it is unlikely that he could command such an important position this early. Furthermore, the ZPB makes no mention of the law code of 1640.

A change in the status of Zaya Pandita can be seen in the supplement to the Mongol-Oirat law code of 1640 promulgated by Dondukh Dashi. As mentioned earlier in the chapter, this supplement begins with a prayer of homage to Zaya Pandita.[60] As has been noted, this same invocation is used to begin the biography of Zaya Pandita, which was written around 1690.[61] The use of this invocation in the Dondukh Dashi supplement would seem to indicate a very real reverence for Zaya Pandita as a true holy personage, and certainly demonstrates the esteem in which he was later held by the Oirats. This use of the same invocation in a biography and a legal code once again demonstrates that the Oirats were well aware of and made use of their own literary traditions.

While it might be open to question as to whether or not Zaya Pandita was a politician of great influence, there can hardly be a doubt about his religious zeal and his religious and cultural accomplishments. As noted previously, the traditional date of 1648 for the creation of the Oirat script has been questioned.[62] This new script called "todu üsüq," or "clear script," was so called because it cleared away the ambiguities of the old Mongol script. This new script most certainly must have increased Oirat nationalistic feelings, and was an event of major cultural importance. Even if Zaya Pandita was not the creator of the Oirat script, and there is no firm evidence to support such a theory, he is the man responsible for making the Oirat script a viable written language through his translation of a vast number of works into Oirat.

There is evidence from his biography that even before the traditional dating of the creation of the Oirat script in 1648, Zaya Pandita was translating works from Tibetan. His biography states that in 1644 he translated the Ma ni bka' 'bum. Without, however, specifying what script he used or what was the language into which this work was translated.[63] The problem is further compounded by the fact that there are two copies of this translation in western libraries, one in Dresden in Oirat script,[64] the other in Marburg, Germany, in Mongol script.[65] This is the only Mongol script work which up until now has been attributed to Zaya Pandita.

From 1650 until the year of his death in 1662, 178 works are listed in the ZPB as having been translated by Zaya Pandita. In addition, another 36 are listed as having been translated by his disciples. This is an enormous amount of material to translate in a period of twelve years, and one might be hesitant to accept the biographer's word at face value. As might be expected, a large portion of Zaya Pandita's works have not survived the 300 or so years since they were translated. However, a sufficiently large volume of translations have survived to give credence to his biographer's figures. This author's studies have revealed that Zaya Pandita was actually responsible for translating more than the number given in the ZPB.[66] The ZPB is a great store of information for anyone considering the history of literature of the Oirats.

Besides being a source for a history of Oirat literature, the ZPB contains much information which would be of use to study political history. It describes very extensively the itinerary of Zaya Pandita, and since he travelled both to the princes of the Khalkha and of the Oirats, one has available valuable notations concerning dates and geographic positions. This is material not duplicated in other Oirat sources. The only connection between the ZPB and other Oirat materials, which has thus far been uncovered has been the invocation to the Dondukh Dashi supplement mentioned above.

Apart from the itineraries and information on Oirat literature, the ZPB also naturally contains much information on religion and religious history. Probably the most interesting and useful material detailing religious history would be the search for the second incarnation of Zaya Pandita.[67] It is clear that the ZPB has much of historical value, and should be considered an important historical source.

Whereas the first three texts discussed in this chapter are normally considered to lie outside the sphere of Oirat historiogrpahy, the GS and DO, are its typical products. They both give extensive genealogical information of the various Oirat tribes, and incorporate legendary material, and maxims attributed to various Oirat leaders. The GS is by far the older of the two, having been composed by Emci Ghabang Shes Rab in 1737.[68] The actual title of this text, which has been noted previously, is Dörbön Oyirodiyin Töüke (History of the Four Oirats). The DO, whose full title is Khoshuud Noyon Batur Ubashi Tümeni Tuurbiqsan Dörbön Oyiradiyin Töüke (The History of the Four Oirats Composed by the Khoshuud Prince Batur Ubashi Tümen), has also been noted in Chapter II, and was composed in 1819.[69]

The GS has been a major influence on the DO. Much of the genealogical information found in the GS is repeated by the DO, sometimes in a distorted fashion.[70] However, this does not mean that the DO should not be viewed as a valuable source. It contains much information on the period after the rule of Ayuuki khan, and also gives fuller genalogies for some of the Oirat tribes, and also mentions and elaborates on other incidents which had earlier been reported by the GS.

Both the GS and the DO begin by giving a breakdown of the tribes constituting the Oirat. This section has been included in the DO as an obvious addition. The Golstunskii text places this as an addendum to the main DO text.[71] At the very beginning of the text, the DO has a lengthy chronology which begins with a mention of the historical Buddha and continues relating the important events of Oirat history through the migration of the Torghuud in 1771.[72] None of the other Oirat primary sources have such a chronology.

After this initial difference between the GS and DO, many corresponding or parallel passages are to be found. In general, both stress the coming of Buddhism among the Oirats and the importance to the Oirats of the Buddhist religion.[73] There is also an emphasis on proper moral leadership. The GS for example warns: "Do not have greed arise in our becoming rich; do not have pride arise in our being good."[74]

This stress on the proper leadership is mentioned in other sections of the GS and the DO. One way in which these earlier Oirat historical sources differ from the later HKK is the great use of maxims and aphorisms by the leaders of the Oirats. One is a good ruler, according to Dayicing, if one knows the time to nurture one's subjects like a mother, the time to act like a prince to one's subjects, and the time to act like a subject to your own subjects.[75] This advice is given to Ayuuki, Dayicing's grandson. Both texts are imbued with a strong sense of morality.

Another aspect discussed and shared by both texts is the idea of inheritance, they outline which of the sons should inherit, and how much they should inherit. The GS entitles the relevant portion: "This was written concerning the nobles of the Four Oirats giving inheritance to their sons"[76] the DO goes so far as to title its discussion of inheritance as follows: "The chapter [in which] the nobles and khans of the Four Oirats [relate] by which means they give inheritance to their own sons."[77] The GS has more information in this matter than the DO, however, the DO does not merely copy the GS. For example, it contains information concerning the inheritance of Bayibaghas and Guusi khan not given by the GS.

These traditional sources, while stressing what actions are proper, do not neglect to report the evil conduct committed by the Oirats. Just as the HKK reveals the times of strife and internecine warfare, so too have these earlier works noted the troubles caused by family feuding. The GS at one point recites a litany of evil deeds perpetrated by one Oirat on another: "Borou khan of Bagha Khoshuud killed his own elder brother and married his sister-in-law. Cecen khan and Abla fought. Torghuud Dayicing destroyed Yeldeng, his own meritorious younger brother."[78] This passage continues in the same manner for a total of twenty-four lines. The DO also mentions some of these same events, but omits the major portion of this section.[79]

Events concerning the Khoshuud and Tibetans are at least noted in the GS and DO. This is rarely done in the HKK. More attention is also given to Guushi khan in these earlier texts than in the HKK. In discussing the Khoshuud, these earlier historical sources give an interesting link between Chinggis and the Oirats. According to both the GS and DO, the genealogy of the Khoshuud tribe began with Khasar, the younger brother of Chinggis.[80]

Perhaps because of this connection between Khoshuud and Chinggis, a story found in the Written Mongol sources is repeated in the GS. This is the only occurrence in any of the Oirat texts in which material not relating to the Oirats is introduced from Mongol sources. Clearly the Oirats had retained a knowledge of the traditional historical beliefs concerning Chinggis and the eastern Mongols. The episode from the Secret History of the Mongols found in the GS is the one in which Alan Qo'a urges her five sons, born of different fathers, to stay united. She shows how one arrow might be easily broken, but five together are hard to break.[81]

The GS uses this incident to show the necessity for families to stay united, and the evils which can ensue if they feud. The incident recorded in the SH in which Chinggis and his brother Khasar kill their half-brother Bekter is also alluded to in this passage in the GS.[82] The motif of using a number of arrows or sticks to demonstrate unity is widespread in Inner Asia. The earliest Inner Asian instance for the use of this arrow motif, as far as I know, dates from 426. A-ch'ai of the T'u-yu-hun demonstrates to his children that a single arrow is easily broken, but that many are not.[83]

Although legends have not been incorporated into the HKK, they are to be found in both the GS and the DO. One instance of a legendary beginning for a tribe is described by both of these texts. It concerns the Coros. A small child was found in the forest lying at the base of a tree. He was being nourished by the tree. A tube-shaped branch was dripping nourishment into his mouth.[84] The Oirat word for tube is corgho,[85] and because of this incident the tribe which was started by this boy became known as Coros. None of the other Oirat tribes are given a legendary beginning in either the GS or the DO, or in any other primary Oirat source.

In many of the examples that have been given in this chapter, the DO has used the GS as a source for information. There are, however, many instances in which the accounts vary and are not related to one another. The account found in the GS concerning the breaking of arrows is found, for example, only in this text. The GS also has stressed greatly the role of Ayuuki in Oirat affairs, a justified emphasis as Ayuuki was one of the great rulers of the Oirats. He ruled for over fifty years, and his reign ended only fifteen years before the GS was written. The DO does, of course, discuss Ayuuki at length, and presents many of his quotations, but not as completely as the GS. Compared to the GS the DO has an added 82 years of history with which to deal.

There are areas covered by both texts in which the DO is more thorough than the GS. This demonstrates that the DO was not simply recording events found in the GS. This is true of both genealogical citations and historical events. A good example is the story linked to the defeat of Ubashi Khün Tayiji, not discussed in the GS. The DO dates and describes the Oirat victory over the Mongols. After this victory, the Oirat were defeated by Mukhur Mujiq, the son of Ubashi Khün Tayiji. Sayin G'ā of the Khoyid devised a plan to avenge this defeat. Twenty-five hundred camels, each loaded with two boxes, were sent to Mukhur Mujiq. Hidden in each box was an armed Oirat warrior. In this way these warriors were able to infiltrate the camps of Mukhur Mujiq and defeat the Mongols.[86]

There is a reason why this event has been presented in such detail in the DO. Sayin G'ā, the hero of this story, is related to the author of the DO, Bātur Ubashi.[87] Sayin G'ā was the son of Sultan Tayishi, Sultan Tayishi's son was Uuzang Khoshuuci, whose son was Bātur Sebten, whose son was Bata Noyon, whose son was Dejīd.[88] Dejīd was the father of Tümen Jirghalang, whose son, Bātur Ubashi, is the author of the DO.[89] The DO is the only Oirat primary source which attaches much attention to the Khoyid line, Bātur Ubashi's way of giving prominence to his family tradition.

Another instance of this stress on Ubashi's family history has been mentioned in Chapter II, the birth of Tümen Jirghalang, which has even been incorporated into the HKK.[90] There is one other episode depicted by the DO which is not noted by other Oirat sources. It also involves Tümen Jirghalang. When Tümen Jirghalang was nine years old, he had an audience with Catherine II in Petersburg. While there, Tümen Jirghalang was afflicted with smallpox, and the Tsarina had him treated by two of her own court physicians, he recovered, and DO praises Catherine for her mercy and compassion.[91]

Besides relating these family episodes, the DO departs from the GS by discussing events which the GS could not report. The main event in Oirat history between the composition of the GS in 1737 and the DO in 1819 was the migration of the Oirats out of Russian territory and into Manchu territory. This event was written about in detail in the HKK.[92] The DO considers this event from a different perspective. The migration and details of the trials and the difficulties are not mentioned by the DO. Nor is the final outcome of the flight, which finds the majority of the Oirats under Manchu control, even noted. Instead the DO only discusses the condition of the Oirats who did not leave Russian territory.

Bātur Ubashi was a loyal subject of Russia, and he described the Russian rule over the Oirats in the best of terms. One does not find dissatisfaction with the Russians. The HKK, on the other hand, as has been shown in Chapter II,[93] voices disapproval of Russian rule. The DO uses many more Russian terms than any other Oirat source. Among these texts; only a very few Russian terms could be found in the HKK. But by the end of the DO, many Russian terms are to be seen. These include: Ghubirnātur ("governor"), Mayor ("mayor"), Astābki ("discharge"), Paten ("patent, warrent"), Poruuciq ("lieutenant"), and Inaral Mayöür ("major general").[94] The DO gives a more favorable view of the Russians and Russian rule than any of the other Oirat histories.

It is clear that the Oirats occupied a significant role in Inner Asian history from the 15th to the 18th centuries, but a competent understanding of Oirat history demands a thorough study of Oirat primary texts. Although the six sources discussed in this work exhibit varied and independent perspectives on the subject, a degree of interrelation between the texts is evident. Although in some cases the actual extent of connections between these works is difficult to ascertain with any accuracy, all six authors shared an awareness of earlier Oirat works, as well as of Mongol historical sources. A more complete utilization and understanding of the earlier sources and their influence on later Oirat histories is a necessary prerequisite of our understanding of Oirat historiography, as well as of Inner Asian history as a whole.

Chapter V - Footnotes

1. See Chapter II above pp. 4-5.

2. See Chapter II above p.5, and also footnotes 14 and 15 to Chapter II for a discussion of the Gomboyev and Jülg texts. Professor Krueger, besides discussing the typeset versions of this work in "Oirat literary resources and problems of Oirat lexicography," also had earlier noted the Laufer and Jülg manuscript copies of the <u>Dörbön Oyirid Monggholi Daruqsan Touji Kemēku</u> in an article entitled, "Catalogue of the Laufer Mongolian Collection in Chicago," in <u>JAOS</u>, vol. 86, pp. 177-178. There is also one printed version of this work which has been set down in Written Mongolian. This work entitled, <u>Mongghol-un Ubashi Khung Tayiji-yin Tughuji</u> is found in Che. Damdinsürüng's work <u>Mongghol Uran Jokiyal-un Degeji Jaghun Bilig Orusibai.</u> pp. 184-188.

3. This passage is taken from the Gomboyev typeset version, which seems to be more accurate than the Jülg text. The latter is lacking several lines in his handwritten copy. Jülg either miscopied the text or the now missing original manuscript was not complete. The manuscript from which Jülg made his copy, Dresden Eb. 404i, is missing, see Heissig, <u>Mongolische Handschriften, Blockdrucke, Landkarten,</u> p. 6. The Jülg version reads as follows: "Oyiridiyin sak'uusun dolon nasutai köböün dü khubilji: Mongghol du caling orkiqsani tere ghal ghakhai jil belei: This passage ends the text folio 7a lines 15-18.

4. Che. Damdinsurung at the end of his Mongol typeset version of the UBXT adds a few lines of commentary. He also has added into the text the date 1587 after the "fire pig year." This date has also been accepted by Kozin in "Oiratskaya istoricheskaya pesn'..."

5. Hidehiro Okada, "Outer Mongolia in the Sixteenth and Seventeenth Centuries," p. 79.

6. Baddeley, <u>Russia, Mongolia, China</u> vol. II, p. 95. See also Bawden, <u>The Modern History of Mongolia,</u> who describes Altan khan and his position as follows: "A fourth important khanate of the seventeenth century; but one which did not long survive, was that carved out for himself by yet another descendant of Geresenje, Sholoi ubasi, known to history as Altan khan - but quite unconnected with the Altan khan of the Tumet - in northwest Mongolia. His pastures touched in the east on the Selenga and Tula rivers, and reached westward as far as Krasnoyarsk." p. 49.

7. See the Gomboyev text p. 210 line 4, and Jülg folio 6b lines 12-14.

8. See DO 24.09-24.10 which states: Ubashi Khung Tayijiyin caq ēce ödögē shoroi tuulai jil kürtele zuun nayan jil boloqsan.

9. For these early relations between Altan khan and the Russians see Baddeley, Russia, Mongolia, China vol. II, "The Altin Khan: Missions of Tumenets and Petroff," pp. 46-62.

10. See Baddeley, Russia, Mongolia, China vol. II, p. 95 for a discussion of these events.

11. See Chapter III above footnote 10.

12. Grousset, Empire of the Steppes, p. 512. Courant, L'Asie Centrale, p. 35.

13. See Lubsanbaldan, "Oiradyn Zaya Pandidyn Orchuulgyn Tukhai Medee," p. 91.

14. Krueger, "Oirat literary resources and problems of Oirat lexicography," pp. 139-140.

15. See UBXT p. 202 lines 2 and 3, in Jülg folio 2b lines 32 and 33.

16. UBXT p. 202 line 9 to p. 204 line 7, in Jülg folio 3a line 19 to folio 4a line 14.

17. UBXT p. 206 lines 10-11, in Jülg folio 5a lines 21-23.

18. UBXT p. 210 lines 4-6, in Jülg folio 6b lines 36-37 and folio 7a lines 1-4.

19. The DO relates these events as follows: Odō zuun nayan dörbödüqci ghal khulughuna jildu oyiradiyin törö sajini ebdeji oyiradiyige olzo kekü sedkil zöüji monggholiyin xān ubashi khung tayiji urangkhani sayin majakh sayitai: emeliyin yeke cerikh yēr dörbön oyiradi dayilaji abkhai ireqsēgi: see DO 37.11 - 37.13. The fire mouse year (ghal khulughuna) is 1636. This date fits the second reference to a period of time in this passage of the DO. Odō zuun nayan dörbödükhci ghal khulughuna jildu, "now it is the 184th year since the fire mouse year." The DO was written in 1819. Thus the year which is 184th from 1819 would be 1635 or 1636, and these dates match the events described. Also note the mention made above in this chapter concerning the confusion of dates surrounding Ubashi Khün Tayiji.

20. See DO p. 37 lines 14 and 15 for the final defeat of Ubashi.

21. See HKK 2.02-2.03 The Forty refers to the Mongols, and the Four to the Oirats.

22. See above Chapter II p. 4

23. Krader, <u>Social</u> <u>Organization</u> <u>of</u> <u>the</u> <u>Mongol-Turkic</u> <u>Pastoral</u>
    <u>Nomads</u>, p. 137. Krader further explains the problem of
    not having actual case materials in a footnote on page
    137: "Adjective law relates to procedure, as
    distinguished from substantive law which is the content
    or "rules of right" of the law itself."

24. Bakunin was also mentioned in the HKK. He attended the
    investiture of Dondukh Dashi in 1757, see chapter II
    above.

25. Riasanovsky discusses the various translations of the law
    codes in his works, <u>Fundamental</u> <u>Principles</u> <u>of</u> <u>Mongol</u> <u>Law</u>
    pp. 77 and 78, and <u>Customary</u> <u>Law</u> <u>of</u> <u>the</u> <u>Mongol</u> <u>Tribes</u>
    (<u>Mongols</u>, <u>Buriats</u>, <u>Kalmucks</u>), p. 33.

26. Krueger, "New Materials on Oirat Law and History Part
    One: The Jinjil Decrees," pp. 194-195 discusses the two
    distinct versions of Golstunskii's translation. The
    second version improves the first.

27. Ibid.

28. Both Riasanovsky's <u>Fundamental</u> <u>Principles</u> <u>of</u> <u>Mongol</u> <u>Law</u>
    and his <u>Customary</u> <u>Law</u> <u>of</u> <u>the</u> <u>Mongol</u> <u>Tribes</u> include
    portions from these law codes. Riasanovsky's work
    include, either sections of the law codes translated from
    Russian translations of the Oirat texts, or summaries of
    various portions of the code.

29. Krueger has more recently translated the last of these
    codes, the Jinjil decrees. This appeared in <u>CAJ</u> vol XVI
    no. 3, 1972 as "New Materials on Oirat Law <u>and</u> History
    Part One: The Jinjil Decrees."

30. The passage in question runs from GS79.02 to 79.07.
    Dörbön oyiridiyin cājiyin bicikh dotoro bayikhci noyodoud
    cuulaghdān küüneldekhsen ügei mongghol kümer cōxor bü
    keye yasu nigetei kümüyigi moujiroulji albutu bolbocigi
    tusa öürsen du bü zarya küükeyini inzadu bü ögüye cōxor
    bü keye: öbörö yasutai albutu kümündü bu ögüye cusu bü
    gharghaya: geji niyidēr kelelceji andaghāraldabai

31. The passage in DO 34.04 - 34.07 is as follows: Dörbön
    oyiradiyin cājiyin bicikh dotodo bayikhci noyoduud
    cuulghadān ukhni mongghol kümer cōxor bu keye: yasu
    nigetei kümüyigi muujiraji albatu bolbacu tusa nüürsün dü
    bu zaruya küükeni inazidu bu ögüye: cōxor bu keye öbörö
    yasutai kümün du bu ögüye: cusu bu gharghaya: geji
    niyider kelelceji andaghāraldabai: A comparison between
    the earlier chronicle GS and the more recent DO
    demonstrates the distortion which have crept into the DO.

32. The translation is from HKK 2.02 and 2.03. For a
    reference to the more exact date for this meeting found
    in the MOZ see footnote 9 in Chapter III above.

33. This passage is found in HKK 2.04-2.05. For a complete

listing of the Oirat and Mongol leaders who are mentioned by the MOZ as having taken part in the law code see footnote 10 in Chapter III above.

34. See also Chapter III footnote 144 above for further information.

35. An English translation of selected passages from the supplemental law code of Dondukh Dashi can be found in Customary Law of the Mongol Tribes, by Riasanovsky, pp. 264-273. Riasanovsky also discusses the various translations of this text and the composing of the work on pp.259-261. See also Riasanovsky, Fundamental Principles of Mongol Law, pp. 77-78.

36. This quotation is taken from HKK 13.09-13.13. The text for the Golstunskii typeset version of the Dondukh Dashi supplement can be found in MOZ 23.04-33.13. The MOZ text more accurately renders the name Donduq Dashi with a spelling more closely transcribing the Tibetan Don Grob bKra sis; see also footnotes 140 and 147 in Chapter III, above.

37. The exact lines in the MOZ from which these quotations were taken have previously been listed in Chapter III, footnotes 148, 149, 150, and 142.

38. The exact lines in the MOZ from which these quotations were taken have previously been listed in Chapter III, footnotes 153, 154, and 155.

39. The transcription given by Tsoloo of the ZPB, folio 1b, lines 1-26, is as follows:
namu gUrU mānzu-ghoshaya
ariün dēdü agnishta ordu xarshi-du:
ariluqsan tabun maxabodi-yēr nasuda orosighchi
amitani itegel ochiro dharādu sögüdümüi:
oqtorghui-lugha ilghal ügei chinar-tu oroshijhi
olon medelgi-yi nige aqshan-dü sayitur ayildun
odxu irekü ügei udagha mashi tögüsüqsen
oghōto teyin ariluqsan nomiyin beyedü sögüdümüi:
erketüyin nomun metü mashi Xōroxui:
eldeb belge üliger-yēr mashi cimeqsen
edügē xamighā sanaxui tende e...ghuqci
eldeb xubilghāni beyedü sögüdümüi ::
erdemiyin usun-i bariqchi baxarqsan dotorōeche
eneriküi aldariyin yeke daghun bükü züqtü dorisun
eshe uxāni nomiyin xorin amitan dalai-yin debeltü-dü
oroüljhi:
erdem biligi-yin üre öüskeqchi klu...xān rab-byam-jāya
pandhidādü sögüdümüi:

The same passage is found in MOZ 23.04-23.10 is given below so that a comparison of the ZPB and MOZ texts might be made. The author of these lines is responsible for the placing of both works in verse form.

namo g'uru manyju-giōshāya:

arium dēdü ag'anistayin ordu kharshidu
arilukhsan tabun maghad-yēr nasuda oroshiji:
argha dēdü dolōn-yer mashi cenggekhci:
amitani itegel ociro dharādu sögödömüi:
okhtaraghoi-lughā saca cinartu oroshiji:
olon züyili nige akhshindu sayitur ayiladun:
odkhu irekü ügei udkha mashi tögösökhsan:
oghōto teyin arilukhsan nomiyin beyedü sögödömüi:
erketüyin numun metü masi ghorokhci:
eldeb belge üligerēr mashi cimekhsen:
ödöge khamighā sanaxui tende urghukhci
eldeb khubilghani beyedü sögödömüi::
erdemiyin usu barikhci bakharakhsan dotorōēce
eneriküi yeke duun bükü zükhtü duurisun:
esi ukhāni nomiyin khurayigi amitan dalai debeltüdü
oruulukhci:
erdem biligiyin üre öüskekhji zāya pandida du sögödömüi::

40. For the dating of the ZPB see Chapter III, footnote 13; the dating for the GS and DO can be found in Chapter II, footnotes 8 and 9 respectively.

41. Krueger, "New Materials on Oirat Law and History Part One: The Jinjil Decrees," p. 194; for an earlier opinion on the dating of the Oirat script see footnote 13 in this chapter.

42. For a complete reference to this work see Chapter III, footnote 3. Both a written Mongol and an Oirat version of the work have been produced. Zh. Tsoloo, besides producing a facsimile of the text, has transcribed and indexed it as well.

43. See Chapter II, footnote 3, for a full reference to the written Mongol text.

44. See footnote 42 above and also Chapter II, footnote 3. Badmaev, in ZayāPandita, p. 14, notes three other manuscripts of the ZPB in Leningrad.

45. For a full discussion of religious biographies (rnam t'ar) and the position and importance of the rnam t'ar as an historical work, see Tucci, Tibetan Painted Scrolls, Vol. I, pp. 150-154.

46. Tucci, Tibetan Painted Scrolls, vol. I, p. 151.

47. Baddeley, Russia, Mongolia, China, vol. I, p. lxxviii.

48. See ZPB, folio 2a, lines 11-14. ZPB, when discussing the actual manuscript, stands for the Tsoloo edition.

49. Benjamin Bergmann, Nomadische Streifereien unter den Kalmücken in den Jahren 1802-03, Riga, 1804-1805; reprinted in 1969 with an introduction by Siegbert Hummel, p.v.

50. A.I. Vostrikov, Tibetskaya istoricheskaya literatura, pp.

181 and 349.

51. A.M. Pozdeyev, Mongolia and the Mongols, p. 272.

52. Rinchen, editor, Rabjamba Cayabandidayin tuguji saran-u gerel kemeku ene metu bolai, introduction by Professor Rinchen, no page number.

53. ZPB, folio 2b.

54. This is the first Panchen Lama, Pang c'en Blo bzang c'os kyi rgyal mts'an. See Tucci, Tibetan Painted Scrolls, vol. I, pp. 72-73 for a listing of the Panchen Lamas.

55. ZPB, folio 3a.

56. Bawden, The Modern History of Mongolia, p. 68.

57. ZPB, folios 12b and 13a.

58. Baddeley, Russia, Mongolia, China, p. lxxix, states: "In this Code Lamaistic influence is strongly marked; and though we do not know that Zaya Pandita was present, we can hardly go wrong in ascribing to him, if not the inception of the Conference, a very large part, at least, in bringing together for the common good such fiercely hostile elements as the princes of the Khalkhas and the princes of the Kalmuks, the main inducement being, it is supposed, fear of the growing Manchu power."

59. See Chapter III, footnote 10, for a complete list of those who are mentioned as having attended the promulgation of the 1640 law code.

60. See this chapter, footnote 39, for a complete transcription of this invocation as found in both the Dondukh Dashi supplement and the MOZ.

61. Che Damdinsurung, Mongghol Uran Jokiyal-in Degeji Jahgun Bilikh Orusibai, p. 327.

62. See this chapter, footnotes 13 and 41.

63. See ZPB, folio 5b.

64. Heissig, Mongolische Handschriften, Blockdrucke, Landkarten, work number 333.

65. Heissig, op. cit., number 334.

66. Halkovic, MA thesis, Indiana University, May 1972, A Comparative Analysis of Zaya Pandita's Bibliography of Translations. This work studies Zaya Pandita's translation output in detail, and also discusses some of the other problems mentioned in the present work.

67. ZPB, folios 30a 30b.

68. See Chapter II, footnotes 8 and 12, for full citations and dating information.

69. See Chapter II, footnote 13.

70. See appendix for line by line comparison of GS and DO.

71. See DO, p. 25

72. DO 24.02-26.11.

73. See GS 79.18-80.01 and 80.03-80.06; DO 32.08-32.11 and 32.03-32.04.

74. Bayajikhu-du mani kharam bü töröül: sayijirakhu-du mani omokh bü töröül: GS 81.11-81.12.

75. GS 82.01-82.04 and DO 33.09-33.11.

76. GS 86.15-86.16.

77. DO 36.08

78. GS 84.18-85.01.

79. DO 35.12-35.17.

80. GS 76.03-76.04 and DO 26.11-26.12.

81. SH, paragraph 22. For the most recent translation of the SH, see Igor de Rachewiltz, "The Secret History of the Mongols," in Papers on Far Eastern History, vols. 4,5,10, and 13.

82. GS 92.06-92.09.

83. Molè, The T'u-yü-hun from the Northern Wei to the Time of the Five Dynasties, pp. 5-6.

84. GS 77.04-77.09 and DO 28.06-28.09. Professor Sinor has pointed out a similar legend involving Bügü khan of the Uighurs, see Juvaini, The History of the World-Conqueror, pp. 55-56.

85. Krueger, Oirat-Written Mongol-English Dictionary, entry nos. 24832 and 24833.

86. GS 78.10-78.15 gives a very truncated version of this story which is presented in detail in DO 37.14-39.11.

87. An earlier instance of the stressing of an event in the DO because of a genealogical connection has been noted in Chapter III; see footnote 131 of that chapter.

88. For this genealogical information see DO 39.14-39.15.

89. See DO 27.16-27.17.

90. See Chapter II, footnotes 50 and 51.

91. DO 41.07-41.11.

92. See the translation of these events in Chapter III. The details of this migration are found in HKK 19.11-22.16.

93. Chapter II, footnote 40.

94. All these terms and titles appear on p. 42 of DO.

List of Abbreviations

CAJ   Central Asiatic Journal

DO   Khoshuud Noyon Bātur Ubashi Tümeni Tuurbigsan Dörbön Oyiradiyin Tüüke

GS   Dörbön Oyirodiyin Tüüke by Emci Ghabang Shes Rab

HKK   Khalimakh Khādiyin Tuujiyigi Khurāji Bicikhsen Tobci Oroshibai

JAH   Journal of Asian History

JAOS   Journal of the American Oriental Society

MOZ   Mongolo-oiratskie zakony 1640 goda, dopolnitel'nye ukazy Galdan-chun--taidziya i zakony, sostavlennye dlja volzhskich kalmykov pri Kalmyckom chane Donduk-dashi.

UAJ   Ural-Altaische Jahrbücher

UBXT   Monggholiyin Ubashi Khun Tayijiyin Tuuji Orshiboi

ZAS   Zentralasiatische Studien

ZPB   Zaya Pandita Biography

APPENDIX I:

Index to the GS, DO and HKK

A

Abagha Ubashi
HKK 12.01

Abida Bolïn Tayishi. cf. Abida Bolo Tayishi

Abida Bolo Tayishi. Dörböd. Son Ongghoco.
DO 28.17
GS 78.02 (Abida Bolïn Tayishi); 79.07 (Tabida Bātur Tayishi)

Abida Buuci. Torghuud. Son of Mangkhai
DO 30.16

Ablai. Khoshuud. One of two sons of Bayibaghas Bātur.
DO 27.01
GS 76.17, 76.18; 84.03?; 85.01?; 85.15?; 90.14?; 91.14?

Ablai. Torghuud. one of Six sons of Örlöq.
DO 33.03; 34.14; 35.12
GS 80.17; 84.03; 85.01?, 85.15?; 87.09; 90.14?; 91.14?

Ablai Sultān. Kazakh.
HKK 20.02; 21.09, 21.12, 21.14.

Adashiri Ghalzuu Cing Tayiji. Khoshuud. Son of Engke Sömör.
DO 26.13
GS 76.05 (Adshri Ghalzuu Cang Tayiji)

Adshri Ghalzuu Cang Tayiji. cf. Adashiri Ghalzuu Cing Tayiji.

Aghudi. Khoshuud. Son of Akhtaixai.
DO 26.15 (Nag'udi. Listed as one of the six sons of Tügüd.)
GS 76.10

Akhalan. Torghuud. Third eldest son of Menggei.
DO 29.16

Akhsarghuldai Noyon. Khoshuud. Son of Saba Shirman.
DO 26.14
GS 76.06 (Aqsu Gholdi)

Akh Sakhal. Torghuud. One of the three sons of Ghaldan Norbo.
DO 30.08

Akhshi Tayiji. Dörböd. Son of Ushkhani Tayiji.
DO 28.14
GS 77.16

Akhsu Gholdi. cf. Akhsarghuldai Noyon.

Akhtaba Ghol. Akhtuiba river.
HKK 4.12

Akhtayikhai. cf. Atakhai.

Aldar G'ā. Dörböd. Son of Öldö. cf. Üledüi Aldar G'ā.
DO 28.15
GS 77.16 (Üledüi Aldar G'ā.); 93.04?

Aldar G'abz'u. Title for a monk. dka' bcu.
DO 25b.08
GS 74.06; 77.10

Aldar Shikhci. Leader of the Torghuud.
DO 25b.14

Alekhsandar Bek'uvici Cirk'āski, (Kines) Prince. Governor of
the Russian army of Kiva.
HKK 7.09, 7.10, 7.14, 7.15; 8.04

Alekhsandra. Khoyid. One of the two daughters of Ceren Dorji,
who also had one son.
DO 28.02

Alekhshē Salba. Dörböd. Son of Dayicing Khoshuuci.
DO 29.08

Alikhsā Mikhalvaci khan. Tsar Alexis (1645-1676).
HKK 2.17

Alikhsei Donduk'ob. Christian name of the son of Zhan.
HKK 12.17; 13.01

Almasai. A monk.
GS 77.10

Altayi. Mountain range.
HKK 23.17
DO 26.10; 36.04
GS 86.11

Amakhai. Torghuud. Son of Noyon Ghabang Namk'a.
DO 31.13

Amidu Cingsan. cf. Ömidö Cingsa.

Aminai. cf. Amini.

Amini. Dzungar. Founder of the Dzungars together with Döbönö.
DO 28.04 (Aminai)
GS 77.07, 77.08

Amughulang Ubashi. Torghuud. One of the four sons of Sanji
Ubashi.
DO 30.11

Amuk'a Sidhi Manyzushri Khutuktu Gegen.

HKK 2.04

Amursana. Dzungar. Defeated by the Manchus in 1755.
HKK 17.14

Andrai Ivanabci G'olican, (Kenes) Prince. Russian minister.
HKK 4.01

Angghasar. Torghuud. One of the three sons of Uubang Khasakh.
DO 30.15
GS 75.09 (Ayighasār)

Āngna Ivanobna, (Tsarina Anna).
HKK 10.12, 10.16; 11.05, 11.08, 11.14

Angshobiye Manyzushiri.
HKK 2.04

Arabbyur. cf. Rabbyuur.

Arabtan. Khoshuud. One of the three sons of Khai.
DO 27.07

Arakh Tömör. Khoshuud. One of the two sons mentioned of
Akhsarghuldai Noyon.
DO 26.14
GS 76.07

Arda. Torghuud. Wife of Sanji.
DO 31.09

Arghan Cingsa. cf. Arkhan Cingsa.

Arkhala Akhatu. Torghuud. One of the ten sons of Cecen Noyon.
DO 30.13

Arkhan Cingsa. Dörböd. Second eldest of the three sons of
Khamukh Tayishi.
DO 28.14, 28. 15
GS 77.15 (Arghan), 77.17 (Arkhan)

Asarai. Torghuud. One of the five sons of Dondukh Wangbo.
DO 30.07

Asarakhu. Torghuud. One of the three sons of Boqshorgho.
DO 30.08, 30.09

Asmana Obakh. Torghuud. One of the ten sons of Cecen Noyon.
DO 30.12

Astābk'ā Uk'as Pirimiyer. Given title Mayor by Tsarina
Catherine.
DO 42.07, 42.08

Ashidayin Sayin
DO 31.17

Atakhai. Khoshuud. Son of Tügüd.

DO 26.15
GS 76.10 (Akhtayikhai. Son of Samulkhu Cecen.)

Ayiciuvakh. Sultan.
HKK 21.07

Ayidarkhan. Astrakhan.
HKK 1.17; 2.07, 2.14, 2.17; 3.03; 7.07; 8.11; 9.16; 10.02,
10.16; 12.03, 12.15; 14.06, 14.09; 17.12; 19.11
DO 24.10; 26.09; 41.12; 42.01, 42.16

Ayighasār. cf. Angghasar.

Ayuuki. Torghuud. Eldest of the three sons of Puncokh.
HKK 3.07, 3.09, 3.13, 3.14, 3.15; 4.01, 4.04, 4.07, 4.08,
4.14, 4.15, 4.16, 4.17; 5.02, 5.03, 5.05, 5.07, 5.09, 5.13,
5.14, 5.16, 5.17; 6.01, 6.04, 6.05, 6.07, 6.09, 6.13, 6.14,
6.15, 6.16, 6.17; 7.01, 7.07, 7.08 (wife), 7.09, 7.12, 7.14,
7.16; 8.01, 8.03, 8.04, 8.06, 8.08, 8.11, 8.12, 8.15 (died);
9.02; 11.17; 15.11.
DO 30.03; 31.06; 33.09; 34.02, 34.10; 35.08, 35.11; 36.07,
36.17
GS 75.02; 79.12; 82.01, 82.14; 84.05, 84.06, 84.15; 85.05;
86.13; 87.13; 89.05, 89.08, 89.12, 89.16; 90.03, 90.04, 90.06,
90.18; 91.02, 91.15; 96.08

B

Badan Tayishi. Dörböd. Founder of clan.
DO 29.03

Badir.
GS 84.16

Bagha Cōxor. Place name and ulus name.
HKK 12.12; 13.02

Bagha Khoshuud. Tribe.
DO 35.13
GS 84.18

Bai. Torghuud. One of the three sons of Dorji.
HKK 12.01
DO 30.05
GS 75.06

Bakhsandai. Torghuud. One of the twelve sons of Phyakhdar Byab.
DO 30.05

Bakhta Girei. Sultan of Kuban.
HKK 7.07, 7.11, 7.16, 7.17; 8.01

Bak'ūnin, (Assessor). Official of Z'ilin.
HKK 14.07, 14.11; 15.11; 16.11, 16.17

Balbu. Nepal.

GS 78.16, 78.17

Balkhashi. Lake Balkash.
HKK 22.09

Balzang. Torghuud. One of the two sons of Ocir.
DO 30.10

Balzuur. Khoshuud. One of the three sons of Dondukh.
DO 27.09

Bargha (Burād). Oirat tribe with Burād in Russia.
DO 25b.10; 33.16
GS 74.05; 78.07, 78.09; 82.09

Bār Köl. Area of Dzungaria.
HKK 23.06

Basang Cedē. Dörböd. One of the three sons of Cö Rashi.
DO 29.10

Bāsu. cf. Bātur.

Bashkir. Turkic tribe.
HKK 3.15; 5.13; 6.02, 6.04

Bata G'a. Khoyid. One of the two sons of Ceren Norbo.
DO 28.03

Bata Noyon. Khoyid. Son of Bātur Sibten of the clan of Yoboghon
Mergen.
DO 27.16; 39.15; 40.06

Batu. Torghuud. One of the twelve sons of Phyakhdar Byab.
DO 30.05

Bātud. Oirat tribe grouped with the Khoyid.
DO 25b.10
GS 74.04; 78.08, 78.09

Bātur. Torghuud. One of the three sons of Uubang Khashakh.
DO 30.15
GS 75.09 (Basu)

Bātur Ercis. River.
DO 37.15

Bātur G'a. Khoyid. One of the two sons of Ceren Norbo.
DO 28.03

Batur Malai. Dörböd. Son of Toyin.
DO 29.05

Bātur Sebten. Khoyid. Son of Uuzang Khoshuuci.
DO 27.16; 39.14

Batur Ubashi. Khoyid. One of the four sons of Tümen Jirghalang.
DO 27.17; 28.01; 42.11

Bātur Ubashi Tümen. Prince of the Khoshuud.
DO 24.01

Bātur Khatun.
GS 85.09

Bātur Khung Tayiji. Dörböd. Eldest of the ten sons of Khara
Khula.
DO 29.01; 35.11?; 36.14?
GS 78.02, 78.03; 83.10?; 91.10?, 91.16?; 92.15?, 92.16?;
95.07?

Bātur Khung Tayiji. Torghuud. One of the six sons of Khō Örlöq.
DO 33.02; 35.11?; 36.14?
GS 80.16; 83.10?; 87.04?; 91.10?; 91.16?; 92.15?, 92.16?;
95.07?

Bayan Darkhan Zayisang.
GS 93.02

Bayar. Torghuud. Son of Sosoi.
DO 29.15
GS 74.11 (Bayir)

Bayarlaghu. Khoshuud. Son of Zerböd.
DO 27.13

Bayi. cf. Bai

Bayibaghas Bātur. Khoshuud. One of the eight sons of (Khan
Noyon) Khongghor. Elder Brother of Zasakhtu Cing Bātur. cf.
Bayibaghas Khan.
DO 26.17; 27.01, 27.13
GS 76.14 (Boyiboghos), 76.16; 80.03, 80.05, 80.08, 80.09,
80.11

Bayibaghas Khan. Khan of the Oirats. Divides inheritance
between his two sons. cf. Bayibaghas Bātur.
DO 32.05, 32.12, 32.13, 32.14; 36.08; 37.14

Bayiliniq. Torghuud. One of the five sons of Rabbyur.
DO 31.09

Bayir. cf. Bayar.

Bayiri. Tangut.
GS 74.06

Bējing. Peiking.
HKK 6.11

Beketob. Governor of Astrakhan, and a major general.
HKK 19.11
DO 42.02 (Bikitob), 42.16

Bek'übci, Kines (Prince). Governor of Astrakhan.
HKK 3.03

Bestene. Torghuud. One of the three sons of Noyon Sanjilai.
DO 31.14

Bikitob. cf. Beketob.

Biri Noyon. Of the Bagha Khoshuud tribe.
DO 35.13
GS 84.18 (Borou Khan)

Blo Bz'ang. cf. Luuzang and Lubzang.
GS 80.08

Blo Bz'ang. Khoshuud. Son of Örlökh.
GS 80.08

Blo Bz'ang Mgonbo. Khoshuud. Son of G'aldama.
DO 27.06 (Luuzang Ombo)
GS 76.18

Blo Bz'ang rdo rje
GS 82.16

Bocin. A zayisang under Bakhta Girei.
HKK 8.02

Bodong. Torghuud. One of the twelve sons of Phyakhdar Byab.
DO 30.06

Bökö Akhari. Torghuud. One of the ten sons of Cecen Noyon.
DO 30.13.

Bökö Mirza. Khoshuud. One of the six sons of Tügüd.
DO 26.15, 26.16
GS 76.11, 76.12 (Bokui. Son of Küsei. One of two sons.)

Bökö Tayiji. Torghuud. Son of Dar(a)shi.
DO 30.15
GS 75.10

Bököi Mirza. cf. Bökö Mirza.

Bolkhan. cf. Bulighan.

Bokhon. cf. Bulighan.

Bolkhuyikh. A monk who spread Buddhism among the Oirats.
DO 32.04

Bokhbōn. Khoshuud. One of the two sons of Zamiyang.
DO 27.14; 42.08

Bokhdo Ezen. Title used for either the Russian tsar or the
Manchu emperor.
HKK 7.05
DO 40.08, 40.09; 42.04

Bokhdo Oula. Mountain.

GS 78.16

Bokhdoyin Gegēn. Dalai Lama.
HKK 4.06
DO 33.14
GS 82.06

Bokhshorgho. Torghuud. One of the two sons of Ghonjib.
DO 30.06, 30.07
GS 75.04 (Boqshorogho)

Bokhshorogho. cf. Boqshorgho.

Boris Matveyebci G'olican.
HKK 4.15; 5.08

Boro Ayalkhu. Dzungar. Son of Östömö Noyon.
DO 28.13
GS 77.13 (Burin Ayoulgha)

Borou Khan. cf. Biri Noyon.

Boryātingski. Russian official.
HKK 10.05, 10.08

Boshokhtu. Khutuktu of Sengge, who became a commoner.
DO 35.06

Boshokhtu Byanong.
GS 89.05

Boshokhtu Khan. Dörböd. Son of Bātur Khung Tayiji. Two of ten
sons are mentioned.
DO 29.01; 34.04; 37.04
GS 78.03, 78.04; 81.06; 83.01, 83.12, 83.18; 84.11; 85.18;
87.09; 88.08; 89.07; 91.13; 93.01

Botoi. cf. Butui.

Boyiboghos. cf. Bayibaghas Bātur.

Boyigho Örlöq. cf. Buyigho Örlöq.

Bulighun. Torguud. Youngest of the six sons of Buyigho Örlöq.
cf. Bolxan, Bolxon.
DO 30.01, 30.02; 31.03
GS 74.15; 75.14, 75.17

Burād (Bargha). Oirat tribe with Bargha in Russia.
DO 25b.11; 33.16
GS 74.05

Burād. Turkic people.
HKK 22.05. 22.07, 22.12

Burin Ayoulghu. cf. Boro Ayalukhu.

Burkhan. Buddha.

HKK 3.04; 19.02, 19.12, 19.14
DO 24.01; 25.03; 32.01, 32.13, 32.15; 33.01; 34.03; 39.03
GS 80.01, 80.10, 80.12, 80.15; 82.15; 89.12; 90.10; 93.14

Burkhani. Torghuud. Son of Saltu.
DO 31.02

Burkhan Sakyi. cf. Burkhan Sanji.

Burkhan Sanji. Khoshuud. Son of Kei Kemnekhtu.
DO 26.13
GS 76.06 (Burkhan Sakyi)

Busuruman Tayiji. Torghuud. One of the twelve sons of Phyakhdar
 Byab.
DO 30.06

Butui. Torghuud.
DO 31.03 (Son of Burkhani.)
GS 75.15 (Botoi. The eldest son of Saltu.)

Buura. Torghuud. Son of Buyigho Örlöq. He is the second eldest
 of six sons.
DO 29.17; 30.11
GS 74.14; 75.06, 75.16

Bukhār. Bukhara.
HKK 4.16; 5.15
DO 26.06

Buyan. Torghuud. Son of Gerel.
DO 30.17; 35.06?
GS 75.11; 84.01

Buyani Tedküqci. Torghuud. Son of Mkhas Dbang, his other name
is Sosii.
DO 29.15

Buyantukh. Torghuud. One of the two sons of Noxōn Köböön.
DO 31.11

Buyan Khatun Bātur. Khoshuud. One of the eight sons of (Khan
Noyon) Khongghor.
DO 27.01
GS 76.15

Buyigho Örlöq. Torghuud. Eldest of nine sons of Menggei. cf.
 Buyigho Orlöq.
DO 29.16, 29.17; 30.11, 30.14, 30.16, 30.17; 31.01
GS 74.12; 75.06 (Buyigho Örölöq)

Buyigho Örölökh. cf. Buyigho Örlöq

Bükü Belgetü. Khoshuud. Half brother of Chinggis.
DO 26.12

Büzē. Torghuud. One of the two sons of Noxōn Köübün.
DO 31.11

Byabulukh.
DO 36.05
GS 86.12 (Byab Buulukhtar)

Byab Buulukhtar. cf. Byabulukh.

Byal. Dörböd. One of the three sons of Solom Darphya.
DO 29.06

Byal. Dörböd. Son of Dorji Noyon.
DO 29.08

Byalba. Dörböd. Son of Shambai.
DO 29.11

Byambai. Torghuud. One of the five sons of Rabbyur, and the elder brother of Coyong.
DO 31.10, 31.12

Byamba Tayishi. Dörböd. One of the two sons of Namēsnikh Cüüci.
DO 29.07

Byamiyang. Ruler of the Khoshuud; stepfather of Tümen Jirghalang. cf. Zamyang.
HKK 12.09, 12.10; 15.13

Byembe. Dörböd. Son of Byalba.
DO 29.11

C

Cāghalai. Torghuud. One of the five sons of Rabbyur.
DO 31.10

Caghān Akha.
DO 35.14
GS 85.02

Caghān Bātur Tayishi.
HKK 4.11

Caghān Khan. Russian Tsar.
HKK 2.01; 3.03; 7.05; 11.07

Caghān Kiciq. Torghuud. One of the two sons of Asarakhu.
DO 30.09

Caghān Malaghai. Moslems.
DO 25.08; 37.09

Caghān Nomiyin Khan.
DO 31.15; 32.05, 32.07, 32.11
GS 79.14, 80.03, 80.06

Caghayang. Khoshuud. One of the two sons of Erke Dayicingghai.
DO 27.05, 27.08

Cangjin. Dörböd. Son of Möngkö.
DO 29.08

Canjin Ubashi. Dörböd. One of the two sons of Öncikh.
DO 29.10

Cayirīcan. City. Tsaritysin.
HKK 4.14; 8.09

Cebekh Dorji. Torghuud. One of the three sons of Ghaldan Norbo.
HKK 17.17; 18.16; 19.13
DO 30.08

Cebekh Ubashi. Dörböd. Son of Ghaldan Ceren.
DO 29.05

Cebekh Ubashi. Torghuud. One of the two sons of Asarakhu.
DO 30.09

Cecen. Turkic tribe.
HKK 5.12

Cecen. Dörböd. Son of Dalai Tayishi. He was not given
inheritance.
DO 36.12; 37.03
GS 87.08; 88.01?

Cecen Bātur. Kills Sengge, his own younger brother.
DO 35.14
GS 85.03

Cecen Khan. Khoshuud. One of the two sons of Bayibaghas Bātur.
DO 27.01, 27.03; 33.16?; 34,12?, 34.14?; 35.01?, 35.12?
GS 76.16, 76.17, 76.18; 82.09?, 82.13?, 83.10?, 83.13?;
84.08?, 84.11?; 85.14?; 85.18?; 87.12?, 87.18?; 88.01?;
90.14?; 91.12?, 91.14?; 94.11, 94.13; 95.07

Cecen Khan. Torghuud. One of the six sons of Khō Örlöq.
DO 33.03, 33.16?; 34.12?, 34.14?; 35.01?, 35.12?; 37.01,
37.03?, 37.06?
GS 80.17; 82.09?, 82.13?; 83.10?, 83.13?; 84.08?, 84.11?;
85.14?, 85.18?; 87.12?, 87.18?; 88.01?; 90.14?; 91.12?, 91.14?

Cecen Noyon. Torghuud. Eldest of the four sons of Buura.
DO 30.12; 31.17; 34.08
GS 75.08; 79.08, 79.17; 83.04; 87.18?; 94.18

Cēgei. Khoshuud. One of the four sons of Duuriskhu.
DO 27.07, 27.09

Cenden Dorji. Dörböd. One of the three sons of Solom Darphyā.
DO 29.06

Cenzē. cf. Ülü Cenzē.

Ceren. Khoshuud. One of the four sons of Dorji Tayiji.
DO 27.05, 27.08
GS 86.17?

Ceren. Messenger of Shikür Dayicing.
HKK 2.15

Ceren Cimid. Khoyid. One of the two sons of Ceren Skyab.
DO 28.02

Ceren Dondukh. Torghuud. Ayuuki's eldest living son after
Phyakhdar Byab dies. Marries daughter of Cevang Rabtan.
Officially loses title of khan in 1735.
HKK 8.12; 9.04, 9.05, 9.07, 9.08, 9.09, 9.12, 9.14, 9.15,
9.16, 9.17; 10.01, 10.04, 10.10, 10.17
DO 30.03 (Ceren Donrob); 31.06
GS 75.03 (Ceren Donrub)

Ceren Dondukh. Khoyid. One of the four sons of Tümen
Jirghalang.
DO 27.17; 28.01

Ceren Donrob. cf. Ceren Dondukh.
DO 30.03

Ceren Donrub. cf. Ceren Dondukh.

Ceren Dorji. Khoshuud. One of the four sons of Kelebe Dalai
Ubashi.
DO 27.04

Ceren Dorji. Khoyid. One of the two sons of Ceren Dondukh.
DO 28.01, 28.02

Cereng Ubashi. Torghuud. Son of Curumi.
DO 31.12

Ceren Nadmid. Khoyid. One of the two sons of Ceren Sphyab.
DO 28.02

Ceren Norbo. Khoyid. One of the four sons of Tumen Jirghalang.
DO 27.17; 28.02

Ceren Rashi. Torghuud. Son of Ceren Ubashi.
DO 30.11

Ceren Sphyabs. Khoyid. One of the two sons of Ceren Dondukh.
DO 28.01

Ceren Tayishi. Oirat prince. He came to the Volga with 10,000
households of Khoshuud, Dörböd Khoyid.
HKK 17.15; 18.05, 18.16; 19.13; 23.14

Ceren Ubashi. Khoyid. Son of Bātur Ubashi.
DO 28.01

Ceren Ubashi. Torghuud. One of the four sons of Sanji Ubashi.
DO 30.10, 30.11

Ceren Ubashi. Torghuud. Son of Tabki.
DO 31.14

Cevang Dorji Namj'al. Son of Ubashi. He became khan at the death of Ubashi in 1775.
HKK 23.15

Cevang Rabtan Khan. Khan of the Dzungars. His daughter becomes the wife of Ceren Dondukh.
HKK 4.09; 5.10; 7.01; 9.06, 9.09

Cilē.
GS 85.12

Cing. Khoshuud. One of the two sons of Marghash.
DO 27.10, 27.12

Cingges Khan. cf. Cinggis Khan.

Cinggis Khan.
DO 24.05, 24.06; 25.02, 25.03, 25.04, 25.10; 26.10, 26.11, 26.15; 37.07; 40.16
GS 74.02, 74.07; 76.04 (Cingges); 92.07

Cingsa Tömör. Khoshuud. One of the three who are listed as being sons of Oröq Tomor. cf. Tögüdei Cingsen Ghorban.
DO 26.15
GS 76.09 (Son of Doureng Docin)

Citer. Dörböd. Son of Möngkö Tömör.
DO 29.04

Ciyicar Turukh. Place name.
GS 92.04

Cokh. Khoshuud. One of the four sons of Kelebe Dalai Ubashi.
DO 27.04

Coros. Tribe.
DO 28.07, 28.09, 28.11
GS 77.06 (Corōs)

Coyong. Torghuud. One of the five sons of Rabbyur.
DO 31.10, 31.11

Cöjib. Khoshuud. One of the four sons of Tarba Ceren.
DO 27.10

Cö Rashi. Dörböd. One of the two sons of Ghakhai.
DO 29.09

Cööker.
DO 32.12

Curumi. Torghuud. Son of Byambai. However, he is raised by Coyong.
DO 31.12

Cüükür. Khoshuud.
DO 35.10

GS 79.07; 80.09; 81.02; 84.14; 85.12

D

Dabsang.
GS 89.09

Dacang. cf. Dasang.

Dacang. Elder brother of Niyiter, whom he seized.
DO 35.15
GS 85.04 (Dayizang)

Daghal. cf. Dayikhal.

Dalai blama
HKK 4.04; 6.07; 11.11
DO 34.11; 39.12
GS 80.18; 81.01, 81.05, 81.07, 81.08; 87.03; 88.04

Dalai Corji. Torghuud. One of the four sons of Buura. cf.
Öbökůi Tayishi Dalai.
DO 30.12

Dalai Khan. Khoshuud. The only son of Dayan Khan listed.
DO 27.05; 29.11
GS 74.06; 77.02; 93.02, 93.05

Dalai Khung Tayiji. Khoshuud. One of the two sons of Guushi
(Nomiyin Khan). He along with his brother Yeke Jiqku was given
the title of prince of Tibet by Guushi.·
DO 27.03; 34.10; 36.09, 36.12
GS 77.02; 79.12; 83.16; 87.01; 88.09; 89.05, 89.08, 89.11,
89.15, 89.16, 89.17; 90.13, 90.17; 91.12; 95.06

Dalai Tayishi. Dörböd. Separates from Badan Tayishi. He has
thirteen sons, only three of whom are mentioned in the
genealogies. A fourth is listed as not receiving an
inheritance. This is Cecen (DO 36.10).
DO 29.03; 32.11; 36.10
GS 79.07; 80.08; 85.11; 86.16; 88.15; 94.17

Dalai Ubashi. Torghuud. One of the ten sons of Cecen Noyon.
DO 30.13

Danar. Torghuud. Younger brother of Dondukh Dashi.
DO 40.17

Dancang. Torghuud. One of the twelve sons of Phyakhdar Byab.
DO 30.05

Danjin. Khoshuud. One of the two sons of Tarba.
DO 27.09, 27.11

Danjin. Torghuud. One of the three sons of Dorji.
DO 30.05
GS 75.06

Danjin Dorji. Torghuud. One of the twelve sons of Phyakhdar
Byab.
DO 30.05

Danjin Wangbo. Seized by his own younger brother Khung Tayiji.
DO 35.15
GS 85.03 (Danjin Wang Bui)

Danjin Wang Bui. cf. Danjin Wangbo.

Danjin Khung Tayiji. Khoshuud. One of the four sons of Kelebe
Dalai Ubashi.
DO 27.04

Darashi. Torghuud. Son of Sübterē.
DO 30.15
GS 75.10 (Darshi)

Darbaghai Ongbu. cf. Darbaghai Wangbo.

Darbaghai Wangbo. Torghuud. Son of Ghaltu of the clan Mangkhai.
DO 30.17
GS 75.12, 75.17 (Darbaghai Ongbu)

Darkhan. Messenger of Shikür Dayicing.
HKK 2.15

Darkhan Noyon. Dörböd. Son of Ölkönö Tayishi.
DO 28.13
GS 77.13, 77.14

Darkhan Tayiji. Khoshuud. He is the only son of Törgön Tayiji
mentioned.
DO 27.14

Darma Bala Khatun. Wife of Ayuuki. She ruled at Ayuuki's death
and married Dondukh Ombu. She refused to attend the
investiture of Dondukh Dashi as khan.
HKK 8.08, 8.12; 9.02, 9.05; 15.11

Darshi. cf. Darashi.

Daruuki. Khoshuud. Son of Bokhbōn.
DO 42.08

Dasang. Torghuud. The eldest son of Phyakhdar Byab.
HKK 8.06, 8.14; 9.04; 10.01, 10.03
DO 30.05

Dashi. Khoshuud. One of the three sons of Khai.
DO 27.07

Dashilai. Khoshuud. One of the three sons of Mönggöd.
DO 27.12

Dashiri. Khoshuud. The only son of Rabzur mentioned.
DO 27.12

David. Dörböd. Son of Cangjin.
DO 29.08

Dayan Khan. Khoshuud.
DO 27.03, 27.05 (One of the two sons of Guushi (Nomiyin Khan)
GS 77.01; 90.13 (Eldest of fifteen sons of Guushi)

Dayicang. Dörböd.
GS 90.13; 91.06; 95.02?, 95.07?, 95.17? 95.18?; 96.02, 96.03,
96.04

Dayicing. Manchu dynasty.
GS 81.18; 82.01; 83.09

Dayicing (Torghuud). Torghuud. Grandfather of Ayuuki. cf.
Shikür Dayicing Torghuud; Shikür Dayicing, Khudai Sukür
Dayicing. He has four sons.
DO 33.08, 33.14; 34.01, 34.17; 35.13; 36.01
GS 74.16, 74.18; 81.18?; 82.07, 82.11; 85.01; 86.07; 87.05,
87.06, 87.07; 88.16

Dayicing Khoshuuci. Dörböd. One of the thirteen sons of Dalai
Tayishi, three are mentioned; he is the middle son of the
three and is given a full share of the inheritance.
DO 29.04, 29.08; 36.11
GS 86.16

Dayikhal. Dörböd. Son of Mongghoi Cecen.
DO 28.15
GS 77.16 (Daghal)

Dayizang. cf. Dacang.

Dayou Tayishi.
GS 95.07

Dayoukha. Wife of (Khudai Shikür) Dayicing.
GS 75.01; 87.05

Debēn. Torghuud. One of the three sons of Arkhala Akhatu.
DO 34.10

Debyed Mergen. Khoyid. One of the three sons of Bata G'a.
DO 28.03

Dejīd. Khoyid. Son of Bata Noyon of the clan of Yoboghon
Mergen.
HKK 12.07, 12.08, 12.09
DO 27.16; 39.15, 39.16; 40.03, 40.04, 40.11, 40.15

Dejid Zambu Tayishi. Dörböd. Son of Erdeni Tayishi.
DO 29.07

Delger. Torghuud.
DO 31.01 (son of Kholoci (one line is dropped from genealogy
as found in the GS)
GS 75.13 (eldest son of Tobokh)

Diba. Torghuud. One of the three sons of Bokhshorgho.
DO 30.07

Dibircub. Khoshuud. One of the three sons of Mönggöd.
DO 27.12

Dodbi. Torghuud. One of the five sons of Dondukh Wangbo.
DO 30.07

Domono. cf. Döbönö.

Don. Don river.
HKK 6.05, 6.06; 10.10; 18.01

Donduk'ob. Christian family name of Zhan.
HKK 12.17

Dondukh. Khoshuud. One of the four sons of Duuriskhu.
DO 27.07, 27.09

Donduhk Dashi. Torghuud. Eldest son of Phyaqkhar Byab, becomes
deputy khan under Dondukh Ombu; writes law code supplementing
1640 code; becomes khan under Elizabeth.
HKK 10.06; 11.02; 12.04, 12.07, 12.14; 13.12, 13.16; 14.04,
14.07, 14.09; 16.02; 17.12
DO 30.05; 31.07; 40.14; 41.01, 41.03, 41.05, 41.07
GS 75.04 (Donrob Rashi)

Dondukh Ombo. Torghuud. One of the two sons of Ghonjib; at
Ayuuki's death he married Darma Bala. cf. Dondukh Wangbo,
Donrob Wang Bo.
HKK 8.13, 8.14; 9.02, 9.13; 10.04, 10.06, 10.09, 10.12, 10.13,
10.14, 10.17; 11.01, 11.04, 11.07, 11.09, 11.10 11.16; 12.03,
12.04; 17.17; 18.10
DO 30.06, 30.07; 31.07; 35.16
GS 75.04, 75.16 (Don Rob Ongbo); 84.07

Dondukh Wangbo. cf. Dondukh Ombo.

Donrob Rashi. cf. Dondukh Dashi.

Donrob Wang Bo. cf. Dondukh Ombo.

Dorji.
DO 35.14
GS 85.02

Dorji. Torghuud. One of the four sons of Nazar. cf. Nazariyin
Dorji, Rdo rje Mgün po.
DO 30.04 (Dorji G'ombo)
GS 75.05 (Rdo rje Mgün po)

Dorji Arabtan. Torghuud. Brings 1,000 subjects to the Volga
from Dzungaria.
HKK 3.07
DO 29.12 (Noyon Dorji Rabtan)
GS 74.08 (Rdo rje Rabtan)

Dorji Arshi. One of the twelve sons of Phyakhdar Byab.
DO 30.06

Dorji G'ombo cf. Dorji.

Dorji Noyon. Dörböd. Father of Byal.
DO 29.08

Dorji Tayiji. Khoshuud. One of the four sons of Düürgeci
Ubashi.
DO 27.02, 27.04

Dorji Ubashi. Torghuud. One of the four sons of Sanji Ubashi.
DO 30.11

Döbönö. Dzungar. Together with Aminai founded the Dzungars.
DO 28.04
GS 77.07, 77.08 (Domono)

Döcin Mongghol. The Mongols.
DO 25b.01

Dörböd. Torghuud. One of the six sons of Khō Örlög.
DO 33.03
ĠS 90.14

Dörböd. Tribe.
HKK 1.10; 3.13; 6.06; 15.13; 17.16; 18.11
DO 25b.11; 25.16; 28.05; 29.02; 36.10
GS 74.05; 77.04, 77.08, 77.11; 78.05, 78.06; 80.17; 85.11;
86.16; 91.06 (Dayicang?); 96.02 (Dayicang)

Dörbön Oyirad.
HKK 1.04
DO 24.01; 25b.01, 25b.04, 25b.12; 26.02; 31.15; 32.01, 32.04;
33.03; 34.11, 34.12; 35.01, 35.02, 35.09; 36.03, 36.08, 36.17;
37.07, 37.08, 37.13, 37.17; 38.07, 38.08, 38.17; 39.07, 39.09
GS Title page; 74.03; 78.10, 78.12, 78.15, 78.17; 79.02,
79.13, 79.14, 79.18; 80.05, 80.17; 81.01, 81.03, 81.10; 82.09;
83.03, 83.13, 83.14; 85.07, 85.09, 85.17; 86.04, 86.05, 86.09,
86.10, 86.14; 87.14; 88.08, 88.12, 88.14, 88.17; 89.17; 90.03,
90.04; 91.02, 91.09; 92.05; 93.02, 93.07, 93.08, 93.12, 93.13,
93.14, 93.17; 94.15; 95.09, 95.13, 95.14, 95.15; 96.01, 96.04,
96.09; 97.06

Düüreng Döcin. Khoshuud. One of the three sons of Örökh Tömör.
DO 26.14
GS 76.08 (only one son listed)

Dughār.
DO 35.08, 35.12
GS 84.03, 84.04, 84.15

Dural. Messenger of Shikür Dayicing.
HKK 2.15

Dural. cf. Dural Dayicin.

Dural Dayicin. Torghuud. One of the four sons of Ezenē Tayiji.
DO 31.04
GS 76.02 (Dural Dayicang)

Duurisxu. Khoshuud. One of the four sons of Dorji Tayiji.
DO 27.05, 27.07

Dünēke. Torghuud. One of the ten sons of Cecen Noyon.
DO 30.13

Düüregeci Ubashi. Khoshuud. One of the eight sons of (Khan
Noyon) Khongghor.
DO 26.17; 27.02
GS 76.14 (The GS lists as one name beginning with Tümüdē
Köndölöng)

Dzungar cf. Zöün Ghar.

E

Ebel. Torghuud. One of the ten sons of Cecen Noyon.
DO 30.13

ē Caghān Khatun.
GS 88.03

Ecüs Kölgön. Torghuud. One of the ten sons of Cecen Noyon.
DO 30.13

Ejil. cf. Ijil.

Elisaveta. Khoyid. One of the two daughters of Ceren Dorji.
DO 28.02

Elizabeth. Tsarina. She is referred to but not actually named
in the following places in the text.
HKK 11.17; 12.02, 12.05

Embe Ghol. Embe River.
HKK 1.12

Enedkekh. India.
GS 96.10

Engke Sömör Tayiji. Khoshuud. Son of Khabutu Khasar.
DO 26.12
GS 76.04

Ercis. Irgiz River.
HKK 20.09

Erdeni. Khoshuud.
DO 26.16 (Son of Obukh Cingsa. cf. Khatai Erdeni)
GS 76.12 (Son of Uur Uuzang)

Erdeni. Torghuud. Son of Caghān Kiciq.
DO 30.09

Erdeni Bātur Khung Tayiji. Attended the 1640 law code.
HKK 2.05

Erdeni Khung Tayiji. Khoshuud. One of the two sons of Cecen
Khan.
DO 27.03, 27.06
GS 76.17

Erdeni Tayishi. Dörböd. One of the two sons of Namēsniq Cüücei
Tayishi.
DO 29.07

Erdeni Zasakhtu Khan.
HKK 2.04

Erempes. Khoshuud. One of the two sons of Zanji Rashi.
DO 27.11

Erke Dayicing. Khoshuud. One of the four sons of Düürgeci.
DO 27.02, 27.05

Erke Skyab Nong. Torghuud. Son of Mergen Skyab Nong.
DO 31.05
GS 76.02

Erke Tayiji. Dörböd. Son of Batur Malai.
DO 29.06

Erketen. Place name and ulus name.
HKK 13.02

Erlikh.
DO 34.09

Eselbe. cf. Eselbei.

Eselbei. Khoyid. Son of Yoboghon Mergen; father of Sayin G'a.
DO 27.15; 37.11; 38.01, 38.06, 38.14; 39.02, 39.07, 39.08,
39.11
GS 78.11; 85.10 (Eselbe)

Esen. Dörböd. Son of Toghon Tayishi.
DO 28.12
GS 77.12 (Yesen)

Eyona Donduk'ob. Christian name for one of the sons of Zhan.
HKK 12.17

Ezenē Tayiji. Torghuud. Eldest son of Ongkho Cabcāci.
DO 31.04
GS 76.01

G

Genden Norba. Khoshuud. One of the two sons of Tukhcu.
DO 27.11

Gengge. Khoshuud. One of the two sons of Tukhcu.

DO 27.12

Genshikhcab. Khoshuud. Son of Ghaldan Dörji.
DO 27.10

Gerel. Torghuud.
DO 30.17 (Son of Abida Buuci)
GS 75.11 (Son of Mongkhai)

Geser Sphyabs. Khoyid. Son of Ser Od Sphyab.
DO 28.01

Gombo Dorji.
GS 91.11

Goyang
GS 79.09

Güncöb Byab. Torghuud. One of the twelve sons of Phyakhdar
Byab.
DO 30.05

Güngge. Khoshuud. One of the three sons of Dundokh (the son of
Duuriskhu).
DO 27.09

Günji Khatun
GS 88.06

Güre. Wife of (Khudai Shikür) Dayicing; he has no children by
her.
GS 75.01

Güüsi Khan. cf. Güüsi Nomiyin Khan.

Güüsi Nomiyin Khan. Khoshuud. One of the eight sons of (Khan
Noyon) Khongghor.
HKK 2.04, 2.13
DO 26.17; 27.03; 32.06 (Khan of Oirats); 33.02 (explains how
he received the title Nomiyin Khan); 34.16; 35.17; 36.04,
36.09, 36.12
GS 76.14; 77.01, 77.02; 80.15, 80.16; 81.03, 81.11; 83.08;
86.06, 86.10, 86.18; 89.14; 91.10, 91.11; 95.01, 95.06

Gh

Ghabang Sharab, (Emci). Dörböd. Son of Khabciq of the clan of
Bolkhon.
DO 29.10
GS Title page; 75.18

Ghakhai. Dörböd. Son of Nima.
DO 29.09

Ghal Bars.
HKK 4.11 (1686)

Ghaldama. Khoshuud. One of the two sons of Cecen.

DO 27.03, 27.06
GS 76.17, 76.18; 88.05 (Noyon Ghaldama); 91.14; 94.13; 95.03, 95.07

Ghaldan Byamco. Khoshuud. One of the three sons of Öbögön.
DO 27.08

Ghaldan Ceren. Dörböd. Son of Lhabang Dorub. He attended the investiture of Dondukh Dashi in 1757.
HKK 15.13
DO 29.05
GS 85.04?

Ghaldan Ceren. Dörböd. Son of Zorikhtu Khung Tayiji.
DO 29.02
GS 78.04; 85.04?

Ghaldan Danzin. Torghuud. One of the four sons of Ayuuki.
HKK 11.17; 12.01
DO 30.04
GS 75.03; 85.07

Ghaldan Dorji. Khoshuud. Son of Erdeni Khung Tayiji.
DO 27.06
GS 76.18 (G'aldan Rdo Rje)

Ghaldan Dorji. Khoshuud. One of the three sons of Öbögön.
DO 27.08, 27.10

Ghaldan Khung Tayiji. Became khan in the territory of Dzungaria.
DO 35.03; 39.15, 39.17

Ghaldan Norba. Khoshuud. Son of Zanji Rashi.
DO 27.11

Ghaldan Norbo. cf. Ghaldan Norbu.

Ghaldan Norbu. Torghuud. One of the five sons of Dondukh Ombu.
cf. Ghaldan Norbo.
HKK 10.10; 11.13, 11.15; 17.17
DO 30.07, 30.08 (Ghaldan Norbo)
GS 96.06

Ghal Ghakhai.
HKK 5.12 (1707)
DO 37.08 (1527)

Ghal Khonin.
HKK 13.01 (1787)

Ghal Khulughuna.
DO 37.12 (1636)

Ghal Luu.
HKK 11.02 (1736), 11.04 (1736)

Ghal Moghoi

HKK 11.02 (1737)
GS 96.07 (1737)

Ghal Tak'ā.
HKK 7.16 (1719)

Ghaltu. Torghuud. Son of Buyan.
DO 30.17
GS 75.12

Ghal Ükür.
HKK 4.14 (1697); 14.04 (1757)
DO 40.05 (1757)

Ghangha Müren. River.
DO 26.01

Gharī Shiri. Khoshuud. Son of Cing.
DO 27.12

Ghonjib. Torghuud. Son of Ayuuki by Darma Bala.
HKK 5.05, 5.07; 8.12
DO 30.03 (Mg'un Sphyabs), 30.06 (G'un Sphyab); 36.17 (G'un
Sphyabs)
GS 75.03 (Mgün skyab); 87.13 (Mgün Byab)

Ghori. cf. Ghoroi.

Ghoroi. Torghuud. Third eldest of the six sons of Buyigho
Örlöq. cf.Ghori.
DO 29.17; 30.14
GS 74.14; 75.08, 75.16

Ghurban. Made a subject of the Dörböd Dalai Tayishi.
DO 36.10

Ghurban Ecige Ghalg'ās. Khoshuud. Son of Tögüdei Cingsen
Ghorban.
DO 35.10
GS 76.09; 84.13

G'

G'a. cf. Sayin G'a.

G'aldan Ceren. cf. Ghaldan Ceren.
HKK 15.13

G'aldan Rdo Rje. cf. Ghaldan Dorji.

G'anuu. Torghuud. One of the two sons of Buyantukh.
DO 31.11

G'ombo. cf. Rdo Rje Mgün po.

G'ombo Yeldeng. Torghuud. One of the six sons of Khō Örlöq.
cf. Yeldeng.
DO 30.02; 34.16

HKK 2.08, 2.12

G'ūdiq. Torghuud. One of the two sons of Bayilinikh.
DO 31.10

G'un Sphyab. cf. Ghonjib.

G'un Sphyabs. cf. Ghonjib.

G'unstantin. Khoyid. Son of Ceren Dorji.
DO 28.02

G'ümbü Sharab. Khoshuud. cf. Mgümbü Sharab.
DO 26.16 (One of four sons of Obukh Cingsa)
GS 76.12 (Mgümbü Sharab. Son of Erdeni)

I

Ijil. Torghuud. One of the three sons of Noyon Sanjilai.
DO 31.14

Ijil Müren. Volga River.
HKK 1.02, 1.14, 1.17; 3.06, 3.09, 3.13; 4.09; 6.01; 7.07;
8.01; 9.01; 10.10; 12.08; 17.16; 19.05, 19.07; 19.12; 22.11,
22.13
DO 24.10; 26.09; 40.13, 40.15
GS 84.03 (Ejil); 95.16

Ikiri Müren. River.
DO 26.01

Ili. Area of Dzungaria.
HKK 23.06, 23.09

Indastani. Place name.
DO 25.12

Inzan Rinbuce Gekīd.
HKK 2.03

Irakh Lob Khomoghal. cf. Irekhlöü.

Irekhlöü (Khomoghol).
DO 36.05
GS 86.11 (Irakh Lob Khomoghal)

Irnali. Sultan of Kazakhs.
HKK 21.11; 22.01, 22.02, 22.03

Ismayilob. Governor of Astrakhan.
HKK 9.16; 10.16

Istanica. Russian name for Zamyang.
DO 42.17

J

Jiteshen. Turkic tribe.

HKK 1.13; 7.11; 8.01

K

Kei Kemnekhtu. Khoshuud. Son of Adashiri Ghalzuu Cing Tayiji.
DO 26.13
GS 76.05 (Kē)

Kē Kemnekhtu. cf. Kei Kemnekhtu.

Kelebe Dalai Ubashi. Khoshuud. One of the four sons of Düürgēci
Ubashi.
DO 27.02, 27.03

Keshiq. Dörböd. Son of Darkhan Noyon.
DO 28.13
GS 77.14

Kiciq. Khoshuud. One of the three sons of Dondukh (the son of
Duuriskhu).
DO 27.09

Kiresen. Torghuud. The third eldest son of Khō Örlökh.
DO 30.02
GS 74.17

Kishangski. Russian official.
HKK 19.09

Kitad. China.
HKK 6.10, 6.15; 7.06; 9.17; 17.14; 22.16; 23.01, 23.02, 23.05,
23.14
DO 26.07, 26.10; 32.17; 33.17; 40.09; 42.15
GS 74.07; 80.14; 82.10, 82.11; 83.17; 84.09; 92.03; 94.14;
96.12, 96.17

Kitad Khan. Chinese emperor.
HKK 6.08, 6.11, 6.12; 23.13

Kīve. Kiva.
HKK 5.15; 7.08, 7.14, 7.15

Kiwang. Ally of Torghuud. cf. Mg'as Dbang.
GS 74.10

Kiyibi Khan.
HKK 20.11

Kiyirib. Torghuud. One of the three sons of Ghaldan Norbo.
DO 30.08

Kökö Nuur. Lake. Ch'ing Hai.
DO 25.17; 26.08
GS 77.01; 78.08

Köndölöng Ubashi. Torghuud. One of the six sons of Khō Örlöq.
DO 33.03, 33.04?, 33.13?; 36.13?; 37.02?
GS 80.17; 81.11?, 81.13?; 87.03?, 87.07?

Köndölöng Ubashi. Tayishi of the Khoshuud.
HKK 3.05
DO 32.12; 36.13?; 37.02?
GS 80.09; 87.03, 87.07

Köndölöng Ubashi Khan.
DO 33.04, 33.13?; 36.13?; 37.02?

Köngköyigi Khoton. Area.
HKK 23.08

Kümeng. Tribe.
HKK 5.12

Küng Tügüdi. cf. Tügüdi.

Küsei. Khoshuud.
DO 26.15 (One of the six sons of Tügüd)
GS 76.11 (Eldest of the eight sons of Aghudi)

Küüken Bātur. Dörböd. Son of Sakil Noyon Khashikha.
DO 28.17
GS 78.01

Küüken Ubashi. Torghuud. One of the ten sons of Cecen Noyon.
DO 30.13

Kyal Bu. cf. Rbyal Bo.

KH

Khabcikh. Turkic tribe.
HKK 1.13
DO 36.07
GS 86.13 (Khabshikh)

Khabcikh. Dörböd. One of the three sons of Byal.
DO 29.09, 29.10

Khabshikh. cf. Khabcikh.

Khabutu Khasar. Khoshuud. Younger brother of Chinggis.
DO 26.12; 40.16
GS 76.04

Khai. Khoshuud. One of the four sons of Dorji Tayiji.
DO 27.04, 27.06

Khai Khulakha. Torghuud. One of the three sons of Arkhala
Akhatu.
DO 30.14

Khalimakh. Kalmyk.
HKK 1.01, 1.03; 2.07, 2.14, 2.16, 2.17; 3.06, 3.08, 3.11;

4.02, 4.05, 4.10, 4.17; 5.01, 5.11; 6.02, 6.03, 6.17; 7.11,
7.17; 8.02, 8.09, 8.10, 8.11, 8.16; 9.01, 9.07, 9.08, 9.12,
9.14, 9.15; 10.15, 10.17; 11.03, 11.04, 11.14; 12.11, 12.14;
13.03, 13.04, 13.05, 13.06, 13.10; 14.04, 14.14; 16.02, 16.03,
16.04; 17.10; 19.02, 19.05, 19.07, 19.08, 19.09, 19.10, 19.17;
20.01, 20.03, 20.05, 20.10, 20.13, 20.14; 21.01, 21.04, 21.05,
21.06, 21.08, 21.12, 21.15, 21.16; 22.02, 22.07; 23.07, 23.13,
23.16, 23.17
DO 24.08; 25.14; 25b.15; 41.16
GS 90.07

Khalkha. Khalkha.
DO 25.12

Khamighai Bekhtu. cf. Khamoughai Bakhtokhoghai.

Khamoughai Bakhtokhoghai. Khoshuud. One of the two sons of
Buyan Khatun Bātur.
DO 27.01 (Khamighai Bekhtu. Listed as one of the eight sons of
Khan Noyon Khongghor)
GS 76.16

Khamukh Tayishi. Dörböd. Son of Örlöq.
DO 28.14
GS 77.14

Khara Kitad.
DO 24.03

Khara K'alpaq. Karakalpak.
HKK 4.16

Kharam. Krim Tatars.
HKK 3.01, 3.03, 3.11; 4.01; 6.02

Kharamlai. Tribe.
HKK 11.05

Khara Sabar. Khoshuud. Son of Zasakhtu Cing Bātur.
DO 27.13

Khara Usun. Area in Dzungaria.
HKK 23.06, 23.08

Khara Khula. Dörböd. Son of Abida Bolo Tayishi; father of Bātur
Khung Tayiji.
DO 28.17; 32.12
GS 78.02 (Khara Khola); 79.10

Kharbad. Tribe: Kabardian.
HKK 7.17; 11.13; 12.14

Khasakh. Kazakhs.
HKK 4.04, 4.16; 6.12; 9.11; 11.03; 12.11; 13.03, 13.04, 13.05,
13.07, 13.08; 14.08; 19.17; 20.02, 20.03, 20.09, 20.14, 20.16;
21.03, 21.04, 21.06, 21.10, 21.11, 21.16, 21.17; 22.01, 22.06,
22.13
DO 36.06

GS 86.14; 94.13

Khatai. Turkic tribe.
HKK 1.13
DO 36.07
GS 86.13

Khatai Erdeni. Khoshuud. cf. Erdeni.
DO 26.16 (One of the four sons of Obukh Cingsa)
GS 76.12 (Erdeni. Son of Uur Uuzang)

Khatāmad. Khoshuud group.
DO 42.09

Khayinakh Tüsētü. cf. Ukh Tüshētü.

Khayirtu. Khoshuud. One of the two sons of Luuzang Ombo.
DO 27.06

Khazaghuud. Cossacks.
HKK 6.06; 15.06; 17.07; 20.05, 20.07

Khazalbashi. Persia.
HKK 3.12; 5.15; 8.07, 8.10; 12.14
DO 25b.07
GS 78.08; 92.04

Khazan. Kazan.
HKK 3.16; 11.15; 12.12; 17.17

Khodai Shükür Dayicang. cf. Khudai Shükür Dayicing.

Kholaghayici. cf. Khulaghāci.

Kholdoi Khosouci. cf. Kholodoi Khosuuchi.

Kholoci. Torghuud. The eldest of the three sons of Ülü Cenzē.
DO 31.01
GS 75.13

Kholodoi Khoshuuci. Dörböd. Son of Ömidö Cingsa.
DO 28.16
GS 77.18 (Kholodoi Khoshouci)

Khongghor Noyon. Khoshuud. Elder son of Bökö Mirza.
DO 26.17 (Khongghor Khan Noyon)
GS 76.13

Khō Örlöq. Torghuud. Son of Zulzugha Örlöq.
HKK 1.05, 1.17; 2.01, 2.05, 2.06, 2.07, 2.08, 2.10; 23.16
DO 30.01; 33.02, 33.07; 34.08, 34.15; 36.15
GS 74.15; 79.01?; 80.16; 81.15; 83.06; 87.05; 95.17 (Örlöq Dayicang)

Khoshuuci. Torghuud. Youngest of the four sons of Butui.
DO 31.03
GS 75.16

Khoshuud. Tribe: Khoshuud.
HKK 1.09; 3.05; 12.09, 12.10; 15.13; 17.16; 18.11; 23.07,
23.08
DO 24.01; 25b.12; 25.16; 26.03, 26.11; 41.13, 41.14; 42.09
GS 74.05; 77.03

Khoton. Tribe. Turkestan.
DO 33.16
GS 78.07; 82.10, 82.11

Khoyid. Tribe: Khoyid.
HKK 12.07, 12.10; 17.16
DO 25b.09; 25.16; 27.15; 33.16; 34.08, 34.17; 37.07, 37.10;
39.16; 42.09
GS 74.04; 78.07, 78.09; 79.09; 82.10; 83.12, 83.14; 90.14;
94.11

Khubun. Kuban.
HKK 3.09; 4.01; 5.15; 7.06 (Sultan), 7.12, 7.17; 8.04
(Tatars); 10.07, 10.09; 11.02, 11.07

Khudai Shükür Dayicing. Torghuud. The eldest of the six sons of
Khō Orlöq. cf. Sikür Dayicing, and Dayicing (Torghuud).
DO 30.01, 30.02, 30.09
GS 74.16, 74.18

Khulaghāci. Torghuud. Son of Bökö Tayiji.
DO 30.16
GS 75.10 (Kholaghayici)

Khumuq. Tribe.
GS 78.08

Khung Tayiji. Seized his elder brother Danjin Wangbo.
DO 35.11, 35.15
GS 84.16; 85.03, 85.07

Khuvangdi, Dēdü Ezen. Huang Ti.
HKK 7.03

K'

K'aspiski Dalai. Caspian Sea.
HKK 13.05

K'aspuyin Dalai. Caspian Sea.
HKK 1.08

K'atai. Turkic tribe.
HKK 7.17

K'rasnoyarski. City.
HKK 10.08

L

Lavang. Torghuud.
HKK 10.07

Lekhbe. Khoshuud. One of the three sons Khai.
DO 27.07

Lesgin. People, allies of Persia.
HKK 8.10

Lhabang Dorub. Dörböd. Son of Citer.
DO 29.05

Lhacang Khan.
GS 85.15

Likhsum Khan. Khoshuud. Son of Dalai Khan.
GS 77.02

Lob Kyā Lubphyȳ.

Lori Damba. Khoshuud. Son of Caghang.
DO 27.08

Lubphyē Torghuud. One of the three sons of Dorji.
HKK 10.04 (Lübci)
DO 30.04
GS 75.06 (Lob Kyā)

Lubzang. Torghuud. The fifth eldest of the six sons of Khō O
Örlöq.
HKK 2.08, 2.11, 2.12
DO 30.02 (Luuzang)
GS 74.18 (Blo Bz'ang); 95.03, 95.16

Luuzang. Khoshuud. Son of Kelebe Dalai Ubashi.
DO 27.04

Luuzang. cf. Örlö̈KH Luuzang?
DO 36.02
GS 86.08

Luuzang Ombo. cf. Blo Bzang Mgonbo.

Lübci. cf. Lubphyē.

M

Makhacin Kered. Torghuud. One of the nine sons of Menggei.
DO 29.17
GS 74.13; 90.01

Makhaciyin Kerēd. cf. Makhacin Kered.

Makhani Sereng.
GS 92.14, 92.17

Malai.
GS 88.03

Manas Yeldeng. Torghuud. Son of Ezenei Tayiji. cf. Manus
Yeldeng.
DO 31.04 (Manus Yeldeng)
GS 76.01

Mangghad. Tatars?
HKK 7.09, 7.12; 8.01; 9.07; 14.09
DO 25b.16; 36.06
GS 95.17

Mangghai. cf. Mangkhai.

Mangghus.
HKK 7.14

Mangkhai. Torghuud. Fourth of the six sons of Buyigho Örlö̈KH.
cf. Mangghai.
DO 29.17; 30.16
GS 74.15; 75.11, 75.17

Mangzi. Manchu.
HKK 7.01

Mangzi Ezen. Manchu emperor.
HKK 7.02; 9.14; 22.17; 23.01, 23.04, 23.07, 23.10

Mangzi Khan. cf. Mangzi Ezen.

Mangzu. cf. Mangzi Ezen.

Mangzushiri. Khan of the Khara Kitad.
DO 24.03

Manus Yeldeng. Torghuud. One of the four sons of Ezenē Tayiji.
DO 31.04
GS 76.01 (Manas Yeldeng)

Manu Tokhoi. Place near Tsaritsyn.
HKK 6.14

Manzushiri. Torghuud. One of the ten sons of Cecen Noyon.
DO 30.12

Manzuukh.
GS 85.12

Marghash. Khoshuud. One of the four sons of Duuriskhu.
DO 27.07, 27.09

Mashi. Torghuud. Son of Ningbo.
DO 30.08, 30.10

Mazan. Torghuud. Son of Ociro.
DO 30.14

Mengge(i). Torghuud. One of the nine sons of Bayar.
DO 29.16; 31.03

GS 74.12; 75.18

Mergen. Khoyid. Lineage to Chinggis Khan.
DO 27.15

Mergen Dayicang. Dzungar.
GS 85.08

Mergeni Erektü. Torghuud. Tibetan name; Mg'as Dbang.
DO 29.15
GS 74.10 (Kiwang)

Mergen Skyo Nong. cf. Mergen Sphyonong.

Mergen Sphyonong. Torghuud. Son of Tenes Mergen Temene.
DO 31.05
GS 76.02 (Mergen Skyo Nong)

Mergen Tayiji. Seizes and kills Puncokh.
DO 35.06, 35.07
GS 84.01

Mgümbü Sharab. Khoshuud. Son of Erdeni. cf. G'ümbü Sharab.
GS 76.12

Mgün Byab. cf. Ghonjib.

Mgün Sphyab. cf. Ghonjib.

Mg'as Dbang. Torghuud. Mongol name; Mergeni Erketü. cf. Kiwang
DO 29.14

Mg'un Skyabs. cf. Ghonjib.

Mila. Khoshuud. Son of Ceren (the son of Dorji Tayiji).
DO 27.08

Modon Bars.
HKK 3.12 (1674); 10.12 (1734)

Modon Ghakhai.
HKK 17.14 (1755)

Modon Khonin.
HKK 2.15 (1655); 7.06 (1715); 23.15 (1775)

Modon Mecin.
GS 86.03 (1644)

Modon Tuulai.
HKK 10.16 (1735)

Modon Ükür.
HKK 13.03 (1745)

Mogileva. Province.
HKK 13.01

Moghoi. Snake Year.
GS 92.14

Mongghoi Cecen. Dorbod. Son of Akhshi Tayiji.
DO 28.15
GS 77.16

Mongghol.
HKK 1.02; 7.04; 8.09, 8.15; 19.01, 19.02; 23.05, 23.07
DO 24.16; 25.11, 25.12, 25.13; 32.17; 34.05; 37.12; 38.01,
38.02, 38.07, 38.09, 38.11, 38.15; 39.04, 39.05, 39.06, 39.10,
39.13
GS 74.03, 74.09; 78.07, 78.10, 78.12, 78.18; 79.01, 79.03,
79.06; 80.06, 80.15; 92.18

Mosk'va. Moscow.
HKK 2.16

Mönggöd. Khoshuud. One of the four sons of Tarba Ceren.
DO 27.10, 27.12

Möngkö. Dörböd. Son of Dejid Zambu Tayishi.
DO 29.07

Möngkön. Khoshuud. Son of Luuzang Ombo.
DO 27.06

Möngkö Nasun. Dörböd. One of the three sons of Byalba.
DO 29.11

Möngkö Tömör Tayishi. Dörböd. Son of Solom Ceren Tayishi.
HKK 5.14, 5.17
DO 29.04

Mughucar. Mountain.
HKK 21.08

Mukhur Mujikh. Mongol. Son of Ubasi Khung Tayiji of the
Mongols.
DO 37.16; 38.07, 38.11, 38.15; 39.04, 39.05, 39.07, 39.09

Muu Kööken. Torghuud. One of the two sons of Bayilinikh.
DO 31.10; 31.11

Muu Kööken. Torghuud. One of the two sons of Mashi.
DO 30.10

N

Naghai Tatar.
HKK 1.13; 2.11; 3.09; 5.12; 7.17

Nag'udi. cf. Aghudi.

Nalxu. Khoshuud. Son of Danji.
DO 27.11

Nama Sereng. cf. Nima Sereng.

Namēsniq Cüücei Tayishi. Dörböd. Son of Tundud.
DO 29.06

Natar. Torghuud. Son of Tukh.
DO 31.14

Nazar. Torghuud. Son of Nima Sereng.
DO 30.04
GS 75.05

Nazarbaq. Khoshuud. Son of Darkhan Tayiji.
DO 27.14; 40.16 (Nazar Bakh)

Nazāriyin Dorji. Tsar Peter's choice as khan after Ayuuki; he
refused khanship.
HKK 8.11; 9.03, 9.04; 10.04, 10.06; 11.17

Neyiter. cf. Niyiter.

Nikhtar. Torghuud. One of the twelve sons of Phyakhdar Byab.
DO 30.05

Nima. Khoshuud. One of the three sons of Mönggöd.
DO 27.12

Nima. Dörböd. One of the three sons of Byal.
DO 29.09

Nima Sereng. Torghuud. One of the four sons of Khudai Shükür
Dayicing. cf. Nama Sereng.
DO 30.02, 30.04; 36.16
GS 75.01, 75.04; 87.06

Nimgen Ubashi. Torghuud.
HKK 15.13

Ningbo. Torghuud. One of the three sons of Bokhshorgho.
DO 30.08

Nitar Ubashi. Torghuud. One of the four sons of Sanji Ubashi.
DO 30.10

Niyiter. Younger brother of Dacang, who seized him.
DO 35.15
GS 85.04 (Neyiter)

Nomiyin Khan Güüsi. cf. Güüsi (Nomiyin Khan).

Noxōn Köböün. Torghuud. One of the five sons of Rabbyur.
DO 31.10, 31.11

Noyon Dorji Rabtan. cf. Dorji Arabtan.

Noyon Ghabang Namg'a. Torghuud. Separated from Rabbyur.
DO 31.13

Noyon Ghaldama. cf. Ghaldama.

Noyon Gholo Cingsa. Dzungar. Son of Onggho.
DO 28.16

Noyon Sanjilai. Torghuud.
DO 31.13

Noyon Tümen. cf. Tümen Jirghalang.
DO 42.10

Noyon Ubashi. Torghuud. One of the four sons of Buura.
DO 30.12

Noyon Khongghor. cf. Khongghor.

Nöür Uuzang Shükür. cf. Uur Uuzang Shükür.

Nurali Khan. Khan of the Kazakhs.
HKK 19.17; 20.07, 20.08, 20.10, 20.11; 21.08

O

Obö. Torghuud. One of the four sons of Bolkhon. cf. Ung.
DO 31.02
GS 75.15 (Oböng)

Obokh Cingsa. cf. Ubakh Cingsa.

Oböng. cf. Obö.

Ocir. Dörböd. One of the two sons of Oncikh.
DO 29.10

Ocir. Torghuud. One of the three sons of Cebekh Ubashi.
DO 30.09

Ocir Dhara Khutuktu. cf. Ociro Dara Khutuktu.

Ocir Erdeni. Torghuud. Son of Amakhai.
DO 31.13

Ociro. Torghuud. One of the three sons of Arkhala Akhatu.
DO 30.13

Ociro Dara Khutuktu.
DO 34.09
GS 79.09 (Ocir Dhara Khutuktu)

Ocir Tayishi. Dörböd. One of the three sons of Cö Rashi.
DO 29.09

Oin Buulukh Tatar. Tribe.
HKK 8.01

Olon Cecen. cf. Ülü Cenzē.

Omba. A <u>zayisang</u> under Bakhta Girei.
HKK 8.01

Oncikh. Dörböd. One of the three sons of Khabcikh.
DO 29.10

Ongasār. cf. Ongghosōr.

Ongghai. cf. Ongghoi.

Onggho. Dzungar. Son of Arkha cingsa.
DO 28.16

Ongghoco. Dörböd. One of the two sons of Arkha Cingsa.
DO 28.16, 28.17
GS 77.17; 78.01

Ongghoi. Dörböd. One of the two sons of Arkha Cingsa.
GS 77.17

Ongghoi. Dörböd. Youngest of the three sons of Khamuq Tayishi.
DO 28.14
GS 77.15

Ongghoi. Torghuud. One of the four sons of Bulighun.
DO 31.02
GS 75.14 (Ongghai)

Ongghon Cabaji. Torghuud. Second son of Mengge. cf. Ongkho
Cabcīci.
GS 75.18

Ongghosor. Torghuud. One of the four sons of Bolkhon.
DO 31.02
GS 75.14 (Ongasār)

Ongkho Cabcīci. Torghuud. The second of the nine sons of
Mengge; he has five sons. cf. Ongghon Cabcaji. Ongkhon
Cabcāji.
DO 29.16; 31.04 (Onggho Cabcāji)
GS 74.12; 75.18

Ongkhon Cabcaji. cf. Ongkho Cabcīci.

Ori. River.
HKK 21.08

Oringburg. Orenburg Province.
HKK 3.16; 19.17; 20.07

Oron Buurg. cf. Oringburg.

Oros. Russia.
HKK 1.03, 1.15; 2.07, 2.14, 2.15, 2.17; 3.02, 3.09, 3.11,
3.12, 3.15, 3.16, 3.17; 4.01, 4.02, 4.03, 4.11, 4.12, 4.14,
4.16, 4.17; 5.01, 5.02, 5.12, 5.13, 5.15; 6.02, 6.04, 6.10,
6.13, 6.15, 6.16, 6.17; 7.08, 7.12, 7.15; 8.03, 8.17; 9.15;
10.06, 10.08, 10.09, 10.10, 10.12; 11.03, 11.04, 11.10; 13.01,

13.03, 13.04; 14.17; 16.01; 17.08, 17.10, 17.15; 18.02, 18.03,
18.04, 18.05; 19.08, 19.10, 19.12, 19.15; 20.01, 20.05, 20.09,
20.11, 20.13; 20.16; 21.16; 22.14; 23.03, 23.13, 23.16
DO 24.13; 26.07; 33.16; 35.08; 40.03, 40.04, 40.07, 40.09,
40.11, 40.14
GS 78.07; 82.09, 82.12; 84.05; 85.05; 92.04; 96.06

Oros Khan. Russian ruler..
HKK 2.16, 3.01, 3.10, 3.14, 3.17; 4.07, 4.11; 5.08

Orski. Fortress.
HKK 20.09

Oyirad.
HKK 1.16; 4.08, 4.11; 13.09; 17.15, 17.16; 19.01, 19.04
DO 24.08; 25.14; 28.12; 29.14; 32.04, 32.06, 32,16, 32.17;
33.15; 34.05, 34.08, 34.15; 35.03, 35.17; 37.12, 37.14, 37.16,
37.17; 38.02, 38.14, 38.16; 39.03, 39.05, 39.10, 39.11, 39.12;
41.06
GS 74.03, 74.10; 78.09; 79.01, 79.09, 79.12; 80.02, 80.14;
81.09, 81.17; 82.08; 83.02, 83.07; 84.13, 84.17; 85.06, 85.16;
87.10, 87.16; 88.03, 88.07, 88.16; 89.06, 89.10, 89.15; 90.06,
90.11, 90.12; 91.01, 91.08; 92.10; 93.17; 94.10, 94.16; 95.05,
95.09; 96.06, 96.12, 96.14; 97.01, 97.02, 97.04

Ö

Öbögön. Khoshuud. One of the four sons of Dorji Tayiji.
DO 27.05, 27.07

Öbögö Tayishi. Torghuud. One of the four sons of Buura. cf.
Öböküi Tayishi Dalai.
DO 30.12

Öböküi Tayishi Dalai. Torghuud. One of the four sons of Buura.
cf. Öbögö Tayishi.
GS 75.08

Öldö. Dörböd. Son of Dayikhal. cf. Üledüi Aldar G'ā.
DO 28.15
GS 77.13 (Üledüi Aldara G'a); 93.04

Ölkönö Tayishi. Dzungar. Son of Boro Ayalxu
DO 28.13
GS 77.13 (Ölökönöi Tayishi)

Ölöd. Tribe. cf. Öyilöd.
GS 74.04; 76.07

Ölökönöi Tayishi. cf. Ölkönö Tayishi.

Ölzöi Oroshikhu. Wife of Dejīd Noyon; her son is Tümen
Jirghalang.
DO 40.03, 40.07, 40.11, 40.17; 41.05

Ömidö Cingsa. Dörböd. Son of Noyon Gholo Cingsa.
DO 28.16
GS 77.18 (Amidu Cingsan)

Önöcin Acīn Khān Tayiji.
GS 88.02

Örlökh. Dzungar. Son of Keshiq.
DO 28.14

Örlökh. khoshuud.
gs 80.08

Örlökh (Luuzang).
DO 36.05
GS 86.12

Örlökh Dayicang. cf. Khō Örlöq

Örlökh Luuzang. cf. Luuzang.
DO 32.12; 36.02?

Örlökh Yeldeng. cf. Yeldeng.

Örlökh Yeldeng Torghuud cf. Yeldeng.

Örökh Römör. Khoshuud. One of the two sons of Akhsarghuldai
Noyon.
DO 26.14
GS 76.07, 76.08

Öröü Salki. Additional name for Darma Bala, q.v.
GS 84.08

Ösh Tomoi Dar Khan Noyon. cf. Öshtömö Noyon.

Öshtömö Noyon. Dörböd. Son of Esen (Yesen).
DO 28.12
GS 77.12 (Ösh Tomoi Dar Khan Noyon)

Öyilöd. cf. Ölöd. Tribe.
DO 24.08; 25b.05, 25b.06, 25b.07, 25.14; 26.03
GS 74.04; 76.07 (Ölöd); 78.08, 78.09

P

Padma. Torghuud. One of the two sons of Ocir.
DO 30.10

Pavrad.
GS 89.04

Penze. Province in Russia.
HKK 5.14; 8.02

Peterbuurg. City.
HKK 10.09; 11.08; 12.06, 12.16; 18.02
DO 41.09, 41.12

Peter Donduk'ob. Christian name of one of the sons of Zhan.
HKK 12.17

Peter Matveyevici Aprakhsin.
HKK 5.16

Peter Tayishi. Younger brother of Dasang.
HKK 10.02, 10.07

Peter Yeke Khan. Tsar Peter the Great.
HKK 4.12; 6.03, 6.10, 6.16; 8.07, 8.09, 8.10; 10.02

Peter Soyimonob. Minister of the Tsarina Anna.
HKK 11.09

Phyakhdar Byab. Torghuud. Eldest son of Ayuuki.
HKK 5.04, 5.06, 5.07, 5.09; 7.16; 8.06, 8.14; 10.01; 12.03
DO 30.03, 30.05
GS 75.03, 75.04; 84.07; 85.05; 91.18; 92.14, 92.16 (Phyaqdar
Skyab)

Phyakhdar Skyab. cf. Phyakhdar Byab.

Pilib Donduk'ob. Christian name of one of the sons of Zhan.
HKK 12.17

Piter. Petersburg.
HKK 12.16
DO 41.12

Pitiyir. Petersburg.
HKK 10.17

Porbo. Dörböd. One of the two sons of Ghakhai.
DO 29.09

Porudcikh. Russian title for warrant officer held by the son of
the governor of Astrakhan, Zhilin.
HKK 16.11

Pöncukh Kyamcub. cf. Puncokh.

Puncokh. Torghuud. One of the four sons of Shikür Dayicing.
HKK 3.02, 3.04, 3.05, 3.06, 3.10
DO 30.03; 35.07; 36.16
GS 75.01, 75.02, 75.06; 84.02; 87.06; 95.08?

R

Rabbyur. Torghuud. cf. Rabj'uur, and Rabp'yur.
DO 31.09, 31.12

Rabj'uuri. Torghuud. Nephew of Ayuuki, and one of the four sons
of Nazar. cf. Rabbyuur and Rabp'yur.
HKK 6.07, 6.08, 6.09, 6.12, 6.15; 7.04
DO 30.04
GS 75.05 (Rab Gbyor)

Rabp'yur. Torghuud. cf. Rabj'uuri.
DO 30.04

Rabtan. Dörböd. One of the three sons of Byalba.
DO 29.11

Rabzuur. Khoshuud. One of the two sons of Marghash.
DO 27.10, 27.12

Randuli. Torghuud. One of the five sons of Dondukh Ombo. cf.
Rangdol.
HKK 11.14, 11.16; 12.02
DO 30.07

Rangdol. Torghuud. One of the five sons of Dondukh Ombo. cf.
Randuli.
DO 30.07

Raniu Li. Torghuud. Son of Cecen Noyon.
GS 94.18

Rashi Gomang. cf. Rashi G'omong

Rashi G'omang. Monastery.
DO 25b.08
GS 77.10 (Rashi Gomang)

Rbyal Bo. Torghuud. Eldest of the four sons of Khudai Shükür
Dayicing.
DO 30.02; 36.16
GS 75.01 (Kyal Bu)

Rdo Rje Mgun po. Torghuud. One of the four sons of Nazar. cf.
G'ombo.
DO 30.04 (G'ombo)
GS 75.05

Rdo Rje Rabtan. cf. Dorji Arabtan.

Rencen.
GS 84.12

Rgyamcoi Khabtai.
GS 95.08

Rnam Rgyal Khatun.
GS 84.11

Rphyalcang. Torghuud. One of the four sons of Khudai Shükür
Dayicing. He is not mentioned as having received any
inheritance (DO 36.16).
DO 30.03

S

Saba Sharmen. cf. Saba Shirman.

Saba Shirman. Khoshuud. Son of Burkhan Sanji.

DO 26.13
GS 76.06 (Saba Sharmen)

Sajin. cf. Sanjin.

Sakil Noyon Khashikha. Dzungar. Son of Kholodoi Khoshuuci.
DO 28.17
GS 78.01

Saltu. Torghuud. Son of Bolkhon.
DO 31.02
GS 75.15

Samden. Russian emissary.
HKK 6.10

Samukhu. Khoshuud. One of the six sons of Tügüdi.
DO 26.15
GS 76.09 (Samulkhu Cecen)

Samulkhu Cecen. cf. Samukhu.

Samur. City. Kubishev.
HKK 1.17

Samur Ghol. River.
HKK 12.05

Sanjib. Son of Ayuuki.
HKK 5.09, 5.11

Sanjin. Torghuud. Fourth of the six sons of Khō Örlöq; younger
brother of Khudai Shükür Dayicing.
DO 30.02; 31.09
GS 74.17 (Sajin)

Sanji Ubashi. Torghuud. One of the two sons of Mashi.
DO 30.10

Sayin Barkul. Mountain pass?
DO 31.16

Sayin G'a. Khoyid. Son of Eselbei; father of Sultan Tayishi.
DO 27.15; 35.10; 37.11; 38.01, 38.06, 38.14; 39.02, 39.07,
39.08, 39.11, 39.14
GS 78.11, 78.14; 84.14

Sayin Tenes Mergen Temene. cf. Tenes Mergen Temene.

Scerbatob. Russian official.
HKK 3.14

Seber. Siberia.
HKK 6.13; 7.04; 20.01 (Sibēr)

Sem Palād. City. Semipalatinsk.
DO 40.09

Sengge. Dörböd. Son of Bātur Khung Tayiji (two of ten sons listed); he was killed by Cecen Bātur.
DO 29.01; 35.05, 35.15
GS 78.03, 78.04; 83.18 (Sengge Raduli); 85.03; 95.07 (Sengge Duradul)

Sengge Duradul. cf. Sengge.

Sengge Raduli. cf. Sengge.

Serdengke. River. cf. Batur Ercis.
DO 37.15

Sered Byabs. Khoyid. One of the three sons of Bata G'a.
DO 28.03

Serkesh. Torghuud. One of the two sons of Buyantukh.
DO 31.11

Ser Od Skhyabs. Khoyid. One of the four sons of Tümen Jirghalang.
DO 27.17

Sīber. cf. Seber.

Sikis. River.
HKK 21.08

Simbiyir. Russian province.
HKK 8.02

Skyab Bi.
GS 86.01, 86.03

Solom Ceren Tayishi. Dörböd. One of the thirteen sons of Dalai Tayishi. cf. Sonom Ceren Tayishi.
HKK 3.13 (Sonom Ceren Tayishi)
DO 29.04
GS 91.15

Solom Cīn Khatun.
GS 88.06

Solom Darphyā. Dörböd. Son of Erke Tayiji.
DO 29.06

Solom Dobcin. Torghuud. One of the twelve sons of Phyakhdar Byab.
DO 30.06

Sonom Ceren Tayishi. cf. Solom Ceren Tayishi.

Sosoi. Torghuud. Son of Mg'as Dbang; Mongol name: Buyani Tedküqci.
DO 29.15
GS 74.11 (Susai)

Soyimonob, Petor. Minister for Tsarina Anna.

HKK 12.17

Söngkö. Torghuud. Youngest of the six sons of Khō Örlökh.
DO 30.02
GS 74.18 (Shüngkei)

Sultan Tayishi. Khoyid. Son of Sayin G'a; negotiated with Cecen Khan.
DO 27.15; 34.17; 39.14
GS 83.12; 90.14; 94.11

Susai. cf. Sosoi.

Sübterē. Torghuud. One of the three sons of Uubang Khashakh.
DO 30.15
GS 75.09

Sh

Shakyamuni (Burkhan). Buddha.
HKK 16.06
DO 34.09 (Shaphyamuni)
GS 74.10

Shambai. Dörböd. One of the three sons of Byal.
DO 29.09, 29.10

Shara Cekē. River.
HKK 3.11; 4.01, 4.15; 14.07

Shara Shuma. Area into which the Ölöd fled.
DO 25b.05
GS 74.04

Shara Tuu. City. Saratov.
HKK 5.07

Shatamal. Torghuud. Son of Delger.
DO 31.01
GS 75.14

Shikur Blama.
HKK 9.08, 9.17

Shikür Dayicing. Eldest son of Khō Örlökh. cf. Khudai Shükür Dayicing, and Dayicing (Torghuud).
HKK 2.10, 2.13, 2.15, 2.16; 3.01, 3.02; 4.06
DO 30.01, 30.02, 30.09; 33.08, 33.14; 34.01; 36.16; 37.01, 37.02
GS 74.16, 74.18

Shirib Maghamed Sultan.
DO 26.06

Shoroi Bar.
HKK 6.07 (1698 not 1678 as printed)

Shoroi Khonin.

HKK 12.05 (1734)

Shoroi Khuluxuna.
HKK 5.16 (1708)

Shoroi Luu.
HKK 1.09 (1628)
GS 95.15

Shoroi Mecin.
DO 42.05

Shoroi Moghoi.
GS 95.16

Shoroi Morin.
HKK 1.07 (1618)

Shoroi Tuulai.
DO 24.02, 24.04, 24.05, 24.07, 24.08, 24.09, 24.11, 24.12, 24.13; all of these citations refer to the year 1819.

Shuubang Khashkha. Torghuud. One of the two sons of Ghoroi.
DO 30.15
GS 75.09

Shüngkei. cf. Söngkö.

Shütē. Torghuud. One of the three sons of Cebekh Ubashi.
DO 30.09

T

Tabida Bātur Tayishi. cf. Abida Bolo Tayishi.

Tabki. Torghuud. One of the two sons of Bestene.
DO 31.14

Tabun Baras. Khoshuud. Senior wife of Noyon Khongghor.
GS 76.13; 79.08, 79.17; 87.17

Tamagha. Region near Dzungaria.
HKK 22.14

Tambuvi. Russian province. Tambov.
HKK 5.14

Tangbad. People.
GS 74.06; 81.02

Tarba. Khoshuud. One of the two sons of Erke Dayicingghai.
DO 27.05, 27.08

Tarba Ceren. Khoshuud. One of the four sons of Duuriskhu.
DO 27.07, 27.10

Tarbaghatai. Area of Dzungaria.
HKK 23.06, 23.07

Tatār.
HKK 1.12, 1.15; 2.09, 2.10; 3.09; 7.09, 7.11; 15.06; 17.06;
22.06

Tatiscib. Governor of Astrakhan.
HKK 12.03, 12.12

Tege. Khoshuud. Son of Cēge.
DO 27.09

Telengged. Khoshuud. One of the two sons of Zamiyang.
DO 27.14

Temene.
DO 34.08
GS 79.08 (Temne Örlökh); 88.01; 94.18 (Temne Khō Örlökh)

Temene Khō Örlökh. cf. Temene.

Temne Örlökh. cf. Temene.

Tenes Mergen Temene. Torghuud. One of the four sons of Ezenē
Tayiji.
DO 31.04, 31.05; 32.02
GS 76.01, 76.02; 80.02

Terkümüd. Tribe. Turkic?
DO 36.02

Teyigēn. Torghuud. One of the six sons of Khō Örlökh.
DO 33.02

Tobokh. Torghuud. One of the four sons of Kholocin.
GS 75.13

Tobol. Tobolsk province.
HKK 12.08

Toghon Tayishi.
DO 28.12 (Dzungar. Chief from whom princely line started.)
GS 76.08 (Ölöd); 77.03 (Khoshuud line), 77.12 (Dörböd of the
Dzungars)

Torghuud. Tribe.
HKK 1.05, 1.09; 2.09; 4.09; 10.07; 15.13; 18.08, 18.10, 18.11;
23.07, 23.08
DO 24.10, 24.12; 25b.12, 25.16; 26.08; 29.11, 29.14; 31.05,
31.09; 33.08; 36.17; 40.13, 40.14; 42.02
GS 74.05, 74.06, 74.08, 74.10; 76.03; 78.09; 80.02; 81.18;
84.03; 85.08; 91.06, 91.07; 95.04; 96.02

Toyin. Dörböd. One of the thirteen sons of Dalai Tayishi.
DO 29.04, 29.05

Töböd. Tibet.

HKK 2.12; 6.08; 9.10; 11.12; 19.03
DO 25.17; 26.03, 26.05; 31.16; 32.15; 33.17; 34.11; 35.17;
36.03, 36.09
GS 79.15; 80.11, 80.18; 81.04, 81.09; 82.10; 86.06; 92.03;
96.07, 96.10, 96.12

Töböi. Torghuud. One of the four sons of Kholocin.
DO 31.01
GS 75.14

Tögüdei Cingsen Ghorban. Khoshuud. Son of Döüreng Döcin. cf.
Cingsa Tömör.
GS 76.09

Tömör Bar.
HKK 6.03 (1710)

Tömör Batur. Khoyid. One of the three sons of Bata G'a.
DO 28.03

Tömör Lang.
DO 24.06; 25.11; 37.10

Tömör Luu.
HKK 2.02 (1640)
DO 31.06

Tömör Mecin.
DO 24.02

Tömör Modon.
HKK 5.03 (1701)

Tömör Moghoi.
HKK 17.13 (1761)

Tömör Morin.
HKK 1.13 (1630)
GS 95.16

Tömör Noghai.
HKK 3.06 (1670)

Tömör Tak'a.
HKK 3.15 (1681); 11.15 (1741); 12.11 (1741)
DO 42.10 (1801)

Tömör Tuulai.
HKK 19.11 (1771)

Tömör Ükür.
HKK 3.02 (1661); 8.06 (1721)

Törgön Tayiji. Khoshuud. Son of Khara Sabar. One son listed.
DO 27.13

Törö Nayiraltu. Manchu emperor.
HKK 23.04

Traubengberg. Governor of Russian forces against the Kalmyks in 1771.
HKK 20.14

Tukh. Torghuud. One of the three sons of Noyon Sanjilai.
DO 31.14

Tukhcu. Khoshuud. One of the two sons of Cēge.
DO 27.09, 27.11

Tundud. Dörböd. One of the three sons of Solom Darphyā.
DO 29.06

Turkhai. River.
HKK 20.10

Turkhai. Area east of Ural river.
HKK 9.08, 9.11

Turukh. Country: Turkey.
GS 92.04

Tuurki.
HKK 6.04; 11.03, 11.07

Tuurki Sultān.
HKK 3.11; 10.07

Tügüdi. Khoshuud. One of the three sons of Örökh Tömör mentioned. cf. Tögüdei Cingsen Ghorban, and Kung Tügüdi.
DO 26.14, 26.15

Tügül. Khoshuud. Son of Lori Damba.
DO 27.11

Tülishin. Chinese emissary.
HKK 6.13

Tümed. Oirat tribe.
DO 25b.12

Tümedi Köndölöng. Khoshuud. One of the eight sons of Khan Noyon Khongghor.
DO 26.17
GS 76.14 (Tümüdē Kündölöng Döürügeci Ubashi)

Tümüdē Köndölöng Döürügeci Ubashi. cf. Düürgēci Ubashi.

Tümüdē Kündölöng Döürügeci Ubashi. cf. Tümedi Köndölöng.

Tümen. City in province of Tobolsk.
HKK 12.08
DO 40.11

Tümen Jirghalang. Khoyid. Son of Dejīd, stepson of Byamiyang; he became ruler of the Khoyid and Khoshuud. He went to Petersburg contracted smallpox, but recovered. He is the

father of the author of the DO.
HKK 12.09, 12.10
DO 27.17; 40.05, 40.12, 40.15; 41.06, 41.07, 41.09, 41.10, 41.13; 42.10; 43.02

Tûrkemen.
HKK 4.04

Tûshêtû Khan.
HKK 2.04

U

Ubakh Cingsa. Khoshuud. cf. Ubukh Cingsa.
DO 26.15 (Obokh Cingsa), 26.16 (son of Tûgûdi)
GS 76.11 (son of Kûsei)

Ubashi. Khoshuud. One of the four sons of Tarba Ceren.
DO 27.10

Ubashi. Dörböd. One of the three sons of Cö Rashi.
DO 29.09

Ubashi. Torghuud. One of the four sons of Nazar.
HKK 12.01
DO 30.04
GS 75.05 (Ubasha)

Ubashi (Khan). Son of Dondukh Dashi; he became khan in 1761.
HKK 14.05; 16.03; 17.14, 17.16; 18.01, 18.02, 18.04, 18.05, 18.08, 18.09, 18.15; 19.11; 20.15; 21.16; 22.01, 22.08, 22.16, 22.17; 23.02, 23.03, 23.04, 23.08, 23.15, 23.16
DO 31.08; 41.16; 42.09, 42.15

Ubashi Khung Tayiji. Khoshuud. One of the four sons of Dûûrgêci Ubashi.
DO 27.02

Ubashi Khung Tayiji. Khan of the Mongols.
DO 24.09; 26.04; 37.12, 37.14, 37.15, 37.16

Ubukh Cingsa. Khoshuud. Son of Kusei. cf. Ubakh Cingsa.
DO 26.15, 26.16 (Obukh. One of the six sons of Tûgûdi)
GS 76.11 (Ubakh Cingsa)

Ukhni Biyi. Torghuud. Son of (Khudai Shikûr) Dayicing.
GS 75.01

Ukh Tûsêtû. Khoshuud. One of the two sons of Buyan Xatun Bâtur.
DO 27.01 (Khayinakh Tûsêtû. Listed as one of the eight sons of Khan Noyon Khongghor.)
GS 76.16

Ulân. Personal name.
GS 78.15

Ulân Zalâtu (Red tassaled). Oirat, Kalmyk, and Öyilöd.
DO 24.08

Ung. cf. Obō.

Unzad Corci. Torghuud. The clan of Ülü Cenzē.
DO 31.03
GS 75.17

Urangkhan Sayin Mazakh.
DO 37.13

Urumci. Region of Dzungaria.
HKK 23.06

Ushkhani Tayiji. Dzungar. The eldest of the three sons of Khamukh Tayishi.
DO 28.14
GS 75.15, 75.16

Usun Bar.
HKK 8.08 (1722)

Usun Luu.
HKK 6.10 (1712); 22.14 (1772)

Usun Mecin.
GS 95.18

Usun Moghoi.
HKK 6.13 (1713)

Usun Noghoi.
HKK 12.13 (1742)

Usun Ükür.
HKK 3.10 (1673)

Utu Nasun. Torghuud. Son of Muu Köüken
DO 31.11

Uubang Khashkha. Torghuud. One of the two sons of Ghoroi.
DO 30.14, 30.15
GS 75.08, 75.09

Uur Uuzang Shükür. Khoshuud. Son of Yadāi Cingsen.
DO 26.16 (Nöür Uuzang Shükür. Listed as one of the four sons of Obokh Cingsa)
GS 76.12

Uuzang Khosuuci. Khoyid. Son of Sultān Tayishi.
DO 27.16; 39.14

Uuzang K'ras Mgömögö dam anduu. Provinces of Tibet: bUs and gTsang etc.
GS 80.13

Ü

Üledüi Aldar G'ā. Dörböd. Son of Daghal. cf. Öldö which
separates Aldar G'ā.
GS 77.17; 93.04

Ülü Cenze. cf. Ülü Cenzē.

Ülü Cenzē. Torghuud. Fifth of the six sons of Buyigho Örlöq.
DO 30.01, 30.17 (Ülü Cenze); 31.03 (Ülü Zenzen)
GS 75.12 (Olon Cecen), 75.17 (Ülü Cēze)

Ülü Cēze. cf. Ülü Cenzē.

Ülü Zenzēn. cf. Ülü Cenzē.

V

Vasilii Kinviyeg'ob. Nephew of the governor Z'ilin.
HKK 16.12

Volīngski. Governor of Astrakhan.
HKK 9.03

W

Wang Khan. Torghuud. Descended from Chinggis.
DO 29.12, 29.13
GS 74.07, 74.08, 74.09

Y

Yabashike. cf. Yabāshki.

Yabāski. Torghuud. Son of Khulaghāci of the clan of Ghori
(Ghoroi).
DO 30.16
GS 75.11 (Yabashike), 75.17

Yabughun Mergen.
DO 24.06

Yadāi Cingsen. cf. Yedei Cingsa.

Yag'aram. Dörböd. One of the three sons of Khabcikh.
DO 29.10

Yaman. Torghuud. Son of Mazan of the clan of Buura.
DO 30.14
GS 75.16

Yandakh. Torghuud. One of the twelve sons of Phyakhdar Byab.
DO 30.06

Yangkhal. City: Chernyi Yar.

HKK 17.11

Yarang Nomiyin Rgyamcula.
GS 81.06

Yedei Cingsa. Khoshuud. One of the four sons of Ubakh Cingsa.
DO 26.16
GS 76.11 (Yadāi Cingsen)

Yeke Abughai. Messenger sent by Torghuud. to Cewang Rabtan.
HKK 9.06

Yeke Jikhku. Khoshuud. Son of Güüsi Khan. Güüsi makes him prince of Tibet with Dalai Khung Tayiji.
GS 86.18

Yeke Mingghan. Khoyid. Group (anggi) of people of the Khoyid.
DO 37.10; 40.07

Yeketerine (Aliqsēyebana). Tsarina Catherine.
HKK 18.09
DO 41.08, 41.09, 41.11, 41.15

Yeke Zuu. Monastery.
DO 37.05; 42.09

APPENDIX II:

COMPARISON OF THE GS AND DO

A Line by Line Textual Comparison between the GS and DO

GS	DO	
GS 74.01 – 74.06		
GS 74.06 – 75.03	DO 29.11 – 30.04	DO distorts and also adds new information.
GS 75.03 – 75.04	DO 30.06 – 30.07	
GS 75.04	DO 30.05	DO lists additional genealogical information.
GS 75.04 – 75.06	DO 30.04 – 30.05	
GS 75.06 – 75.07		
GS 75.07 – 75.08	DO 30.11 – 30.12	DO changes information.
GS 75.08 – 75.16	DO 30.14 – 31.03	DO distorts but also adds new information.
GS 75.16 – 75.17		
GS 75.17 – 75.18	DO 31.03	
GS 75.18 – 76.03	DO 31.03 – 31.05	DO drops material.
GS 76.03 – 76.07	DO 26.11 – 26.14	DO adds material.
GS 76.07 – 76.08		
GS 76.08 – 76.17	DO 26.14 – 27.02	DO has great disparity in information.
GS 76.17	DO 27.03	
GS 76.17 – 76.18	DO 27.06	DO drops phrases.
GS 76.18		

GS 77.01	DO 27.03	
GS 77.01	DO 27.05	
GS 77.02		
GS 77.02	DO 27.03	
GS 77.03 – 77.04		
GS 77.04 – 77.07	DO 28.06 – 28.09	DO contains some variations.
GS 77.07 – 77.08	DO 28.04 – 28.05	DO lacking some information.
GS 77.08 – 77.09		
GS 77.10 – 77.11	DO 25b.08 – 25b.09	DO distorts material.
GS 77.11 – 77.12		
GS 77.12 – 78.04	DO 28.12 – 29.02	GS presents more complete information.
GS 78.04 – 78.07		
GS 78.07	DO 33.16	
GS 78.07 – 78.08	DO 33.16 – 33.17	
GS 78.08	DO 25b.07 – 25b.08	DO only partially the same.
GS 78.08 – 78.11		
GS 78.11 – 78.18	DO 38.06 – 39.11	Texts roughly parallel, however, DO more complete.
GS 78.18 – 79.02		
GS 79.02 – 79.07	DO 34.04 – 34.07	DO drops some words distorts others.
GS 79.07 – 79.08		
GS 79.08 – 79.14	DO 34.08 – 34.11	GS is more complete.

GS 79.14 - 80.02   DO 31.15 - 32.03

GS 80.02 - 80.03

GS 80.03 - 80.05   DO 32.05 - 32.06

GS 80.06 - 80.12   DO 32.09 - 32.15

GS 80.12 - 80.15

GS 80.16 - 80.18   DO 33.02 - 33.03

GS 80.18 - 81.10

GS 81.10 - 81.17   DO 33.03 - 33.08   DO   reverses
several of the

                                                         lines of the
GS and also
drops some
material.

GS 81.17 - 81.18

GS 81.18 - 82.16   DO 33.08 - 34.04   DO changes and
omits material
found in the
GS.

GS 82.16 - 83.03

GS 83.03 - 83.06   DO 34.12 - 34.14   DO adds
material.

GS 83.06 - 83.10   DO 34.15 - 34.17

GS 83.10 - 83.12

GS 83.12 - 83.15   DO 34.17 - 35.03

GS 83.16 - 83.17

GS 83.18 - 84.03   DO 35.05 - 35.08

GS 84.03 - 84.04

GS 84.04 - 84.06   DO 35.08 - 35.09

GS 84.06 - 84.13

GS 84.13 - 84.15   DO 35.09 - 35.11   DO changes
text of GS.

GS 84.15   DO 35.11 - 34.12

GS 84.16   DO 35.11

GS 84.16 – 84.18		
GS 84.18	DO 35.13	
GS 85.01 – 85.04	DO 35.12 – 35.15	
GS 85.04 – 86.06		
GS 86.06	DO 35.17	
GS 86.06 – 86.07	DO 36.01	DO is lacking some information.
GS 86.07 – 86.08	DO 36.01 – 36.03	DO presents some different information.
GS 86.08 – 86.10		
GS 86.10 – 86.12	DO 36.04 – 36.05	DO greatly distorts GS.
GS 86.13	DO 36.07	
GS 86.14 – 86.15	DO 36.06 – 36.07	DO slightly changes GS.
GS 86.15 – 86.16	DO 36.08	
GS 86.16 – 86.18	DO 36.10 – 36.12	
GS 86.18 – 87.01	DO 36.09	
GS 87.01 – 87.02	DO 36.12 – 36.13	
GS 87.02 – 87.03		
GS 87.03 – 87.06	DO 36.13 – 36.16	
GS 87.06 – 87.09	DO 37.01 – 37.04	
GS 87.09		
GS 87.09 – 87.13	DO 37.04 – 37.07	
GS 87.13 – 97.15		

BIBLIOGRAPHY OF WORKS CITED

Ahmad, Zahiruddin. _Sino-Tibetan Relations in the Seventeenth Century._ Serie Orientale Roma, vol. XL. Rome: Istituto Italianod Per Il Medio Ed Estremo Oriente, 1970.

Alexander, John T. _Autocratic Politics in a National Crisis: The Imperial Russian Government and Pugachev's Revolt 1773-1775._ Russian and East European Series, vol 38. Bloomington: Indiana University Press 1969.

_____. _Emperor of the Cossacks: Pugachev and the Frontier Jacquerie of 1773-1775._ Lawrence, Kansas, 1973.

Apollova, N.G. _Ekonomicheskie i Politicheskie Svyazi Kazakhstana s Rossiej v XVIII-nachale XIX v._ Moscow: 1960.

Atlas Astrakhanskoi Oblasti, Glavnoe upravlenie geodezii i kartografii. Moscow: 1968.

Atlas SSSR. Glavnoe upravlenie geodezii i kartografii. Moscow: 1969.

Baddeley, John F. _The Rugged Flanks of the Caucasus._ 2 vols. London: Oxford University Press, 1940.

_____. _Russia, Mongolia, China: Being some Record of the Relations between them from the beginning of the XVIIth Century to the Death of the Tsar Alexei Mikhailovich A.D. 1602-1676._ 2 vols. reprinted, New York: Burt Franklin, no date.

_____. _The Russian Conquest of the Caucasus._ London: Longmans, Green and Co., 1908.

Badmayev, A.V. editor, _Kalmytskie istoriko-literaturnye pamyatniki v russkom perevode._ Elista: 1969.

_____. _Zaya-Pandita (spiski kalmyckoj rukopisi "Biografiya Zaya-Pandity")._ Elista: Kalmyckoe Khiznoe izdatel'stvo. 1968.

Barkman, C.D. "The Return of the Torghuts from Russia to China." _Journal of Oriental Studies_ vol. II, (1955). pp. 89-115.

Bawden, C.R. _The Modern History of Mongolia._ New York: Frederick A. Praeger, 1968.

_____. "A Mongol Document of 1764 Concerning the Repopulation of Ili." _ZAS_ vol. 5, 1971. pp. 79-94.

Bayanova, D.N. _Kratkaya istoriya Kalmytskikh Khanov._ Paris: 1974. pp. 7-29.

Bell, John of Antermony. _Travels from St. Petersburg in Russia_

to Diverse Parts of Asia in two volumes. Glasgow: Robert and
Andrew Foulis, 1763.

Bergmann, Benjamin. Nomadische Streifereien unter der Kalmüken
in den Jahren 1802 und 1803. Riga: 1804. reprinted with an
introduction by Siegbert Hummel, Oosterhout, Netherlands:
Anthropological Publications. 1969.

Cahen, Gaston. "Deux Ambassades Chinoises en Russie au
commencement du XVIIIe siècle." Revue Historique, CXXXIII,
1920. pp. 85-89.

_____. History of the Relations of Russia and China under Peter
the Great 1689-1730. Translated by W. Sheldon Ridge. Russian
Series vol. 4. Bangor, Maine: University Prints and Reprints.
1967.

Conolly, Violet. Beyond the Urals: Economic Developments in
Soviet Asia. London: Oxford University Press. 1967.

Courant, Maurice. L'Asie centrale aux XVIIe et XVIIIe siècles.
Empire kalmouk ou empire mantchou? Annales de l'Université de
Lyon N.S. fasc. 26. Paris-Lyon: 1912.

Curtiss, Mina. A Forgotten Empress: Anna Ivanova and Her Era
1730-1740. New York: Frederick Ungar Publishing Co., 1974.

Damdinsürüng, Ce. Mongghol Jokiyal-un Degeji Jaghun Bilig
Orusibai. Corpus Scriptorum Mongolorum vol. XIV. [Ulan Bator],
1959.

Das, Sarat Chandra. A Tibetan-English Dictionary. Delhi:
Motilal Bandarsidass. 1973 reprint.

De Mailla, Joseph-Anne-Marie De Moyriac. Histoire Générale de
la Chine, ou Annales de cet Empire; Traduites du
Tong-Kien-Kang-Mou. Paris: 1777. Reprinted in Taipei:
Ch'eng-wen Publishing Co., 1969.

De Quincey, Thomas. The Revolt of the Tatars: or flight of the
Kalmuck khan and his people from the Russian territories to
the frontiers of China. edited with notes and introduction by
Charles Sears Baldwin. New York: Longmans, Green, and co.,
1897.

De Rachewiltz, Igor. translator of the Secret History of the
Mongols. Papers on Far Eastern History. Canberra: Australia
National University. vols. 4, 5, 10, and 13. 1971, 1972, 1974,
and 1976.

Donnelly, Alton S. The Russian Conquest of Bashkiria 1552-1740:
A Case Study in Imperialism. New Haven: Yale University Press,
1968.

Fletcher, Joseph. "An Oyirod Letter in the British Museum."
Mongolian Studies, edited by L. Ligeti, Bibliotheca Orientalis
Hungarica, Budapest: 1970. pp. 129-136.

Geiger, Bernard; Tibor Halasi-Kun; Aert H. Knipers and Karl H. Menges. Peoples and Languages of the Caucasus: A Synopsis. 's-Gravenhage: Mouton & Co., 1959.

Golstunskii, K.F. Mongolo-oiratskie zakony 1640 goda, dopolnitel'nye ukazy Galdan-chun-taidziya i zakony, sostavlennye dlja volzskich Kalmykov pri kalmyckom chane Donduk-Dashi. St. Petersburg: 1880.

Gomboyev, G. Altan Tobchi. Mongol'skaya letopis'. Trudy vostochnago otdeleniya Imperatorskago Russkago Arkheologicheskago Obshchestva. St. Petersburg: 1858.

Grousset, René. Empire of the Steppes: A History of Central Asia. translated by Naomi Walford. New Brunswick, New Jersey: Rutgers University Press, 1970.

Halkovic, Stephen A. A Comparative Analysis of Zaya Pandita's Bibliography of Translations. M.A. thesis, Indiana University, May, 1972.

Hambly, Gavin. Central Asia. London: Weidenfeld and Nicolson. 1969.

Haneda, Akira. "L'histoire des Djounghar aux 16e et 17e siècles, Origine des Eleutes." UAJ XLII (1970), pp. 119-126.

Hangin, John Gombojab. Köke Sudur (The Blue Chronicle): A Study of the First Mongolian Historical Novel by Injannasi. Asiatische Forschungen vol. 38. Wiesbaden: Otto Harrassowitz, 1973.

Heissig, Walther. Mongolische Handschriften, Blockdrucke, Landkarten. Verzeichnis der Orientalischen Handschriften in Deutschland vol. 1. Wiesbaden: 1961.

Holt, P.M., Ann K.S. Lambton and Bernard Lewis. The Cambridge History of Islam, 2 vols. Cambridge: Cambridge University Press, 1970.

Howorth, Henry H. History of the Mongols from the 9th to the 19th Century: Part 1. The Mongols Proper and the Kalmuks. London: Longmans, Green and Co., 1876.

Hummel, Arthur W. Eminent Chinese of the Ch'ing Period (1644-1912). Washington: United States Government Printing Office, 1943.

Hunczak, Taras, editor. Russian Imperialism from Ivan the Great to the Revolution. New Brunswick, New Jersey: Rutgers University Press, 1974.

Illeritskii, V. "Ekspeditsiia Kniazia Cherkasskogo v Khivu." Istoricheskii zhurnal, no. 7, 1940. pp. 40-51.

Imanishi, Shunjū. Tulisen's I-yü-lu Revised and Annotated, 1964.

Juvaini, 'Ata-malik. The History of the World Conqueror. Translated by John A. Boyle. Cambridge: Harvard University Press, 1958.

Koehne, Carl. "Das Recht der Kalmuken." Zeitschrift für Vergleichende Rechtswissenschaft, 1891, vol. 9, pp. 445-475.

Kolmash, Josef. Tibet and Imperial China; a survey of Sino-Tibetan relations up to the end of the Manchu dynasty in 1912. Canberra: Centre of Oriental Studies, Australia National University, 1967.

Kozin, S.A. "Oiratskaya istoriceskaya pesn' o razgrome Khanlkhasskogo Sholoi-ubashi khuntaidji v 1587 godu." Sovetskoe Vostokovedenie vol. 4, Moscow: 1947.

Krader, Lawrence. Social Organization of the Mongol-Turkic Pastoral Nomads. Indiana University Publications. Uralic and Altaic Series, vol. 20. Bloomington, Indiana: 1963.

Krueger, John R. "Catalogue of the Laufer Mongolian Collection in Chicago." JAOS, vol. 86, 1966. pp. 156-183.

_____. "The Ch'ien-lung Inscriptions of 1755 and 1758 in Oirat-Mongolian." CAJ, 16 no. 1, 1972. pp. 59-69.

_____. "A Decree on the Origins of Lamaism among the Kalmyks (1756)." in Tractata Altaica: Denis Sinor, sexagenario optimo de rebus Altaicis merito dedicata. edited by Walther Heissig et al. Wiesbaden: Otto Harrassowitz, 1976. pp. 355-364.

_____. "New Materials on Oirat Law and History Part I: The Jinjil Decrees." CAJ, 16 no. 3, 1972, pp. 194-205.

_____. "New Materials on Oirat Law and History Part II: The Origin of the Torgouts." CAJ, 18 no. 1, 1974, pp. 30-42.

_____. "Oirat Literary Resources and the Problems of Oirat Lexicography." American Oriental Society, Middle West Branch, Semi-centennial volume. edited by Denis Sinor. Bloomington, Indiana. 1969. pp. 134-157.

_____. Materials for an Oirat-Written Mongol-English Citation Dictionary. 3 volumes, Publications of the Mongolia Society. Bloomington, Indiana. 1978 and 1984.

_____. "Three Oirat-Mongolian Diplomatic Documents of 1691." CAJ, 12 no. 4, 1969. pp. 286-295.

_____. "Two Imperial Decrees to the Kalmyks (1735 and 1828)." UAJ, vol. 47, 1975, pp. 119-123.

_____. "Written Oirat and Kalmyk Studies." Mongolian Studies vol. II, 1975. pp. 93-113.

Lessing, Ferdinand, general editor. Mongolian English Dictionary. Berkeley: University of California Press, 1960.

Lewis, B., Ch. Pellat and J. Schacht, eds. The Encyclopaedia of Islam. New edition. Vol. II. Leiden: E.J.Brill, 1965.

Longworth, Philip. The Three Empresses: Catherine I, Anne and Elizabeth of Russia. New York: Holt Rinehart and Winston, 1972.

Luvsanbaldan, Kh. "Oiradyn Zaya Bandidyn orcuulgyn tukhaj medee." Khel Jokiol Sudlal, VI, fasc. 6, Ulaan Bator: 1969.

Mancall, Mark. Russia and China: Their Diplomatic Relations to 1728. Cambridge, Massachusetts: Harvard University Press, 1971.

Mathews, R.H. Mathews' Chinese English Dictionary. Cambridge, Massachusetts: Harvard University Press, 9th printing, 1969.

Mish, John L. "The Return of the Turgut." JAH, vol. 4, 1970. pp. 80-82.

Molè, Gabriella. The T'u-yü-hun from the Northern Wei to the Time of the Five Dynasties. Serie Orientale Roma vol. XLI. Roma: Istituto Italiano Per Il Medio Ed Estremo Oriente, 1970.

Okada, Hidehiro. "Outer Mongolia in the Sixteenth and Seventeenth Centuries." Ajia-Afurika Gengo Bunka Kenkyu.

Pallas, P.S. Sammlungen Historischer Nachrichten uber die mongolischen Volkerschaften. St. Petersburg, vol. I, 1776; vol.II, 1801.

Pelliot, Paul. Notes critiques d'histoire Kalmouke. Paris: Librarie d'Amérique et d'Orient. 1960.

Petech, L. China and Tibet in the Early 18th Century: History of the establishment of Chinese protectorate in Tibet. Monographies du T'oung Pao vol. I. Leiden: 1950.

Pipes, Richard. Russia under the Old Regime. New York: Charles Scribner's Sons. 1974.

Poppe, Nicholas. "Stand der Kalmückenforschung." Wiener Zeitschrift für die Kunde des Morgenlandes LII, 1955. pp. 346-379.

Posch, Udo. "The Syllabic Groups and their Further Development in the Written Oirat Language: Part I." CAJ, III, 1957-1958. pp. 206-219.

Pozdneyev, A. Kalmyckaja Khrestomatija dlja chtenija v starshikh klassakh Kalmyckikh narodnykh shkol. 1st edition St. Petersburg, 1892; 2nd edition St. Petersburg, 1907; 3rd edition St. Petersburg, 1915.

Pozdneyev, A.M. Mongolia and the Mongols: Volume I - 1892. Indiana University Publications, Uralic and Altaic Series vol. 61. Bloomington, Indiana: 1971.

Radna-bhadra. Biography of Caya Pandita in Oirat Characters. with introduction, transcription and index by Zh. Tsoloo. Corpus Scriptorum Mongolorum vol. V, fasc. 2-3, edited by Y. Rinchen. Ulanbator, 1967.

Ramstedt, G.J. Kalmückisches Wörterbuch. Helsinki: Suomalais - Ugrilainen Seura. 1935.

Ratnabhadra. Rabjamba Cay-a bandida-yin tuguji saran-u gerel kemeku ene metu bolai. Corpus Scriptorum Mongolorum, vol. V, fasc. 2. edited by Y. Rinchen, Ulanbator: 1959.

Redhouse, Sir James. New Redhouse Turkish-English Dictionary. Istanbul: Redhouse Press, 1974.

Riasanovsky, V.A. Customary Law of the Mongol Tribes (Mongols, Buriats, Kalmucks). Harbin, China: 1929.

_____. Fundamental Principles of Mongol Law. Indiana University Publications, Uralic and Altaic Series, vol. 43. Bloomington, Indiana: 1965.

Rubel, Paula G. The Kalmyk Mongols: A Study in Continuity and Change. Indiana University Publications, Uralic and Altaic Series, vol. 64. Bloomington, Indiana: 1967.

Sarkisyanz, Emanuel. Geschichte der orientalischen Völker Russlands bis 1917. München: Oldenbourg Verlag. 1961.

Serruys, Henry. Genealogical Descendants of Dayan-Qan. Central Asiatic Studies vol. III. 's-Gravenhage: Mouton & Co. 1958.

Sumner, B.H. Peter the Great and the Emergence of Russia. London: The English Universities Press Ltd., 1966.

Tucci, Giuseppe. Tibetan Painted Scrolls. Roma: La Libreria Dello Stato: 1949.

Tu-li-shin. Narrative of the Chinese Embassy to the Khan of the Tourgouth Tartars in the years 1712, 13, 14 & 15; by the Chinese Ambassador, and Published by the Emperor's Authority at Pekin. translated by Sir George Thomas Staunton. London: 1821. reprinted Arlington, Virginia: University Publications of America, Inc. 1976.

Ustjugova, N.V., et al, editors. Ocherki istorii Kalmyckoj ASSR, Moscow: 1967.

Vernadsky, George. Political and Diplomatic History of Russia. Boston: Little, Brown, and company. 1936.

Vostrikov. A.I. Tibetskaya istoricheskaya literatura. Bibliotheca Buddhica Vol. XXXII. reprinted Osnabrück, West Germany: Biblio Verlag, 1970.

Wawilow, S.I. et al, editors. Grosse Sowjet - Enzyklopädie. Berlin: Verlag Kultur und Fortschritt, 1952.

Weigh, Ken Shen. Russo-Chinese Diplomacy 1689-1924. reprinted in The Russian Series vol. 3. Bangor, Maine: University Prints and Reprints. 1967.

Zlatkin, I. Ja. Istorija Dzhungarskogo Khanstva (1635-1758). Moscow: 1964.